LAND OF DISENCHANTMENT

LAND OF DISENCHANTMENT

Latina/o Identities and Transformations
in Northern New Mexico

Michael L. Trujillo

University of New Mexico Press
Albuquerque

Library of Congress Cataloging-in-Publication Data

Trujillo, Michael L., 1971–
Land of disenchantment : Latina/o identities and transformations in
northern New Mexico / Michael L. Trujillo.
         p. cm.
Includes bibliographical references and index.
ISBN 978-0-8263-4736-7 (pbk. : alk. paper)
 1. Hispanic Americans—New Mexico—Espanola Valley—Ethnic identity.
2. Hispanic Americans—Race identity—New Mexico—Espanola
Valley. 3. Hispanic Americans—New Mexico—Espanola Valley—Social
conditions. 4. Hispanic Americans—New Mexico—Espanola
Valley—Intellectual life. 5. Ethnology—New Mexico—Espanola Valley.
6. Political culture—New Mexico—Espanola Valley. 7. Regionalism—
New Mexico—Espanola Valley. 8. Espanola Valley (N.M.)—Ethnic relations.
9. Ethnicity—United States—Case studies. 10. United States—Ethnic
relations—Case studies. I. Title.

         F802.E8T78 2009
         305.868'078952—dc22

                                        2009029167

FOR MY FATHER

(1936–2005)

"*¿La risa de Dios?* The laughter of God?" Flaco laughed.
There's an articulate beauty to the words. The gracefulness
and the intangibility of the words lifted and gave them
an interconnected musical attribute. Somewhere between
consciousness and darkness lay the secret of why God laughs

—G. Benito Córdova, *Big Dreams and Dark Secrets in Chimayó*

It is a cardinal error to believe that, of "Surrealist
experiences," we know only the religious ecstasies or the
ecstasies of drugs. The opium of the people, Lenin called
religion, and brought the two things closer together than
the surrealists could have liked. . . . But the true, creative
overcoming of religious illumination certainly does not lie
in narcotics. It resides in a *profane illumination*, a materialistic,
anthropological inspiration, to which hashish, opium, or
whatever else can give an introductory lesson

—Walter Benjamin, "Surrealism"

No estás, Miguel condenado
ni esperes ir al infierno
cuando Dios, amante tierno,
cuanto has escrito te ha dado

—Miguel de Quintana,
Defying the Inquisition in Colonial
New Mexico

You know what brother? Believe
nothing you hear and half of what
you see. Okay? That's how
I look at it around here.

—Joey Jaramillo, Española, New Mexico

You are not damned, Miguel,
nor need to fear going to hell,
since God, like a tender lover,
has given you all that you have written

—Translation by Francisco A. Lomelí
and Clark A. Colahan

TABLE OF CONTENTS

Preface   XI

Acknowledgments   XVII

Introduction   I

Chapter One: Remembering and Dismembering   27

Chapter Two: Good Friday   57

Chapter Three: A Northern New Mexican "Fix"   74

Chapter Four: A Time for Bitterness   96

Chapter Five: Appearances Teach   127

Chapter Six: Cuando Hablan los Enamorados   156

Chapter Seven: The Secret of Why God Laughs   183

Conclusion   209

Notes   214

Bibliography   230

Index   254

PREFACE

When I first wrote my proposal for this project, I planned a thematic focus on the complex and often-fraught relationship between emerging and traditional or residual aspects of northern New Mexican Latina/o or Chicana/o ethnic/racial identity. I believed a geographic focus in the Greater Española Valley of north central New Mexico to be an excellent location for such research. This ethnography has retained these thematic and geographic foci. The text I wrote has changed from the one I planned in most other respects. At the time I wrote the proposal, mostly sitting at a desk in my studio apartment in Austin, Texas, I imagined a far shorter research period and producing a very different sort of text. The ethnographic writing that I foresaw was more in line with the previous ethnographies written on the region. As so often happens, my fieldwork, research, and writing became more profound and drawn out than I first planned. What emerges is not an ethnography in the traditional sense. Rather it is an exploration of New Mexican Latino identity, ethnographic representation, and the complexity each evokes through its multiplicity, silences, and contradictions.

A Personal Journey

I first began seriously to imagine this book after a car ride from New Mexico's Tierra Amarilla to southern Colorado's San Luis Valley with community and political organizer María Varela. At that time, 1997, I was researching community mobilization based in the ongoing land movement in northern New Mexico. The land movement seeks the return of land often swindled from the area's Latino population following the American annexation of the Southwest. In that conversation, Varela described a gap between northern New Mexico's youth and older generations that she had seen grow since her arrival in northern New Mexico in the 1960s. My interest in this gap led me to switch my research interest from the villages of northern Rio Arriba County, where my relatives still live, to southern Rio Arriba County's city of Española. In the late 1990s, when the Española Valley began to appear in regional and national headlines for extraordinarily high rates of fatal drug overdoses, the significance of this issue and its importance in this particular location became even more urgent.

This project has also become a personal intellectual journey. In my research and writing, I have confronted my own visions of New Mexico. Although New Mexican by "blood," I grew up in central Washington state rather than the northern New Mexican communities where my family has lived for hundreds of years. Nevertheless, through my parents' stories, their assertions of "who we are," and countless trips to see relatives, New Mexico played a major role in my childhood and young adulthood. I also spent some of my twenties living in New Mexico and, in the course of my undergraduate and graduate education, the extensive ethnographic literature by scholars such as Charles Briggs, Miguel Gandert, Paul Kutsche, Enrique Lamadrid, Sylvia Rodríguez, and Brenda Romero began to play a role in my thinking.

In my actual experiences in northern New Mexico in the 1990s and 2000s, I did not find the communities my parents described or the communities I remembered from the countless family trips "home." Similarly, the objects of my ethnographic analysis are not the people who populate the more romantic ethnographies of the region, as these representations seemed to be incomplete. In my research and wider experience, I found instead something "more," or perhaps, "less," that required inclusion in my text—a something I would eventually recognize as negativity both in a popular and philosophical sense. I believe the following ethnographic text will evoke this something else.

This Project

I moved to Española in the summer of 2000 and spent 2000–2001 as a reporter for the newspaper *The Rio Grande Sun*. This locally owned newspaper is well known for its gritty reporting, has a paid circulation of more than eleven thousand, and is closely monitored by the state's larger news outlets. Under the tutorship of then News Editor Beth Velásquez and General Editor Robert Braiden Trapp, I gained a strong knowledge of Española's political order and social issues. I spent 2001–2 working full time on my research. During 2001–2, a University of Texas Thematic Fellowship afforded me this luxury. At this time, I formulated many of the chapters of this text, and I conducted most of my research into the chapters' subjects: the work of embroiderer Policarpio Valencia, the previous ethnography of Española and other area communities, the oeuvre of local author Jim Sagel, and the 1998 vandalism of a statue of supposed city founder and conquistador don Juan de Oñate.

In 2002–3, I was employed as a detox attendant and facilitated drug treatment groups at an Española-based treatment facility and worked on a University of New Mexico (UNM) study of drug treatment, a subject that also appears in this book (Willging, Trujillo, and La Luz 2003). The treatment study received widespread attention, including articles in the *Albuquerque Journal* and *Santa Fe New Mexican* (Davis 2003; Lenderman 2003b).

My journey continued over the course of the two years I primarily devoted my time to writing. In that time, I lived in Oaxaca, Mexico; Austin, Texas; and Colorado Springs, Colorado; spent a summer as an Ethel-Jane Westfeldt Bunting Fellowship at the School of American Research (SAR) in Santa Fe; taught at the University of Texas at Austin (UT); and served as a Riley Fellow for the Center of Southwest Studies and Department of Anthropology at Colorado College (CC). I revised several chapters as assistant professor at the University of Oklahoma and drafted the final chapter as an assistant professor of American Studies and Chicano/Hispano/Mexicano Studies at the University of New Mexico. Versions of chapter 1 and chapter 3 appeared as articles in *Aztlán: A Journal of Chicano Studies* and *Cultural Dynamics* (Trujillo

2006, 2008). In the process, I threw out countless pages of written text and reformulated and discarded entire chapters.

What emerged from this journey was an ethnographic text that focuses on the "negative" and "positive" aspects, in the philosophical or semiotic sense, of New Mexican racial/ethnic identity, its assignment, or both. New Mexicans are increasingly defined by these dialectical notions of what *they are* and what *they are not*. Implicated within this dialogue are tropes such as visions of New Mexico as the "Land of Enchantment" and jokes about Española's residents. In this exploration, I have come to envision my project as a social and creative anthropological commentary on the Española Valley. It is the interdisciplinary nature of such work and its sojourns into literary criticism and the realms of cultural studies that led me to my current formation as an American Studies scholar. In this book, my intent is to evoke some aspects of these issues rather than attempt to create an exhaustive or complete rendering. As will become apparent, such a full rendering remains a tremendous and complex undertaking that is only begun in this work.

Such issues of representation, identity, and nonidentity are not new to academic and popular works concerned with New Mexicans. For the most part, this conflicted history has taken the form of disagreement over terms of racial/ethnic identity and assignment for the people descendant from New Mexico's pre-1848, Spanish-speaking population. Nearly any academic work focused on northern New Mexicans and their communities must be preceded with a justification for the author's chosen racial/ethnic term for this population. This ethnography is no exception.

Terms of Identity

Academics and other members of this community often assert that particular terms of identity are the best or most correct terms of self-identification and that there is a consensus that supports their view. As I will show in this text, however, their assertions can usually be contradicted by another made with equal authority and fervor. Often a single individual will make contradictory assertions depending on moment, audience, and language spoken. As I will show in the body of this text, any term must be understood within its particular context, and no term fully captures New Mexican Latino identity and nonidentity. Rather, all use the term that seems to best fit their views, time, and place. In Española alone, I have heard people use the terms Chicana/o, Spanish, Latina/o, Mexican, Mexicano, *raza*, and *la plebe*. In formal situations, most northern New Mexicans self-identify as Hispanic, Chicano, or Spanish/Spanish American. In contrast, when speaking Spanish, many use terms such as *mexicanos de aquí* (Mexicanos from here). My experience with a diversity of terms was further confirmed by the ethnic/racial identifications given by individuals in interviews conducted in a treatment study I co-wrote with Cathleen E. Willging and Azul La Luz (Willging, Trujillo, and La Luz 2003). Perhaps epitomizing the complexities of these terms is the entry for "Mejicano" in Rubén Cobos's venerable dictionary of New Mexico and Southern Colorado Spanish. Cobos writes:

> **mejicano,-na** adj. [Sp. Mexicano, Mexican] Col. and Terr. N.M. Sp., a New Mexican of Indo Hispanic descent; a Mexican national; the Indian language of the Valley of Mexico (Aztec or Náhuatl); the Spanish language in New Mexico and Southern Colorado; *hablar en mejicano,* to speak Spanish. (Cobos 1983, 109)

Like many anthropologists, Angela García used the term Hispano in a recent *Cultural Anthropology* article (García 2008). In contrast, I eschew that term, although many anthropologists have favored it, as I rarely hear it in conversation and have found that some members of the population are actually unfamiliar with it. In other words, as there is no single correct popular term, there is no exclusively correct academic term either.

Like the northern New Mexicans that deploy multiple terms, I will follow suit and use the term that seems to best fit the particular sentence and its context. As a result, I will use terms such as Latino, Chicano, Hispanic, New Mexican, and northern New Mexican to refer to the same population. In contexts where other terms do not seem to be a better fit, I use the Spanish-language regional identifier *nuevomexicano* that parallels the Texas Mexican identification tejano. I choose this term simply because, I believe, all members of the population it describes know and understand it, and I have never heard anybody object to being called Nuevomexicano. I will also tend to avoid some terms like Spanish, Spanish American, or Hispano. In common usage, the self-identification of Spanish and Spanish American is in decline and is largely being replaced by the less controversial term Hispanic that also fits better with national identification/assignment. Through the notion of negativity, this book will explore the multiplicity and proliferation of these terms as well as their transformations. As is appropriate when speaking of the negative, rather than attempt to simply assert a more perfect description, I will instead explore the complexity of its implications. Also particularly pertinent to this project are popular discussions of negative representations.

Focusing on the Negative

In the course of my ethnographic study, many people told me that they were pleased by my interest in the communities' social problems. Others worried about the potential "negative" depictions of their hometown. Along these lines, the vernacular usage of "the negative" is a particularly loaded description of one aspect of my time in Española, the year I spent working as a reporter for the *Rio Grande Sun*. The newspaper's longtime owner, Robert E. Trapp, and the managing editor, Robert Braiden Trapp, are often accused of "focusing on the negative." In particular, community leaders who accuse these editors of overlooking the "positive" often state this view. In this sense, my ethnographic writing could be subject to the same criticism. Nevertheless, I am encouraged by Theodor Adorno's view that the popular praising of those who are "positive" is a fetish of the Hegelian notion of the positive-in-itself. In this sense, focusing on the negative is a refusal to sanction things as they are (Adorno 1973, 159). This book's focus is thus intended to both evoke and employ a certain oppositional politics. Citations of the negative are an incitement to negate blockages and closures and assert an openness and affirmation that resist the violence and denial required to sustain the very real processes of domination.

ACKNOWLEDGMENTS

I am indebted to many people and institutions for assistance in the various stages of this project. My first thanks must go to the people of north central New Mexico who often took me under their wing and sometimes challenged me. This project is my effort to work through their diverse and often-profound lessons. Because of the sensitive nature of my research, many of the people who played an important role cannot be named. Of those who can, I owe a special thanks to Teresa Archuleta, James Espinoza, Angel Espinoza, John Garland, Fr. Julio Gonzales, Michael Trujillo, and Beth Velásquez. Teresa in particular has opened her home and heart. She is a relative of mine, although a very distant one, and I hope this work has begun to do her life and art justice.

I am particularly grateful to the University of Texas at Austin and UT's Department of Anthropology for their generous support of my academic preparation, research, and writing. A 2001–2 UT Thematic Fellowship and University Federal Credit Union Fellowship were instrumental in the funding of my initial field research. Key sections of this text were written when I was as an assistant professor of honors and anthropology at the University of Oklahoma, a Riley Fellow and visiting assistant professor at Colorado College, and when I was an Ethel-Jane Westfeldt Bunting Fellow at the School of American Research (SAR) in Santa Fe, New Mexico. During 2002 and 2003, I was a member of a team in a New Mexico Department of Health-funded ethnographic study. Over the course of my time in Española, other institutions played an important role in my intellectual development. I was employed at the local newspaper, the *Rio Grande Sun*; at the University of New Mexico at Los Alamos (UNMLA); and at the Hoy Recovery Program.

At UNMLA, Carlos Ramírez and Juanita Jabbanema encouraged me in the tough, early days of this project. The *Rio Grande Sun*'s Robert E. Trapp and Robert Braiden Trapp taught me to see Española with the critical eye of a journalist. At the Hoy Recovery Program, my employers, Sherrijean Padilla, John Garland, and Ben Tafoya, exemplified integrity and empathy. Cathleen E. Willging and Howard Waitzkin showed me how to study drug use with both a deep sense of understanding and academic rigor.

Colorado College folklorist and anthropologist Mario Montaño mentored me in through the completion of my doctorate and the start of my teaching career. Also at CC, Claire García, Anne Hyde, Victor Nelson-Cisneros, and Sarah Hautzinger provided support and welcomed me into the college's community of scholars. The SAR's Nancy Owen Lewis provided insight at a crucial time in my dissertation's development. At the University of Oklahoma, conversations with Randolph Lewis and Sarah Tracy were particularly influential. At UT, Richard Flores, Kathleen Stewart, Pauline Turner Strong, and Martha Menchaca taught me to be an anthropologist and cultural critic, and to them I will always be grateful. José E. Limón supervised my dissertation and deserves my profoundest gratitude for shepherding me through this process of becoming an academic. He pointed the way to American studies and showed me how to be a scholar. I continue to be inspired by his work.

I completed this book as an assistant professor of American Studies and Chicano/Hispano/Mexicano Studies at the University of New Mexico. In Albuquerque and over the past several years, conversations with a fine group of Chicana/o and New Mexico scholars, including first and foremost Enrique Lamadrid, Gabriel Meléndez, and Sylvia Rodríguez, as well as Jennifer Alvarez, James Brooks, Robert Con Davis Undiano, Miguel Gandert, Manuel García y Griego, Peter García, Felipe Gonzales, Sarah Horton, Troy Lovata, Ann Massman, Anna Nogar, Genaro Padilla, Laura Padilla, Estevan Rael-Gálvez, Tey Marianna Nunn, Tey Diana Rebolledo, Brenda Romero, and María Varela among others. Gandert and Teresa Archuleta kindly allowed me to include images of their art in this text. The University of Texas Benson Latin American Collection's Margo Gutiérrez and Museum of International Folk Art librarian Ree Mobley have been very helpful. Comments by Gabriel Meléndez and Ben Chappell were critical to the completion of this text. In UNM's American Studies Department, I am particularly fortunate to work with a committed and diverse group of scholars, including Alex Lubin, Amy Brandzel, Alyosha Goldstein, Laura Gómez, Laura Hall, Vera Norwood, Rebecca Schreiber, and Gerald Vizenor. Among my best and most valuable teachers have been my students at the University of New Mexico, the University of Oklahoma, and Colorado College. My editor, Lisa Pacheco, shepherded this manuscript to completion.

My family has supported me throughout my life and work and was often working on this project with me in spirit. My uncle, Manuel Ferran, and aunts, Sister Carmela Trujillo and Cleo Ulibarrí, deserve my great gratitude for the kindness they have shown me over the years. I must also thank my wife and partner, Ronda Brulotte. She has read parts of this text countless times, showing great patience, and this project could not have been completed without her. Finally, I could not have done any of this without the years of guidance and tremendous patience of my parents, Gladiola Eleanor Trujillo and Gregory Trujillo. It is a great joy for me that my father read many of this book's essays and offered his thoughts and insights. His counsel and example were precious gifts. They have shaped me in ways I am only now, in his absence, beginning to fully understand. It is to him that this book is dedicated.

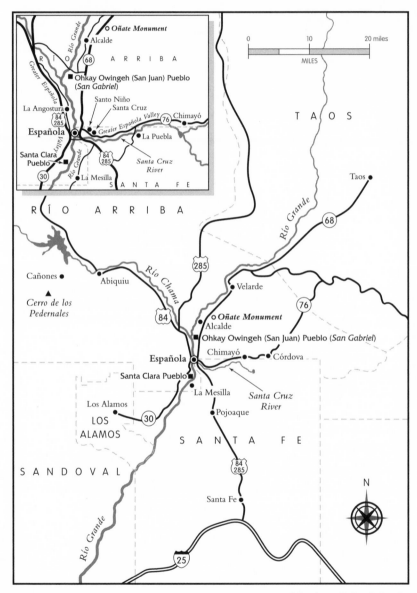

Map by © Deborah Reade

INTRODUCTION

He was born with a gift of laughter
and a sense that the world was mad.
And that was all his patrimony

—Rafael Sabatini, *Scaramouche: A Romance of the French Revolution*

G. Benito Córdova's book, *The 3½ Cultures of Española*, speaks to the ethnic jokes that people tell about the author's primarily Latino hometown. He suggests such seeming ridicule may sometimes be a strategy instigated by "insidious" Española Valley residents seeking to repel the forces of gentrification that have ruined neighboring cities for many Nuevomexicanos (88). With apparent irony and perhaps a gleam in his eye, such an ironic joke-teller might ask, "Who discovered Española?" This question addresses the fact that this was the first site of Spanish colonial settlement in the current Southwest of the United States: in 1598, don Juan de Oñate led a group of approximately 500 colonists, including 129 soldiers, into what would become the Española Valley.[1] Today, surrounded by the art-tourism centers of Santa Fe and Taos and the high-tech laboratory town of Los Alamos, the Española Valley is largely populated by descendants from the Spanish and Mexican periods of settlement. As will become apparent throughout this book, Española and Oñate's descendants occupy a key place in anthropological and folkloric study.

This joke cites a different figure from don Juan de Oñate as Española's founder. The answer is, of course, Marco Cholo—apparently, the New Mexican cousin of the famous Italian explorer of the Orient. In this punch line, this joke teller addresses Española's special status in northern New Mexico's discursive geography. For those who do not know, cholo is a Latin American term long used for indigenous people who are partially acculturated to the dominant Spanish-speaking culture. In the United States, cholo is an often-used (and sometimes derogatory) term for a particular working-class Chicano style (stereo)typified in its male variant by closely cropped hair, tattoos, and slang.[2] In northern New Mexico, cholo refers to a part Nuevomexicano, part mainstream American, but an entirely shifty way of being that is considered somehow illicit and menacing by those passing through Española and other working-class Latino areas on their way home to neighboring communities. Much like the cholo who supposedly discovered Española, the valley's social geography must be viewed as shifting and contradictory, and like cholos, Española, as almost all New Mexicans know, has a questionable reputation in the larger social milieu. Nevertheless, by virtue of the valley's location between the art-tourism Meccas of Santa Fe and Taos,

Billboard in Arroyo Seco. An Española Valley Chamber of Commerce billboard trumpets the Española Valley just before you enter the area from the south. *Photo by author.*

San Gabriel. A modest marker and cross mark the site of New Mexico's first capital. This site is located within the boundaries of Ohkay Owingeh Pueblo. *Photo by author.*

Española is centrally located in a regional discursive geography defined by state and popular discourses of the "Land of Enchantment." Thus, the valley is steeped in its Nuevomexicano roots and the romanticism that accompanies them. It should be no surprise that in such a place identity is complex in its multiplicity, silences, and contradictions.

The valley is also a place of suffering and tragedy. In particular, in the late 1990s a shocking series of newspaper articles and news stories in both the regional and national media described the area's high rates of death resulting from overdoses from illegal drugs. Indeed, Española's Rio Arriba County had the highest statistical rate of illicit drug overdoses of any county in New Mexico, with New Mexico in turn having the highest rate of illicit drug overdoses of any state (Morgan and Morgan 2002, 172, 176, 184–85, 187–88). In other words, Española is a place where discourses of tradition and the most painful aspects of modernity seem to intermingle, boil, and saturate the landscape.

In this experimental monograph, I explore the qualities of Española that imbue a subversive humor into Marco Cholo's supposed discovery of it. This exploration is premised on Mary Douglas's contention that a joke is a play upon form that brings into relation disparate elements. This play subverts each by presenting an alternative element hidden in the other (Douglas 1968, 366). Along these lines, I suggest that Española is, in part, the object of jokes because it represents the negative hidden within and necessitated by positive narratives of New Mexico as the "Land of Enchantment."[3] In each of this book's chapters, I will explore the dialectical construction of narratives of Española and New Mexico. My goal is to present a vision of Española that encompasses both the positive and negative, thus using dialectical tension to enter their implicit critique and employ certain oppositional politics. I will heed the calls of cultural critics such as Slavoj Žižek, Diana Coole, Gaspar Martínez, and Michael Taussig, who tell us to tarry with the negative and, thus, privilege the condition of struggle and pain that pushes plainly to the surface between Santa Fe and Taos's more recently painted and safely contained geographies (Coole 2000; Martínez 2001; Taussig 2004, 2006; Žižek 1993). This, I believe, is the subversive power that may be found in the ironic tellings of the Española joke. Before I delve into negativity, however, I will first briefly describe the positive narratives of enchantment that serve as Marco Cholo's straight man.

The Land of Enchantment

Premised on the notion of Native American-Latino-Anglo "tricultural harmony," the popular conceptualization of New Mexico as the "Land of Enchantment" powerfully fuses race, landscape, architecture, and food into romance and commodity (Lomelí, Sorell, and Padilla 2002; Rodríguez 2003). Precursors may be found in the late nineteenth-century writings of Charles Lummis (Gutiérrez 2002). In New Mexico, Lummis found a primitive, primordial place that compared favorably to both the Orient and the "heart of Africa" (Lummis 1893; Gutiérrez 2002, 21). He wrote:

> Sun, silence, and adobe—that is New Mexico in three words. If a fourth were to be added, it need be only to clinch the three. It

is the Great American Mystery—the United States which is *no* United States. Here is the land of *poco tiempo*—the home of "Pretty Soon." Why hurry with the hurrying world? The "Pretty soon" of New Spain is better than the "Now! Now!" of the haggard States. The opiate sun soothes to rest, the adobe is made to lean against, the hush of day-long noon would not be broken. Let us not hasten—*mañana* will do. Better still *pasado mañana*. (Lummis 1893, 3)

A 1950s school textbook titled *New Mexico: Land of Enchantment* written by E. B. Mann and Fred E. Harvey pays special attention to the contributions and magical aspects of the state's landscapes and its "Indian," "Spanish," and Anglo population. They write the "Land of Enchantment" means "New Mexico—The state . . . which delights and charms our hearts and sense" (Mann and Harvey 1955, iv):

and so this book is the story of "The Land of Enchantment." It is a story partly of the past, partly of the present, partly of the future. It is not a complete story in any of those parts; it would take many books much larger than this to tell the complete story—and if this book is well written, it will make you want to read more of that story in the many, many books that are available. We hope it does; because the story of New Mexico is a fascinating story, as strange in parts as any fairy story, more exciting than a wild-West movie. The more you know about it, the better you will be able to understand the land and its people, the better you will be able to see and appreciate and profit from the great resources that are your heritage. (Mann and Harvey 1955, v)

The publication of such views has not diminished with time.

While the fantasy and condescending qualities of many of these works are apparent, the conceptualization of the valley in terms of the successive groups that have occupied it has some utility. Indeed, much of the valley's social geography may be understood within this vision. The Greater Española Valley is largely located within Rio Arriba County and is situated at the center of the Rio Arriba region of northern New Mexico and southern Colorado. This region has long maintained a concentrated and long-term resident Latino, Native American, and Anglo-American population.[4] Based on fieldwork completed in the mid-1960s, cultural geographer Lynn Rubright's thesis, "A Sequent Occupance of the Española Valley, New Mexico," outlines the historical and tricultural constitution of the valley as well as the historical evidence that can still be seen in the landscape.[5] Rubright states that she first became interested in the valley when she drove through and saw landscape elements that seemed to belong to past centuries. At the time of this first impression, she thought the valley seemed to exist in a small world of its own (Rubright 1967, vii–viii).

Despite the existence of the valley in the minds of most of northern New Mexico's residents and the reality of institutions such as the Española Valley School District and Española Valley Chamber of Commerce, the valley lacks any exact political or census designation. Rather the valley extends far beyond the limits of the city of Española and reaches from Española's Rio Arriba County into northern Santa Fe County. In terms of census data, the valley is perhaps best understood in terms of a collection of census units including the "Española, NM Urban Cluster," Ohkay Owingeh (San Juan Pueblo), and Santa Clara Pueblo.[6] Even this inclusive definition is problematic, though, as neighboring communities such as Pojoaque share similarities in terms of ethnic makeup.

As Rubright sees it, the valley extends north and south from the Rio Grande, to the east along the Rio Grande's Santa Cruz River to the village of Chimayó, and to the northwest up the Chama River toward the village of Abiquiú. The history of many valley communities dates to the Spanish and Mexican period of colonization, while the Native American pueblos of Ohkay Owingeh and Santa Clara are far older. Located just outside the valley are the more rural and isolated villages made famous by popular novels such as *The Milagro Beanfield War* and *Red Sky at Morning* and paintings by Georgia O'Keeffe. To the east rise the impressive Sangre de Cristo Mountains, and to the west are the Jemez Mountains. Today, the valley contains a diversity of residents including a large Native American population, an influential "Anglo" or "non-Hispanic" "white" minority, and an emerging Mexican immigrant community. Still, northern New Mexican Latinos remain the majority, control city and county politics, and are the most easily identified actors in the local social scene. Accordingly,

Santa Cruz. The seventeenth-century Iglesia de Santa Cruz de la Cañada is
the historic heart of the village of Santa Cruz. The village was one of the
most important settlements in colonial New Mexico and is now largely
surrounded by the city of Española. *Photo by author.*

the 2000 United States Census describes 84.4 percent of the 23,272
people who live within the "Española, NM Urban Cluster" as "Hispanic."
Similar to Española, the census counts 72.9 percent of the 41,190 people
who live in Rio Arriba County as "Hispanic" and another 13.9 percent
as "Native American" (United States Census Bureau 2005).

Many Española residents—especially politicians and members
of the valley's emerging middle class—assert a vision of the valley
that conforms to notions of tricultural harmony and the Land of
Enchantment. Many proponents of this view cite the evidence of
tradition—such as the Santuario de Chimayó, the small-scale farms
of Velarde, and adobe homes that dot the landscape—as proof that the
valley fits within this idealized vision of New Mexico. Española native
and then New Mexico Department of Health Secretary Alex Valdez
made the following statement to the visiting U.S. Senate Subcommittee
of the Committee on Appropriations. In 1999, the subcommittee met

in Española to discuss the valley's reputed drug problem and methods for combating it. In the face of such negative publicity, Valdez said:

> We are gathered here in Española, my hometown, where I was born and raised and where I have chosen to raise my family. I have always cherished my upbringing in the Valley with its grand vistas, wonderful culture and rich history. Anyone who enters the valley need only look to the Sangre de Cristo Mountains, with their snow caps, to our centuries old churches, to our Rio Grande River to understand what the Valley means to its inhabitants. (U.S. Congress. Senate. Committee on Appropriations. Subcommittee on Commerce, Justice, State, the Judiciary, and Related Agencies 1999, 65)

Next, Valdez slipped into the local brand of multiculturalism that elides the area's simmering conflict along ethnic and racial lines. He said:

> Throughout our history, many have been captivated by its beauty, people, and way of life and have elected to stay. We welcome all who come and who bring good will. New Mexico is known as the Land of Enchantment. When you look out upon this valley, it is a microcosm of all this State has to offer. (U.S. Congress. Senate. Committee on Appropriations. Subcommittee on Commerce, Justice, State, the Judiciary, and Related Agencies 1999, 65)

The Anti-Santa Fe

Despite such championing of the valley by politicians and civic boosters such as Valdez and the longtime mayor, Richard Lucero, Española remains off the well-beaten tourist path that runs from Santa Fe to Taos and, ironically, down Española's Riverside Drive. Unlike its neighboring communities, Española has not seen an influx of Anglo immigrants.[7] Española has instead become even more "Hispanic" in recent censuses, and the Española Valley School District's student population has become 90 percent Latino, as both Anglos and even Native Americans have found alternatives to the public school system.[8]

This marginalization in terms of tourism and Anglo immigration sets Española apart from other northern New Mexican communities and likely results from the fact that Española's working-class economy has constituted an accompanying social geography. On closer look, the cultural geographer Rubright saw a landscape "marred" by its mixture of cinder-block and stucco homes, vehicles, and the television antennas sprouting like "silver weeds" from roofs (Rubright 1967, 103). This thoroughly modern landscape is matched by a local economy that is similarly defined by regional and national economic processes. Area residents now form a large part of the secondary labor force in a segmented labor market for Los Alamos and Santa Fe and, in 2009, the burgeoning casino industry of Ohkay Owingeh, Santa Clara, and Tesuque pueblos (Kosek 2006, 228–54).

Furthermore, the area now conceptualized as the Española Valley did not become known by that name until the twentieth century, and, in many ways, the valley is the creation of modern and increasingly postmodern circumstances and the specifics of American socioeconomic penetration and development. In previous times, this area was more or less recognized as a loose conglomeration of agricultural villages and Native American pueblos under the ecclesiastical authority of the parish of Santa Cruz (Ellis 1980). Robert D. Shadow and Maria J. Rodríguez-Shadow describe the Spanish- and Mexican-era settlers of what would become the American Southwest as "an agrarian-based civil population of rancher-farmers, 'common' everyday men and women whose livelihood rested on exploiting family labor, raising livestock and tending crops" (Rodríguez-Shadow and Shadow 1994, 1998; Shadow and Rodríguez-Shadow 1997, 173).

In May 1846, the United States declared war on Mexico and proceeded to invade its southern neighbor in a war that would prove bloody and dramatically expand the boundaries of the United States. As part of that invasion, the U.S. Army arrived in Santa Fe on August 18, 1846, after a two-month trip over the Santa Fe Trail from Fort Leavenworth, Kansas (Weber 1982, 273). A few days before, New Mexico's governor, Manuel Armijo, judged the situation hopeless and abandoned all defenses. The invaders raised the American flag over the Santa Fe Governor's Palace, and Kearny announced the annexation of New Mexico. Many residents continued to fight the Americans, including a battle near the Española Valley community of Santa Cruz and another just to the north of Española Valley near the village of Embudo. American forces did not gain full control until January 1847 (Weber 1982, 275). After the 1848 signing of the Treaty of Guadalupe Hidalgo, New Mexico and the rest of Mexico's north became a part of the southwestern United States. Following the firm establishment of U.S. authority, much of northern New Mexico was appropriated from Mexican- and Spanish-era communities by the machinations of the government and land speculators (Ebright 1994). Ultimately, most of the land in Española's Rio Arriba County became federal and state lands, and much of the remainder now is reservation and private lands owned by Anglo-American ranchers and developers or seasonal homes for Anglo-American retirees and artists.

The city of Española's founding in the nineteenth century and growth in the twentieth are the result of two symbols of American economic and technological power. Española was founded in 1881 as a railroad stop on the Denver and Rio Grande Railway and has since served as the area's commercial center (Gjevre 1969).[9] In the second half of the twentieth century, Española became economically bound to the Los Alamos National Laboratory—the inventors of the atomic bomb (Kosek 2006, 228–75; Masco 2006). The valley has also become the labor source for the blue-collar and service-sector elements of Los Alamos's thriving economy. I attribute the reconceptualization of the area as the Española Valley to the rise of the city of Española, the 1950s founding of the area's weekly newspaper, the *Rio Grande Sun*, the creation of the Española Valley School District in the 1960s, and the consolidation of Española High School and Santa Cruz High School into Española Valley High School in the 1970s.[10]

Today, driving on the highway into Española from the south, the town first appears to be a collection of fast-food restaurants, hotels, gas stations, and both adobe and mobile homes. Few tourists stop in Española proper as they do in the Native American pueblos and Latino weaving village of Chimayó.[11] On the highway to Taos, Española is dominated by a Wal-Mart Supercenter, Lowe's home improvement center, the Dreamcatcher Cineplex, and two casinos, Santa Clara Pueblo and Ohkay Owingeh enterprises, respectively. In the city itself, much of the architecture bears a resemblance to the combination of aging commercial buildings and both professionally built and vernacular architecture common to many working-class barrios in the western United States. The recognizable hearts of the centuries-old villages with their predominately adobe architecture and Native American pueblos are off the highway.

This thoroughly modern landscape is matched by a local economy that is similarly defined by regional and national economic processes. Most area Latinos' income comes from the government, service, and retail sectors. According to figures for 1997, only 982 people in Rio Arriba County were in farm employment compared to 12,719 people who were employed in other jobs (Bureau of Economic Analysis 1999). Of those 2,159 were employed in retail trade, 4,725 were employed in service jobs, and 3,028 were employed in the government or government enterprises (Bureau of Economic Analysis 1999). I cite these figures cautiously because I suspect that in a place where people must often patch together a living from various sources of income, the actual contribution and need for agricultural income and subsistence as well as forest resources are underestimated.[12] I believe, however, that the larger lesson holds true: the traditional economy of agriculture, ranching, and the collection of forest products has been superseded. Today, area residents form the labor force for the state and federal governments and tourist and recreation industries.

Moreover, this economy has often provided an uneven living for the Española Valley's population. For many, the day-to-day effort to cobble together a living is a constant struggle. Some area families make ends meet through a precarious combination of wage labor in Los Alamos or Santa Fe, government support, small-scale agriculture, and the harvesting of forest resources. According to the 1990 census, the annual per capita income of people of "Hispanic origin" in Rio Arriba County was $7,496, compared to a national average of $15,687 for "whites" not of Hispanic origin and $8,400 for Hispanics. Indeed, Rio Arriba County is among the poorest counties in New Mexico, and New Mexico maintains some of the worst poverty rates in the United States (Dalaker 1999; United States Census Bureau 2000).[13]

The present social and economic geography of the Española/Los

Alamos/Santa Fe economy represents a regional variant of a broader pattern of ethnically/racially segmented labor/geographies comparable to other so-called postmodern aggregates such as Los Angeles, Palo Alto, and Austin/San Antonio. Key to this analysis is the fact that the United States is the wealthiest country in the world and at the same time the nation-state with the greatest economic inequality between the rich and poor and the most disproportionate wealth distribution of all so-called developed countries, as evidenced by the differences between contiguous neighborhoods and neighboring towns. Indeed, Víctor Valle and Rodolfo Torres's descriptions of Los Angeles in their book *Latino Metropolis* often reads disconcertingly like descriptions of Española/Los Alamos/Santa Fe. On second thought, such commonalities should not be surprising. Northern New Mexicans have a long history of immigration and, sometimes, return to and from California that is similar to that of Mexican nationals.[14]

Interestingly, the valley is also known for the local retooling of one American icon, the car, into a symbol of Latino identity, the lowrider. Over the last three decades, the modified cars have become inseparable from Española's wider reputation. The community is often called the lowrider capital of the world. Brenda Jo Bright's 1998 article in *American Ethnologist* and a chapter in her widely cited dissertation, "Mexican American Low Riders: An Anthropological Approach to Popular Culture," focus on lowrider culture in the greater Española Valley community of Chimayó (Bright 1994, 1998). In the late 1990s and early 2000s, the Ohkay Casino in the pueblo of Ohkay Owingeh hosted a major lowrider show that attracted attendees from all over New Mexico and southern Colorado and featured major national music acts such as South Park Mexican. The show was prominently featured in the August 2001 issued of *Lowrider* magazine (Gilbert 2001, 105–6, 216–18).

In reference to the irrefutable realities of such a landscape, the recent Lonely Planet guide to Santa Fe and Taos succinctly describes Española as a sort of anti-Santa Fe (Penland 2004). Paige Penland, the guide's author, contrasts Española's seemingly authentic social milieu with the simulated adobe, art galleries, and expensive nouveau New Mexican cuisine of the popular tourist destination and artist colony to the south.[15] She states that in Española, the adobes are real and restaurants are "authentic and inexpensive." In reference to lowriders, she wrote that "masterpieces" are exhibited at "Sonic drive-ins rather than museums" (Penland 2004, 122). She further states:

> At the heart of the northern Rio Grande Valley, Española was designed for commerce, not postcards. Sure the setting is stunning, book ended by the Jemez Mountains and Truchas Peak, with the lush farms of the Rio Grande as a dramatic centerpiece but the city itself feels absolutely no need to gussy itself up for sightseers. (Penland 2004, 121–22)

A View of the Valley and Mountains. This picture looks down toward the city of Española's historic center. *Photo by author.*

The guide's author is not alone in her view of the valley. Some thirty years earlier, an academic writer confessed to a similar but more negative, in the popular sense, first reaction to Española. In the only anthropological monograph focused on Española proper, Spanish anthropologist Alfredo Jiménez Núñez's *Los hispanos de Nuevo México* made an initial critical assessment of Española as a field site. Jiménez wrote that although he soon discovered the enchantment of Española's people and the treasure of unforgettable friendships, "en estas primeras visitas la ciudad se me aparece fea, impersonal, carente de toda armonía. La comparación con Santa Fe o con esos pequeños pueblos cercanos a Española la hacen todavía menos atractiva" (on those first visits, the city appeared ugly, impersonal, lacking in all harmony. The comparison with Santa Fe and those small villages near Española made it even less attractive) (Jiménez Núñez 1974, 71). More recently, University of New Mexico anthropologist and Taos native Sylvia Rodríguez commented that "to the tourist gaze, Española is all class, lower class that is, and no culture, therefore invisible and uninteresting but slow to drive through, on the way from one site of greater attraction to the other."[16] She also rightly described Española's particular sociogeographic position as the working-class labor source for the wealthy and overwhelmingly Anglo Los Alamos. Along these lines, her comments suggest that Española's uniqueness in the northern New Mexican context rests on the relative ease of the perceived congruence of race-ethnicity (Nuevomexicano) and class (working class, underemployed, and unemployed) in the area's character.

While agreeing with the conditions that Rodríguez insightfully elaborated, I would prefer to emphasize that Española retains continuity with the remainder of the upper Rio Grande Valley. After all, if Española is the supposed geographic locus that marks the eruption of the haunting inverse of the northern New Mexican myth, there is a little bit of Española in every New Mexican community. Rodríguez's comments would seem to allow for this. Drawing on the work of Sherry Ortner (1998) and Karen Brodkin (1998), Rodríguez said that in New Mexico, as in the rest of the United States, discourses of ethnicity, race, and gender displace, submerge, and simultaneously fuse with those of class. In this vein, Rodríguez says that in the upper Rio Grande Valley, normative discourses of traditional Nuevomexicano culture such as honor-*respeto*, religion, family, and nation are not merely traditional Latino values. Instead, she says, they are also middle-class values. She contends that multiple social foils set the parameters for this construct. The specific foils she cites, the *surumato*, or undocumented Mexican worker; the *tecato*, or drug addict; the *borracho perdido*, or hopeless drunk; and the gang-banger represent lower-class embodiments.[17] Thus, New Mexican Latinos are discursively divided into two groups: the normative (often corresponding to the emergent middle class) and the deviant (often corresponding to the emerging working-underemployed-unemployed class). Rodríguez's comments suggest continuity with broader regional and national Mexican American class/racial contestations that are often mapped divisions between the resident Mexican-descent population and immigrants (De Genova 2008; Durán 2007; Ochoa 2004; Vila 2000).

Ambivalent Laughter

Community leaders such as Alex Valdez continue to assert a vision that employs the imagery of the Land of Enchantment and tricultural harmony. It is the anxiety of this social contradiction that makes Española jokes so effective for both Anglos and a surprising number of Nuevomexicano joke tellers alike. In other words, it is the unmasking of the discursive overlay that makes Española jokes both amusing and, if told by working-class Chicanos themselves, potentially subversive. A 1984 *New York Times* story chronicled the nonironic form of the phenomenon and explicitly referenced the art of lowriding:

> These are always question-and-answer jokes. Few of them are nice and fewer still are free of an obvious anti-Hispanic bias. A printable sample: "How can you tell when it's winter in Española? When the fur on low rider dashboards grows longer," Printable, but ethnically hostile: "Why are low rider steering wheels so small? So you can drive them handcuffed." (Peterson 1984, A14)

In a 1985 paper, Museum of New Mexico curator Charlene Cerny developed a typology of the jokes that included the following categories:

sexual mores, the Española girl, stupidity/ignorance/lack of sophistication or education, Española the town, crime in Española, and car culture/lowriders (Cerny 1985). In the 1980s and 1990s, the then mayor, Richard Lucero, launched a crusade against the jokes (Lenderman 2003a).

In the introduction to Córdova's book, *The 3½ Cultures of Española*, local writer and scholar Juan Estevan Arellano states that we will observe in Córdova's text "how intelligent, observant and astute these [Española Valley High School] students are. Nothing escapes their probing minds" (Córdova 1990, iv). As noted previously, though, Córdova's claims for Española are wider. Just like the swan of the "Ugly Duckling" folktale, Española is the object of ridicule for other than any internal failings. Instead, Española jokes reveal the ugliness of those who tell the jokes without irony and the world that makes such jokes possible. Córdova writes:

> The youngest, the weakest, and the ugliest of ducklings is always held
> in contempt, such as you, Española, are today being laughed at and
> held up to ridicule. And why is that so? Is it that like all underdogs,
> you Española, represent something that those who seek to keep
> you down lack? Do they fear that one day, Española, as king of the
> mountain, will expose them for what they are? (Córdova 1990, 79)

Córdova states that people from Española can and do laugh at themselves, but they are not the fools, or *pendejos*, that outsiders make them out to be. In seeming response to the *New York Times* joke that references lowrider steering wheels and supposed criminality, Córdova writes satirically:

> No attempt will be made to argue against the belief that the *Cholo*
> uses a small steering wheel, so that he can drive while handcuffed.
> But, it can be confirmed that a *Cholo*, who was hugging his *Chola*,
> while cruising through West Española was pulled over by an angry
> city policeman. Asked by the policeman why he did not use both
> hands, the *Cholo* answered that, he needed at least one hand to drive.
> (Córdova 1990, 46)

Perhaps most provocatively, Córdova asserts the centrality of Española's experience in his epigraph to the body of the book. He asks, "Have you ever wondered why the Messiah appeared at a backward, country town such as Española, and not at an enlightened, scientific center like Los Alamos?"

Américo Paredes saw similar intraethnic joking in south Texas during the 1960s (Paredes 1993). There, he found that some socially conscious members of south Texas's Mexican American middle class parodied members of their own ethnic/racial group. These joke tellers were impatient with the slow acculturation of the average Mexican American and his low economic and social status. Simultaneously, though, they strongly identified with the unacculturated Mexican who was the subject of their jokes (Paredes 1993, 60). It is this ambivalent attitude that is the source of the south Texas jokes' humor for some Mexican Americans.

Mary Douglas outlines a notion of jokes drawn from Sigmund Freud's *Jokes and Their Relation to the Unconscious* that is particularly pertinent to this discussion of Española jokes (Freud 1960; Douglas 1968, 361–76). Within this model, a joke is an image of the relaxation of conscious control in favor of the subconscious. Douglas states:

> As I see it, all jokes are expressive of the social situations in which
> they occur. The one social condition necessary for a joke to be
> enjoyed is that the social group in which it is received should
> develop the formal characteristics of a "told" joke: that is, a
> dominant pattern of relations is challenged by another. (Douglas
> 1968, 366)

As already mentioned, the ironic telling of the Española joke enacts a form of Mikhail Bakhtin's symbolic degradation and ambivalent laughter. This ironic telling is at the same time cheerful and annihilating. It brings down to earth lofty and often hegemonic values, ideas, and sentiments. Bakhtin writes:

> Alongside direct representation—laughing at living reality—there
> flourish parody and travesty of all high genres and of all lofty models
> embodied in national myth. The "absolute past" of gods, demigods,

and heroes is here, in parodies and even more so in travesties, "contemporized": it is brought low, represented on a plane equal with contemporary life, and in an everyday environment, in the low language of contemporaneity. (Bakhtin 1981, 21)

Returning to the Marco Cholo joke, if we know anything of this subversive founding figure, we know that he is not Santa Fe's mythic conquistador don Diego de Vargas or Los Alamos's physicist Robert Oppenheimer. Neither is he the figure with which some historians and most of Española's civic boosters would want us to identify as Española's founder, the conquistador don Juan de Oñate. Nor is the Española that Marco Cholo discovered located within the "Land of Enchantment," for here there is little or no "tricultural harmony." Marco Cholo and his Española instead subvert and threaten all the above.

In this sense, Marco Cholo suggests negation, resistance and transgression, absence and lack, and, thus, an opposition that is political in more than a linguistic sense. This is the source of the subversive nudge and wink I imagine the ironic telling of the joke. Specifically, each neighborhood in the Española Valley and throughout northern New Mexico exists on a continuum between Española and the more traditional villages that anthropologists and tourists so admire. In the popular conceptualization of Española, however, negativity emerges and saturates the landscape and—if we believe the theorists of negativity—disrupts the stabilizing, classifying logic of the positive.

Tarrying with the Negative

Among the great theorists of negativity are Georg Wilhelm Friedrich Hegel, Karl Marx, Georg Lukács, Maurice Merleau-Ponty, and Theodor Adorno. More recently, a number of intellectuals have tarried with the negative, among them, Slavoj Žižek, Judith Butler, and Michael Taussig.[18] In *Negativity and Politics*, Diana Coole argues that critical modern and poststructuralist discourses are all motivated by an ambiguous political opposition to the positive that lends all philosophies of negativity a radical political ethos (Coole 2000, 10–11):

The positive here refers to those institutions—language, subjectivity, metaphysics, positivist knowledge as well as mode of production, state structures, social stratifications, modern culture—that have become reified, ossified, totalized. The positive is the given; what has presence. As far as philosophers of negativity are concerned, the structures of modernity deny their own genesis and contingency in order to preserve themselves unchanged. (Coole 2000, 10)

A Conquistador on Riverside Drive. A man dressed in colonial-era garb rides in Española's 2004 Fiesta parade. *Photo by author.*

Española Parade Spectators. A family watches the 2004 Española
Fiesta parade. *Photo by author.*

To Coole's list of positive forms I would add the particular vision of a
Nuevomexicano Latino culture understood in terms of, among other
things, "Spanish foods," adobe construction, a particular agropastoral
economy, and the Spanish language. To invoke negativity is a political
intervention and performs a political act that destabilizes illusions of
perfection, presence, and permanence by associating the positive with
petrified and illegitimate structures of power (Coole 2000, 11–12). For
Adorno, negation is the refusal to accept the rules of the game in which
the dice are loaded (Adorno 1973, 159). Like all negativities, Española's
are located in the spacings, intervals, differences, gaps, and coincidences
with which the positive is riven. In the pages that follow, it will take the
form of a place where a statue's foot should have been, a body in the
path of a pilgrimage, narratives of drug use, supposedly unbelievable
embroideries, and a trickster tale.

In such places, the positive and negative, form and excess, reason
and its other, are imbricated. They meet, clash, and incite one another.
Here, negativity is a creative–destructive force that engenders as well as
ruins positive forms and is implicated in the positive. In this dialectical

view, positive and negative are interwoven: a thing is affirmed as what it is through denial of what that thing is not. It is articulated rather than defined, and it is not simply given but moves toward its potential as its relationships expand. That which it negates becomes an integral part of its identity. The other is, thus, other and not other. The thing is self and not self. In the negation of the negation, the alterity of the other is taken into the thing for itself. identity thereby emerges as a complex and dynamic unity, a differentiated, mediated phenomenon contingent on negativity.

The most sustained and perhaps the most confounding examination of negativity within the disciplinary boundaries of sociocultural anthropology is the work of Michael Taussig. Indeed, negativity may be considered central—if you may use such words as central in reference to Taussig's writings—to nearly all of Taussig's texts from 1983's *The Devil and Commodity Fetishism in South American* to 2004's *My Cocaine Museum* and 2006's *Walter Benjamin's Grave* (Taussig 1983, 2004, 2006). Perhaps most convincingly, in his second book, *Shamanism, Colonialism, and the Wild Man*, Taussig explores and textually performs a form of wildness that "white" or mestizo Colombians see in indigenous Colombians.[19] This wildness is at once liberating and horrible and is most definitely opposed to order and positivity (Taussig 1987). It is the spirit of the unknown and the disorderly that is loose in the forest encircling the city and the agricultural lands and disrupts the conventions upon which meaning and the shaping function of images rest. In the first half of the book, Taussig convincingly elaborates how white Colombians' vision of indigenous wildness was created in terrible and genocidal forms of oppression. In the second, healing section of this ethnography, Taussig shows that in colonizing myths of wild Indians, white Colombians project an antiself and uncover a healing power. In other words, Taussig finds that the colonizers reify their myths about the savage, become subject to their power, and thus seek salvation from the civilization that torments them as much as the "savage." Thus, the dialectic churns onward.

University of New Mexico folklorist Enrique Lamadrid's *Hermanitos Comanchitos: Indo-Hispano Rituals of Captivity and Redemption* explores Nuevomexicanos' confrontation with native ancestry and neighbors in similar terms (Lamadrid 2003). He approaches these topics through a "ritual complex" of historical and present New Mexican and Pueblo folkloric forms, including ceremonial dances, Nativity plays, and folk dramas. The strongest moments in Lamadrid's text mark New Mexican Latinos' confrontations with their own Native American ancestry, understood here as Comanche others and Comanche selves. In the context of the Nativity plays, he states that paying homage to the Christ Child is commonplace for a Christian, whether Indian, mestizo, or European. When a Comanche expresses similar homage, however, a special power and even more intense sanctity are evoked. Lamadrid states that this spiritual power of the savage stems from the redemption that emanates from defeat. He cites Taussig's contention that wildness is incessantly recruited and tamed to the needs of order so that it may serve as order's counterimage. In this same process of taming, though, wildness is infused with the difference, force, and autonomy that it requires to serve as order's opposition (Lamadrid 2003, 102; Taussig 1987, 220). Lamadrid shows that this power of negativity lends strength and blessings to the spirit and is particularly efficacious in restoring health.

Taussig's most concentrated focus on negativity, *Defacement: Public Secrecy and the Labor of the Negative*, is perhaps even more pertinent for my ethnographic project (Taussig 1999). Relying on a notion of negativity that owes as much to Friedrich Nietzsche as to the Frankfurt School, Taussig explores what happens when something sacred is defaced. He finds that defacement imbues the sacred with its power. He shows us that defacement works on objects the way jokes work on language, bringing out their inherent magic, and nowhere more so than when those objects have become routinized and social, like money or the nation's flag in secular societies (Taussig 1999, 5). Taussig found that when the human body, a flag, or statue is defaced, a surplus of negative energy is aroused within the defaced thing itself. He said that the resulting desecration is the closest thing that many of us will come to the sacred in the modern world (Taussig 1999, 1). In passages such as these, Taussig tells the reader that defacement is like enlightenment because it brings insides outside, unearths knowledge, and reveals mystery. As it does this, defacement also spoliates and tears; it animates the thing defaced, and the mystery revealed may become more powerful (Taussig 1999, 3–4).

In this monograph, I will similarly explore negativity, although in a somewhat more traditional essay format than does Taussig. The starting point I wish to convey is that I am as interested in Marco Cholo's Española as don Juan de Oñate's, and when I discuss Oñate, it will always be in reference to Marco Cholo and the other forms of negativity that he implies. This is a difficult task, as I cannot explicitly dissect negativity. To ask what something "is" or what something "means" is already to find oneself implicated in the questions and paradoxes negativity provokes. In this sense, negativity bears connotations of alterity, the nonrational, and unrepresentable. It is, in my view, a structure of feeling, in Raymond Williams's sense, that exists in tension with a formal system of signs (Williams 1977, 128–35). To name negativity renders it positive, ideal, and thus destroys it at the very moment of its apparent success. To place it within the specific realm of language destroys its generative power. My dual strategy is instead to evoke it through the choice of topics and in the discursive and performative aspects of this ethnography. In this task, I am encouraged by Diana Coole's admission of similar difficulty. She states, "I have found myself groping for words or phrases where none is adequate, yet persevering because negativity is not nothing" (Coole 2000, 2).

Modernist Ethnography

This ethnography is written as a series of essays, a form designed to address such complex and often-indefinable subjects. George Marcus and Michael Fischer have termed this once-radical and now reasonably common style "modernist ethnography" (Marcus 1998, 1999; Marcus and Fischer 1986; Rabinow and Marcus 2008). It is perhaps best exemplified by the works of Michael Taussig (2006, 2004, 1999, 1987, 1983) and, perhaps, most radically represented in Kathleen Stewart's most recent work (2007). Much of the experimentation of this writing and ethnographic method lies in the revealing of the intertextual nature of contemporary ethnography, an intertexuality that includes reference to views of both the so-called observed and supposed observers (Marcus 1998, 197). This sort of ethnography is aware of the historical and contemporary connections that link it to the objects of its gaze and both makes revisions of the ethnographic archive and remains conscious of its complex intertextuality. In an unconventional passage, Taussig describes this as turning reality back on the writing. He writes a conversation between "reality" and "writing":

> "What have you learned?" the reality asks of the writing. "What remains as an excess that can't be assimilated and what are you going to do with the gift that I bestow, I who am such strange stuff?" (Taussig 2006, viii)

Indeed, Taussig finds these prior representations are an integral part of modernist ethnographic writing and fieldwork.[20] He sees that these previous, often-flawed interpretations are themselves also powerful tools (Taussig 2006, viii).

Marcus prescribes the "modern essay" as the appropriate textual mode for writing modernist ethnography (Limón 1994, 9–11; Marcus and Fischer 1986, 191–92). The essayist writes from a rhetorical position of profound half understanding and half bewilderment with the world in which both the ethnographer and his or her subject live (Marcus and Fischer 1986, 192). Such ethnography remakes and re-presents other representations and resists the desire to unmask or defrock some larger or deeper truth (Taussig 2006, x). Marcus suggests that this form of ethnographic writing is well suited to a time and place when paradigms are in disarray, problems intractable, and phenomena are only partly understood. As Taussig writes:

> It goes like this: reality is a shell game; our writing should be too. For a moment they interlock, but then a new pattern of ordered disorder forms, always the one before the last . . . (Taussig 2006, xi)

In this skeptical vein, an Española drug user named, for the purposes of this ethnography, Joey Jaramillo told me to believe nothing of what I hear and only half of what I see.[21]

This Ethnography

The remainder of this text is divided into two sections and an interchapter that focus on both my original ethnography and previous ethnographic representations and on Española residents' own cultural production. The first section contains three chapters that explore the notion of negativity through two acts that deconstructed positive visions of the valley and narratives surrounding specific forms of embodied negation. Chapter 1 examines an act of monumental vandalism that was of enormous symbolic importance in the Española Valley and captured the imagination of the national media: the 1998 desecration of a statue devoted to don Juan de Oñate near the Española Valley village of Alcalde. The second chapter investigates the 2000 murder of two area youths as they walked in the annual Good Friday pilgrimage. Both these acts, the second in a truly horrible way, clearly evoked the surplus of negative energy that Taussig so cleverly described and performed in *Defacement*. The third chapter investigates current drug use in the Española Valley and demonstrates that the high of heroin or crack cocaine may itself be understood as a visceral, embodied form of negativity. In Española drug users' descriptions of their experiences, I find a powerful, open, and sometimes terrifying overcoming of social and economic contradictions, an overcoming that embraces the most horrible power of negativity.

The interchapter contains a single essay that examines previous anthropological and cultural analysis of the Española Valley. This essay explores the ethnographic writings of two cohorts of anthropologists who both conducted fieldwork in the Española area in the 1960s and 1970s. The interchapter first focuses on the ethnography of Paul Kutsche, John R. Van Ness, and Charles Briggs in the Rio Arriba County villages of Cañones and Córdova and second on the largely overlooked work of University of Oklahoma anthropologist Joseph Whitecotton, his student Stewart Ellis, and Spaniard Alfredo Jiménez Núñez in the semiurban Española Valley proper. In this chapter, I contend that the village ethnographers' focus on positive forms, in both the dialectical and popular sense, elided the more complex and often-emergent forms of Nuevomexicano identity—forms that may be characterized in terms of negativity. Ultimately, their efforts to describe New Mexican identity are incomplete, and the most popular works often produced a stifling positivity.

The second section of this book plumbs local residents' efforts to represent the valley and themselves. The fifth chapter reaches back into time to the 1920s and 1930s through the embroidery of Española Valley native Policarpio Valencia. This artist worked at the time of the city of Española's consolidation as the area's commercial center. Born shortly after the end of the Mexican American War and living until the Great Depression, Valencia experienced both the incorporation of New Mexico into the national economic and social infrastructure of the United States and the rise of the railroad town and commercial center of Española. The sixth chapter examines both the life and writings of author Jim Sagel and his love for a New Mexican woman, artist Teresa Archuleta. Throughout Sagel's work, one sees a repetition of positive and negative oppositions such as Anglo versus Chicano, masculine versus feminine, and wholeness versus alienation. Moreover, in the landscape that surrounded him, Sagel experienced moments where these dialectical oppositions were momentarily unified and others where their contradictions were laid bare. The seventh and final chapter will focus on the fictional ethnography *Big Dreams and Dark Secrets in Chimayó* by scholar and Española resident G. Benito Córdova. In this novel, Córdova confronts issues of alcohol and drug addictions. It is also a trickster tale that levels a profound critique of American society and calls Nuevomexicanos to become the agents of their own history.

Ultimately, I do not intend this text to be a better or more accurate representation of Española in the common understanding of ethnography. I instead use the notions of positive and negative to constitute a social and anthropological commentary on aspects of Latino identity, which are themselves too complex to be fully represented in any text. I take exception to classic norms of comprehensive holism, even as I seek to paint a picture that is somehow more whole than previous ethnographies. Moreover, as will also probably become apparent, the dialectical use of the philosophical and semiotic notions of the positive and negative appeals to my somewhat modernist, Marxist or at least neo-Marxist, perhaps Roman Catholic aesthetic: I find something sublime and fulfilling in their juxtaposition.

CHAPTER ONE

Remembering and Dismembering

Viva Oñate. ¡Viva!
Viva la historia de ese gran señor.

—Ángel Espinoza and James Espinoza, "El Corrido de Don Juan de Oñate"

Long live Oñate. Long may he live!
Long live the history of this great man.

(My translation)

We cut his foot off on the darkest, coldest night of the year.

—The Friends of Acoma, in a message to the *Albuquerque Journal*, 1998ᴌ

Michael Taussig writes that when the human body or a public statue is defaced, a surplus of negative energy is aroused within the defaced thing itself. Such acts cut into the circle of understanding, and out of the breach spills a contagious, proliferating force (Taussig 1999, 1). This chapter uses Taussig's insights to examine an act of monumental dismemberment. During the final days of 1997 or the first days of 1998, some people—it required more than one—drove toward the Oñate Monument and Visitors Center just north of the town of Española, New Mexico. The chilling air of a northern New Mexican winter night must have bitten them as they removed the power equipment from their vehicle somewhere along the side of Highway 68. They planned well. The state trooper who lived in the neighboring mobile home was out of town, and there was no one watching over the seemingly deserted center. They must have stood among the timbers that served as pillars for the monument and looked at the larger-than-life bronze statue of New Mexico's first Spanish colonial governor. Perhaps after a few moments of hesitation, if any, they began to cut off Oñate's right foot. Early the next morning, they sent a message and a photo of the amputated foot to the *Albuquerque Journal*'s northern bureau in Santa Fe. The statue cutters were never caught, and the foot was never found.[1]

This chapter explores the crisis the foot cutting provoked and thus enters the complex realm of Nuevomexicanos' embodied ethnic/racial identity. Among Nuevomexicanos, divergent ethnic/racial identities such as Hispanic, Chicano, and Spanish compete and contest with one another (Gonzales 1993). Such battles are not exclusive to New Mexico, as notions of race and racial mixture play a dominant role in discussions of Latin American and U.S. Latino identity and culture. The Oñate icon's Spanish body is a similarly hotly contested site of signification. This chapter's arguments are informed by three mysterious messages sent to New Mexico newspapers by the person or persons claiming to represent the statue vandals (Calloway 1998; Larry Calloway, personal communication with author, 1999; *Santa Fe Reporter* 1998). I conclude that in his dismembered state, Oñate is an "open" icon that dynamically and provocatively represents the complexities and contradictions of New Mexican Chicana/o or Hispanic identity.

Moreover, the implications of this essay are not limited to New Mexico. In both Latin American and Chicana/o literature and popular culture, the mixed race or mestizo body is a site of contestation that both signifies and incarnates the multiple forces at play upon and within it (Lima 2007; Pérez-Torres 2006). The identity politics of the national Chicano movement of the 1960s and 1970s and much of the energy of Chicana/o studies today may be understood as an effort to counter such broad-based views and investigate these fraught and interpenetrating identities. In the current moment, the controversy surrounding the recent installation of a larger statue in El Paso, Texas, has garnered national attention and a nationally televised documentary (Pérez and Ortega 2008; *The Last Conquistador* 2008; Hendricks 2009). Michigan State University professor Sheila Marie Contreras recently chronicled the fraught relationship between Chicana/o literature and anthropological and Mexican national discourses on race and hybridity. She writes that her own Chicana/o students often expressed such tensions. She writes, "An anecdote a student once told in class sums it up brilliantly: After being the last one in the family served dinner, her father asks with indignation, *'Qué soy, indio o qué?'"* (Contreras 2008, 77). With such comments in mind, this chapter begins by narrating the events of 1598 and 1998 that the statue's dismemberment so profoundly collapses.

The *Cuartocentenario*

In 1598, don Juan de Oñate led a group of approximately 500 colonists, including 129 soldiers, into what would become the Española Valley. His expedition included Spaniards, other Europeans, mestizos, and indigenous peoples from what was then New Spain. Upon their arrival, the colonists occupied the current pueblo of Ohkay Owingeh and then founded a capital called San Gabriel across the Rio Grande (Barrett 2002, 47; Kraemer 2006, 80–81; Simmons 1993, 111, 117; Hendricks 2009). Four hundred years later, Ohkay Owingeh is located north of the city of Española and just several miles west of the Oñate Monument and Visitors Center.

In 1998, the commemoration of the founding of the Spanish colony of New Mexico aroused great excitement and often focused on the conquistador. A man dressed in colonial-era Spanish costume emulated Oñate's expedition by walking from Zacatecas, Mexico, to Española, and the song "El Corrido de Don Juan de Oñate," by Española-based musician Ángel Espinoza, was prominently featured on radio stations such as Española's bilingual KDCE (pronounced ¿Qué dice?). Riding the wave of her Oñate corrido, Espinoza had a good year. She won eight awards at the 1998 Hispano Music Awards, held fifteen miles south of Española at Tesuque Pueblo's Camel Rock Casino. With reference to Española's annual fiesta or festival, which crowns a community member as Oñate, Espinoza sang:

> Y cada año celebramos nuestra herencia
> Y recordamos todos a Don Juan
> Y dedicamos nuestras fiestas en su nombre
> Y conservamos esta bella tradición.
> (Espinoza and Espinoza 1996)

Every year we celebrate our heritage
Everybody remembers don Juan
We dedicate our fiestas in his name
And preserve this beautiful tradition.
(My translation)

Statues such as the one near Española also played a central role in the cuartocentenario, the four-hundredth anniversary of Oñate's arrival in New Mexico and the advent of Spanish colonization. A similar statue was planned further south in Albuquerque (Friese 2007; Gonzales 2007). A lawyer and Oñate descendant from Madrid, Spain, Manuel Gullón de Oñate, was flown in to unveil yet another bronze statue near Santa Fe. Finally, inspired by the anniversary, a massive three-story statue of Oñate was planned for El Paso, Texas.

Partly in anticipation of the anniversary, the Oñate Monument and Visitors Center opened in the early 1990s near Ohkay Owingeh, featuring as its main attraction a monumental equestrian statue of Oñate by Albuquerque artist Sonny Rivera. Longtime state senator and New Mexico power broker Emilio Naranjo introduced a bill in the state legislature that proposed the center and statue. The legislature approved the bill, the county donated the land, and funding was appropriated through tax bonds, grants, and the Small Business Bureau (García 1998, 3). According to an Oñate center pamphlet from the mid-1990s, the statue cost $108,000, and the center's total cost was $1.5 million. Today, the center is largely funded by the Rio Arriba County Commission, and in 1998 Juan Estevan Arellano, a Nuevomexicano intellectual and artist, served as its director. In coordination with the county commissioners, he planned a series of events to commemorate the cuartocentenario. The founding of the Spanish colony of New Mexico was soon commemorated in a way neither Arellano nor the commissioners intended, however.

During the first week of January 1998, a reporter from the *Albuquerque Journal* called Arellano at the Oñate Center and asked if somebody had cut off the statue's foot. Arellano replied with a pun, "I think somebody is pulling your leg," because he had seen the statue intact the previous day (Arellano 1999).[2] Arellano told me, "When I

The don Juan de Oñate Monument and Visitors Center as it appeared in 1998. *Photo by author.*

looked from the building, believe me, it looked like nothing was wrong, but I might as well go all the way around to look at the sculpture. When I went, I saw right away [that the foot] was missing!" (Arellano 1999). That morning Larry Calloway of the *Albuquerque Journal*'s northern bureau in Santa Fe received a message in the mail, along with a photo of the amputated foot. The first message read:

> We invite you to visit the Oñate Distortion Museum and Visitor Center. Located eight miles north of Española. We took the liberty of removing Oñate's right foot on behalf of our brothers and sisters of Acoma Pueblo. This was done in commemoration of his 400th year anniversary acknowledging his unasked for exploration of our land. We will be melting his foot down and casting small medallions to be sold to those who are historically ignorant.

With cutting wit, the repressed memory of the Native Americans killed and oppressed in the process of colonization returned to haunt the monument. Indeed, the amputation of the statue's foot caused great excitement and captured the most coverage of any cuartocentenario event. Arellano was soon fielding calls from the *Dallas Morning News*, *Los Angeles Times*, *New York Times*, *Christian Science Monitor*, *People* magazine, and Mexican and Spanish newspapers. Arellano says he was even interviewed live by a radio station in Madrid, Spain (Arellano 1999).

Yet the wit of the statue's dismemberment demands further explanation, and this essay seeks to acknowledge the exhortations of the statue cutters themselves. In their second message to the *Albuquerque Journal*, the Friends of Acoma wrote, "We see no glory in celebrating Oñate's fourth centennial and we do not want our faces rubbed in it. If you must speak of his expedition, speak the truth in *all* its entirety." In particular, they are referring to events that occurred in December 1598 and January 1599.

Skillful Reapers

During the first cold day of December 1598, a nephew of Oñate named Juan de Zaldívar and a small force of thirty-one men arrived at the base of the 357-foot-tall mesa that is the site of Acoma Pueblo (Gutiérrez 1991, 52–55; Knaut 1995, 38–40; Simmons 1993, 135). The stores of the colonists, on a quest for an outlet to the Pacific Ocean, had fallen short of what was required for the trip. Eight men, led by Capt. Gerónimo Márquez, visited Acoma Pueblo and demanded supplies (Knaut 1995, 39–40; McGeagh 1990, 34; Simmons 1993, 135–36; Villagrá 1992, 199–208). Although the Pueblos had judged the Spaniards' demands too great, the colonists nevertheless decided to enter the village. Leaving three men to guard the horses, Zaldívar and fourteen other colonists and several indigenous servants climbed the difficult trail to the village and eventually dispersed. When a soldier named Vivero stole two turkeys, a bird sacred to the Pueblos, and violated a Pueblo woman, Acoma's warriors attacked (Gutiérrez 1991, 53). Most of the Spaniards were killed; at the end of the brief battle, Zaldívar, two of his captains, eight soldiers, and two servants were dead.

Fearing the possibility of a widespread revolt, Oñate conducted judicial proceedings to decide the "just" course of action. Upon the court's verdict against the Pueblos' village, Oñate declared a "war by blood and fire" against the Pueblos at Acoma (McGeagh 1990, 35). On January 21, 1599, Juan de Zaldívar's younger brother, Vicente Zaldívar, led a force of seventy men armed with two cannons in an attack on the pueblo. In 1610 the battle was glorified as the finale of Gaspar Pérez de Villagrá's epic poem *Historia de la Nueva México* (Villagrá 1992, 215–302). In somewhat archaic Spanish, Villagrá painted a grisly scene:

No tienden, apañando, con más ayre
La corba hoz los diestros segadores
Quando apriessa añudan sobre el brazo
Vna y otra manada y assí, juntos,
Lebantan por mil partes sus gavillas,
Como estos bravos y altos combatientes,
Que, en vn grande ribazo tropezando
De cuerpos ya difuntos, no cessaban
De derramar apriessa grande suma
De fresca y roja sangre, con que estaba
Por vna y otra parte todo el muro
Bañado y sangrentado, sin que cosa
Quedase que teñida no estuviesse.
(Villagrá 1992, 267)

No skillful reapers do more swiftly wield
Their curving sickles, flashing rapidly,
Then they do quickly knot within their arms
One handful after other and do so
Set up their sheaves in a thousand places,
As these brave, haughty combatants
Who, stumbling upon a lofty mound
Of bodies now dead, never ceased
To shed apace a mighty sum

Of fresh red blood, by which the wall
Was everywhere, upon all sides,
Bathed and ensanguined, and nothing
Remained that was not sprent with it.
(Villagrá 1992, 267; translation by Miguel Encinas, Alfred Rodríguez,
and Joseph P. Sánchez)

In the hard-fought battle (some would call it a massacre), eight hundred
Pueblos were killed, no colonists died, and only a few colonists were
wounded (Knaut 1995, 45). The approximately five hundred surviving
Pueblos were taken prisoner and sent to San Juan, where they arrived on
February 9, 1599 (Knaut 1995, 45).

At San Juan, Oñate presided over a trial of the survivors; his
sentences for their supposed crime of rebellion and the murder of Juan
de Zaldívar, ten Spaniards, and two servants were stiff (Gutiérrez 1991,
53–54; Knaut 1995, 46; McGeagh 1990, 37; Simmons 1993, 144–46).
Oñate ruled the children younger than twelve to be free of guilt. He
placed the girls under the charge of fray Alonso Martínez and the boys
under the charge of Vicente de Zaldívar for a Christian upbringing.
Sixty of the small girls were later sent to Mexico City to be parceled
out among the convents. Women older than twelve were condemned
to twenty years of personal servitude. Young men between twelve and
twenty-five were sentenced to twenty-five years of personal servitude.
Two Hopis captured in the fight were sentenced to have their right
hands cut off and to be set free to take home news of their punishment.
Finally, the men older than twenty-five were sentenced to twenty-
five years of servitude and *to have a foot cut off*. According to Simmons,
twenty-four people suffered this punishment. For maximum effect and
as an example of the dangers of rebellion, this sentence was carried out
over several days in nearby pueblos.

In this way, the present act of vandalism evokes Oñate's brutal
sentence and a wider history, and the icon of a heroic Oñate is
deconstructed by both the statue cutters and the Native Americans
his soldiers long ago punished and killed. Moreover, the Acomas
proved more resilient than Oñate imagined. Within a year or two
most of them had escaped their servitude, fled back to the rock, and

rebuilt the pueblo (Simmons 1993, 146). Today, the village of Acoma endures, and this is a powerful counterpoint to positive assertions of colonization and progress.[3] As the foot cutters wrote in their second message to the *Albuquerque Journal*, "This land was ours long ago before the Conquistadors, Mexicans, or Anglos came here. We know the history of this place before their time and we have not forgotten it since their arrival." They proclaimed that, unlike the Oñate Center's director, they "are not taken in by Eurocentric history/thinking." They further elaborated on the ongoing significance of Oñate and used this icon to illustrate the wider brutality of colonization:

> From the beginning our goal has been about acknowledging the truth. We visited the museum three years ago. No one attempted to talk to us or show us around. The one brochure about Oñate said only to look at the positive aspects of his expedition. What about our culture, our way of life? His expedition destroyed it. Catholicism is not the end all of all religions. Who was forced to work the mines, forced to plant the crops, and forced to build the missions?

In another message to the *Santa Fe Reporter*, the Friends of Acoma wrote:

> New Mexico was poised for a grand celebration of the cuartocentenario and we could not let that happen without voicing our existence. Outside of "Indian art" and "gaming," we have become an invisible people, even to ourselves. Our Hispanic brothers have forgotten on whose land they dwell. We have been here for thousands of years and there was plenty to share, but they claimed it all in the name of some faceless King or God, claiming it as theirs. Our people had learned not to overpopulate, not to overuse the land. We lived within our needs. Since then, all newcomers have taken from us and told us what to believe and how to think. Many of our people have forgotten how to live. Our actions were to redirect the thinking of those who have forgotten us. (*Santa Fe Reporter* 1998)

This criticism of Oñate had begun even in his own time. Many of his colonists abandoned New Mexico because of its lack of precious metals, harsh climate, indigenous resistance, drought, and famine. In direct reference to Oñate, they often claimed he was selfish, power hungry, and an elusive manager of colonial affairs (Gutiérrez 1991, 54). The Franciscan missionaries charged that Oñate lived dishonorably and scandalously with married and unmarried women and was excessively harsh with indigenous peoples. His alleged excesses included extracting food and clothing through torture and allowing soldiers to abuse women. The viceroy ordered him to resign his governorship. He left New Mexico in 1610 (Simmons 1993, 184–85), and in 1614 the viceroy tried Oñate and found him guilty of excesses and abuses of his leadership. His crimes included unjustly hanging two Indians and using excessive force in putting down the Acoma rebellion (Simmons 1993, 188). Ultimately, Oñate was banned from New Mexico, and he died in Spain (Hendricks 2009, 104).

Awakening the Dead

From their statements, it would seem that the statue cutters believed the statue's supporters to be mere dupes deluded by a Eurocentric vision. Literary scholar Elizabeth Archuleta would seem to agree in her article about the Oñate controversy (Archuleta 2007). Frank G. Pérez and Carlos F. Ortega make a similar argument in a related article about the installation of a thirty-six-foot statue in El Paso, Texas (Pérez and Ortega 2008). Nevertheless, the significance of the Oñate icon in northern New Mexico for many Oñate supporters may, in part, be found in Nuevomexicanos' own experience as colonized and subjugated people.

Referring to another Southwest Borderlands location, Richard Flores's *Remembering the Alamo: Memory, Modernity, and the Master Symbol* explores the significance and meaning of San Antonio's Alamo as a symbol (Flores 2002). His analysis offers several lessons that are useful for our examination of the Oñate icon. On the one hand, the Alamo is both the location of an 1836 siege of Texan rebels by Mexican government army regulars and the site of the Texan defenders' deaths and the deaths of a much larger number of Mexican troops. Flores is more concerned, however, with the way the Alamo grew into an icon that shaped social relations between Anglos and Mexican Americans. Engaging the work of James Fernández, Terrence Turner, and Clifford Geertz, Flores shows that the symbolic is not merely reflective or passive. It is also assertive, and symbols, through practice and their association with metaphor, produce meaning and therefore shape social identities. Citing Geertz, Flores states that symbols are both "models of" and "models for" a social order (Flores 2002, 156; Geertz 1973).

Strongly influenced by critical theory, Flores finds support for his views in a work that precedes the writings of anthropologists. He cites Karl Marx's *The Eighteenth Brumaire of Louis Bonaparte* (Marx 1978). In this text, Marx notes that nineteenth-century revolutionaries and demagogues used Roman costumes and phrases to set up modern bourgeois society (Marx 1978, 595; Benjamin 1968, 261). Here, Marx uses the famous and apt metaphor that the tradition of dead generations weighs like a nightmare on the brain of the living. Similarly, symbols such as the Alamo and Oñate have more to do with current struggles than the times of their original referent. Marx wrote:

> The awakening of the dead in those revolutions therefore served
> the purpose of glorifying the new struggles, not of parodying the
> old, of magnifying the given task in imagination, not of taking flight
> from their solution in reality, of finding once more the spirit of
> revolution, not of making its ghost walk again. (Marx 1978, 596)

Along these lines, Flores shows that the Alamo was enshrined as a monument late in the nineteenth century and early twentieth century rather than in 1836. A parallel analysis of the Oñate statue may be made. The Oñate icon is also shaped by social relations and has more to do with the twentieth and twenty-first centuries than the colonial period.

New Mexico's George Washington

The desire for an Oñate icon follows from Nuevomexicanos' struggle to retain their community's integrity. Moreover, this nostalgia is constituted in a discursive field long dominated by Anglo America. Most Nuevomexicanos are painfully aware that the United States is imagined as an Anglo-American nation, that the American nation's history began with the *Mayflower*, and that Hispanics are people from south of the border. At the time of Oñate's dismemberment, invoking common Nuevomexicano surnames, Arellano told a journalist, "When we go to school, we are told that our ancestors came from the East. Well, I don't know of many Martinezes, Arellanos, or Archuletas who had any ancestors who landed at Plymouth Rock" (López 1998). In this way, the dominant American iconography of the frontier, pioneers, and westward expansion represses the reality of Chicano/Hispanic claims to the Southwest.

It should therefore be no surprise that Nuevomexicano discursive self-constructions often simultaneously oppose, mimic, and transform these Anglo-American nationalist narratives. Such a view, which asserts a Nuevomexicano Spanish identity, was honed in New Mexico's battle for statehood. New Mexico did not achieve statehood until 1912—one of the last two contiguous forty-eight states to do so—because of widespread suspicion of its "Mexican" population (Lamar 2000; Montgomery 2002). In opposition to such views, statehood boosters often asserted a Spanish identity that echoed the East's narrative of colonization. Charles Montgomery writes that one official, W. A. Fleming Jones, told his audience upon the occasion of Pres. William Howard Taft's 1909 visit that New Mexicans were not peons. Instead, he asserted that both Anglo and Hispanic New Mexicans partake in a history of which they may be proud. He told his audience, "Before a Saxon set foot in New England, Juan de Oñate had firmly established European civilization in Santa Fe" (Montgomery 2002, 76). In the midst of a similar debate over an Oñate monument in Albuquerque, Phillip Gonzales states that Nuevomexicano activists and Hispanophile historians such as Marc Simmons describe Oñate as New Mexico's George Washington (Gonzales 2007, 220–21). This comparison of

Oñate to America's founding figure contests assertions of Anglo-American primacy in the Southwest because Oñate's arrival predates that of the Anglo-American pioneers, the United States' independence, and even George Washington's birth (Gonzales 2000). Moreover, the assertion that Oñate is the so-called "father" of New Mexico raises a further question: who, then, is New Mexico's "mother"? Many believe that mother to have lived in Acoma or other places like it.

Borderlands Relations

In the Spanish colonial and Mexican era as well as the first years of U.S. control, New Mexico was interconnected through a vast array of reciprocal relationships and blood ties that reached beyond the zones of colonial or national control (Brooks 2002; Bustamante 1991; Rael-Gálvez, 2002). Chief among the binding forces was a slaving economy where native, Spanish colonial, and Mexican women and children were ransomed or purchased as war captives. In other words, innumerable Navajo, Comanche, Ute, Kiowa, Pueblo, and other native people were incorporated in Spanish colonial, Mexican, and American-era Hispanic New Mexico through warfare, kidnapping, servitude, adoption, ransom, and friendship. These processes created a population of Hispanicized native peoples termed *genízaros* (Córdova 1979, 52–59; Swadesh 1974, 214) and a truly hybrid society in both ancestral and cultural terms (Brooks 2002; Farago and Pierce 2006; Rael-Gálvez 2002). Ramón Gutiérrez states that colonial New Mexico village populations contained three groups: a large number of landed peasants of mestizo origin, a nobility that consisted of fifteen to twenty families that intermarried, and detribalized native peoples called genízaros (Gutiérrez 2003, 8–9). By one estimate, genízaros were a third of New Mexico's population in 1776 (Córdova 1979, 59; Schroeder 1972, 62).

In his article, "'The Matter was Never Resolved': The Casta System of Colonial New Mexico," Adrián Bustamante illustrates New Mexicans' descent from a diverse colonial population, in both ethnic and racial terms (Bustamante 1991). The article describes a colonial society of complex *castas*, in which only a limited portion of the population called itself *español*, or Spanish. Others, eager to move up the prestige ladder, assumed the racial/ethnic status of those above them. According to Bustamante's description, only part of the population could legitimately belong to the higher rungs of the ethnic/racial ladder in interior Mexico, much less pass for Spanish in Spain. This valorization of European rather than indigenous ancestry did not end in 1848. In the 1970s, Hispanophile intellectual Fray Angélico Chávez denigrated mixed race peoples such as genízaros in his effort to distance himself, and his people, from "Mexicans" and assert *his* Nuevomexicanos' Spanish status. He stated:

> They [genízaros] had Spanish surnames, many had Spanish blood, and all knew only the Spanish language. Generally, they were the "poor ignorant Mexicans" described by American writers and travelers of these times. (Chávez 1973, xiv; Córdova 1979, 57)

Nevertheless, many Nuevomexicanos continue to remember indigenous ancestry and their centuries-long history of warfare and kinship with native peoples through ritual, oral narrative, and fiction (Gandert et al. 2000; Lamadrid 2003; Córdova 2006). As will be seen in chapter 6, nearly the entire career of New Mexico scholar G. Benito Córdova may be read as an argument with Chávez's distancing and perceived denigration of genízaros. With reference to this ongoing process of identity formation, Bustamante concludes his article by relating a short quote by ninety-year-old Seferina Quintana of Pecos, which he believes may be an expression of the New Mexican collective unconscious's recognition of this complex history: "The matter was never resolved. Some say we are Spanish, others that we are Indians, and others that we are Mexican" (Bustamante 1991, 163).

New Mexican Identity and Nonidentity

Such questions of representation are not new to New Mexicans, as is evident from the fact that the terms for Nuevomexicanos are fraught with tension and difficulty, as I suggested in this book's preface. Academics and the popular media have argued over them extensively for far more than one hundred years (Campa 1979; Espinosa 1985; Farago and Pierce 2006; Gómez 2007; Gonzales 2007, 1997a, 1997b, 1993; Meléndez 1997; Mitchell 2005; Montgomery 2002; Nieto-Phillips 2004; Nostrand 1992; Zavella 1997). The exploration of these terms reveals the complexities of Nuevomexicano self-conceptions and ethnic/racial assignment as they each positively identify what New Mexican Latinos *are* and negatively *are not*. The more recent academic debates are waged over claims to an exceptional and isolated New Mexican Latino culture and gene pool and another vision that finds greater continuity with Mexico and the indigenous Southwest in terms of descent and culture. In popular terms, this debate is framed in battles over terms of identification: Spanish or Spanish American versus Chicano and Mexican or Mexican American.

For those interested in the academic battles, two examinations of New Mexican ethnic/racial identity/assignment resulted in particularly enlightening discussions. The first erupted over an article in the *Annals of the Association of American Geographers* and eventual book by University of Oklahoma geographer Richard Nostrand, who contended that northern New Mexicans view themselves as culturally separate from Mexicans (Blaut and Ríos-Bustamante 1984; Chávez 1984; Gonzales 1997b; Hall 1984; Hansen 1981; Meinig 1984; Nostrand 1980, 1981, 1992; Rodríguez 1992). The second followed a study of working mothers by Louise Lamphere, Patricia Zavella, Phillip B. Gonzales, and Peter B. Evans that included Latinas in Albuquerque who largely identified themselves to social scientists as Spanish (Lamphere et al. 1993). In the wake of this study, Gonzales published several articles exploring New Mexican identity, and Zavella wrote an extraordinarily interesting article describing the conflict between her own expectations and her informants' answers concerning Chicana/o and Spanish terms of identity (Gonzales 1993, 1997a, 1997b; Zavella 1997).

Suggesting the complexities of the issue, University of New Mexico anthropologist and Taos native Sylvia Rodríguez used the term Hispano in much of her earlier work and more recently seems to favor the term Nuevomexicano (compare Rodríguez 1987 to Rodríguez 2007). Similarly, Charles Briggs, who worked in the Española Valley

School District village of Córdova, moved from Spanish American and Hispano to the Spanish-language identifier mexicano (compare Briggs 1974 to Briggs 1988). Geographer Jake Kosek recently used the term Hispano (Kosek 2006). In perhaps the most authoritative recent account, Gonzales uses the term Nuevomexicano in the title of the edited volume, *Expressing New Mexico: Nuevomexicano Creativity, Ritual, and Memory* (Gonzales 2007). Within the text's chapters, however, the authors use diverse terms, including, among others, Nuevomexicano, Chicano, Hispano, and Mexican American (Gonzales 2007).

Much of the seeming confusion results from New Mexicans themselves using multiple terms depending on the context of the discussion and the sociopolitical orientation of the speaker. Most responded that they were Hispanic, while others responded, in the following order of frequency, that they were Chicana/o, Latina/o, or Spanish. Often the same person will state a different term of self-identification depending on the context. For example, I have heard people who would clearly prefer the term Spanish in ethnically/racially mixed group settings call themselves Mexican in in-group situations. It therefore seems to me that in both popular and academic usage there is no single proper popular term for this population's racial/ethnic assignment and identity.[4]

For academics working in the Española Valley proper, similar confusion prevails. For example, volume 2 of the 1935 Tewa Basin Study originally described Spanish American villages (Weigle 1975). When edited and reprinted with supplementary material by well-known New Mexico folklorist Marta Weigle, however, these communities were rechristened Hispanic villages (Weigle 1975). Spanish anthropologist Alfredo Jiménez Núñez termed Española's residents Hispanos in his monograph *Los Hispanos de Nuevo México* (Jiménez 1974). Focusing on the ritual matachines dance in the Española Valley's Ohkay Owingeh and village of Alcalde, ethnomusicologist Brenda Romero termed Wiegle's Hispanic villages as Mejicano villages and has more recently used the term Hispano (Romero 1993, 2006, 2007). Anthropologist Brenda Bright seemed undecided about which term best described the cultural artifacts she found in the Española area. She titled her 1998 *American Ethnologist* article about area lowriders "'Heart Like a Car': Hispano/Chicano Culture in Northern New Mexico" (Bright 1998).

Enrique Lamadrid did not settle on one specific term in his descriptions of currently practiced rituals based on captivity narratives. In describing these folkloric events, many of which take place in the Española Valley, he switched between Hispano and Mexicano and, judging from the title of his book, seems to prefer Indo-Hispano (Lamadrid 2003).[5]

A Legacy Foretold

One of the most productive insights of Gloria Anzaldúa, Cherríe Moraga, and the Chicana feminism that emerged as the central trend of Chicana/o studies in the 1980s and 1990s is a sustained assertion of the significance of this complex, internally riven, racial experience (Anzaldúa 1987; Dávalos 2001; Esquibel 2006; Moraga 2000; Moraga and Anzaldúa 1984). In their wake, Chicana/o historians cast Spanish colonialism as a gendered act of domination and sociocultural interpenetration. For example, writing of the Spanish colonization of California in terms of sexual violence, Antonia Castañeda states that the architect of California's colonization, missionary Junípero Serra, recommended to the viceroy that colonial soldiers be encouraged to form formal, permanent unions with native women. Such matches were aimed to create a bond between colonists and natives (Castañeda 1993, 20). She also states that native women were the common objects of assaults by soldiers (Castañeda 1993, 25–26). In New Mexico, Ramón Gutiérrez has provocatively described this aspect of Spanish colonial relations (1991, 2003).[6] Citing colonial archives, Gutiérrez states that native peoples within colonial households could be abused without fear of retaliation, "for as one friar lamented in his 1734 report to the viceroy, Spanish New Mexicans justified their rapes saying: 'an Indian does not care if you fornicate with his wife because she has no shame [and] . . . only with lascivious treatment are Indian women conquered'" (Gutiérrez 2003, 10). With such a history of sexual domination, it should be no surprise that today's Nuevomexicanos have both European and indigenous ancestry (Esquibel 2006; Kraemer 2006).

Indeed, whispers of the inauthenticity of pure Spanish ancestry run back to the time before Oñate and his conquistadors journeyed north and implicated the colonists themselves. Martha Menchaca finds that Juan de Oñate recruited from different regions of Mexico, and his colonists included *peninsulares* (Spaniards born in Spain), *criollos* (Spaniards born in the New World), mestizos, Indians, and approximately five Blacks (Esquibel 2006, 80; Menchaca 2002, 83). Colonial authorities paid close attention to the sorts of men and women who filled Oñate's ranks, and they required him to register all people of mestizo blood. These authorities also barred him from taking "negro slaves, who mistreat the Indians and whom they fear for the harm they cause them" (quoted in Knaut 1995, 32). Even Oñate's own ethnic/racial ancestry was in doubt because of allegations that he was a mestizo assuming the position of a criollo. The poet Villagrá investigated these rumors and wrote that Oñate's mother could not have been the peninsular woman who was recorded as his mother because that woman lived in Spain, not Mexico, at the time of his birth (Cornish 1917; Menchaca 2002, 82). Instead, Villagrá claimed that on Oñate's mother's side, Oñate was a descendant of the Aztec emperor, Moctezuma II (Menchaca 2002, 82). Furthermore, the conquistador had married into indigenous bloodlines. Oñate's wife, doña Isabel de Tolosa Cortés Moctezuma, was a granddaughter of both Hernán Cortés and Emperor Moctezuma II (Chipman 1977; Cornish 1917; Menchaca 2002, 82). When Oñate himself is understood as a product of a Spanish-native encounter, his complex legacy seems almost foretold. It is a legacy still fought over through the terms of identity and their multiplicity.

Conquering Cultures

With New Mexicans' contested self-identification as a reference point, a growing body of scholarship powerfully historicizes the creation of New Mexican Spanish identifications epitomized by claims to descent from conquistadors in the particular U.S. context of Nuevomexicano history (Farago and Pierce 2006; Gómez 2007; Meléndez 1997; Mitchell 2005; Montgomery 2002; Nieto-Phillips 2004). In the social sciences, Phillip B. Gonzales's work offers the most sustained analysis of Nuevomexicano Spanish identifications (Gonzales 2007, 2001, 1997a, 1997b, 1993, 1986).

Gonzales argues that New Mexican Spanish or Spanish-American identity has two chief manifestations. The first Spanish identification rose to prominence in the late nineteenth and early twentieth centuries. Gonzales views it as a protest-oriented identity that confronted Anglo-American prejudice by providing the ideological ammunition to argue that no one had the right to subjugate Nuevomexicanos in a homeland they, as Spaniards, had colonized first (Gonzales 2001, 1997a, 1993, 1986). A second, more conservative version of Spanish American identity arose during the Great Depression and in the course of the New Deal. According to Gonzales:

> Rather than confront prejudice and discrimination, [the more conservative form of Spanish identification's] interest lay more in emphasizing the core commonalities between Spanish American culture and American culture. Both, for example, were conquering cultures. Thus, in place of a poverty-stricken people, the icons now favored elite conquistadors. (Gonzales 1997b, 125)

This is the aspect of the statue—"both were conquering cultures"—that so many find disturbing.

The oppositional aspect of Spanish American identity is demonstrated in one New Mexican intellectual's assertions. Historian Joseph P. Sánchez traces the negative stereotypes of U.S. Hispanics to the colonial-era depictions of Spaniards as bloodthirsty and morally deficient (Sánchez 1990). Sánchez writes, "The main premise upon which the Black Legend rested was the fear, envy, and dislike—or even hatred—of Spain by those nation-states that clashed with Spanish power shortly after Columbus's New World discoveries" (Sánchez 1990, 1). Thus, in revering Oñate and the other Spanish- and Mexican-era colonists and settlers, these Nuevomexicanos support a claim to the Southwest that preceded that of the Anglo-American "pioneers" who supposedly settled the West. They are also asserting an icon and view of history that flies in the face of at least one sort of Anglo-American prejudice.

Pierre Nora tells us that memory is often located in specific sites such as monuments. He describes these as sites where "memory crystallizes and secretes itself at a particular historical moment" and "a turning point where consciousness of a break with the past is bound up with the sense that memory has been torn" (Nora 1989, 7). For some Nuevomexicanos, statues of Oñate are sites where their past is reinscribed or refaced on the landscape and the reality of their own subjugation is momentarily repressed. In revering Oñate and the other Spanish- and Mexican-era colonists, these Nuevomexicanos transgress the dominant political imagining of the United States as an Anglo nation. The Oñate Center's then director, Estevan Arellano, supports such a position: "All this statue represents is that this area—for good or bad, whatever—it was colonized by Spain, and here is our reminder that the colony was led by this man, Juan de Oñate" (Arellano 1999).

Benjamin refers to such locations and moments in his "Theses on the Philosophy of History" (1968). For him, to articulate the past is to seize hold of a memory as it flashes up at a moment of danger. He writes:

> Historical materialism wishes to retain the image of the past which unexpectedly appears to man singled out by history at a moment of danger. The danger affects both the content of the tradition and its receivers. The same threat hangs over both: that of becoming a tool of the ruling classes. In every era the attempt must be made anew to wrest tradition away from a conformism that is about to overpower it. The Messiah comes not only as the redeemer, he comes as the subduer of the Antichrist. Only that historian will have the gift of fanning the spark of hope in the past who is firmly convinced that *even the dead* will not be safe from the enemy if he wins. And this enemy has not ceased to be victorious. (Benjamin 1968, 255)

In sum, in these statues many Nuevomexicanos preserve a sense of historical continuity with their past, and the troubled reality of the present is momentarily repressed. Nevertheless, as Flores writes, "Memory is not only forgetful; in attempting to preserve the past, it selectively silences those elements that attempt to rupture the quiet" (Flores 2002, 20). In this way, Oñate momentarily represses the reality of a decidedly nonvictorious present. It seems that Arellano might acknowledge such an argument. "We value [the Oñate statue] because we have very little left about us here," he said. "We have been here for such a long time. [The statue is] something we can at least identify and say that's ours" (Arellano 1999). As we have already seen, however, remembering Spanish origins is not only an act of remembering, it is also an act of forgetting—an act of negation. The statue cutters reminded us of this in the last sentence of their note to the *Santa Fe Reporter*. "Finally, to those of you who delude yourselves into believing you are of pure Spanish blood, shake that family tree and you will find many limbs with Pueblo roots" (*Santa Fe Reporter* 1998).[7] What the note writers may or may not realize is that many Nuevomexicanos have long been engaged in such tree shaking.

Indo-Hispano Heart

The Española Valley is a place marked by the Chicano movement and Chicano ideologies of mixed racial identity. More significantly for our discussion, Española's Rio Arriba County was the center of the land-grant struggle that sought the return of Spanish and Mexican land grants to their heirs. Furthermore, Rio Arriba's county seat, Tierra Amarilla, was the site of one of the most dramatic events of the Chicano movement era: The 1967 courthouse raid by land-grant activists. Sensationalist stories of the raid made the national press, complete with images of the National Guard's deployment and tanks rolling through Rio Arriba County villages. In the mid-1990s a group of political activists with roots in this era, including county commissioners Alfredo Montoya and courthouse raider Moisés Morales, defeated longtime area political powerbroker Emilio Naranjo, the chief force behind the Oñate monument. One suspects that these then-new leaders, especially Alfredo Montoya, who is married to a woman from Ohkay Owingeh, would not have chosen Naranjo's monument to a Spanish conquistador.

This ongoing political mobilization is accompanied by a related, politicized sense of ethnic/racial identity. Interestingly, the Oñate Center director, Juan Estevan Arellano, advocated such a view in his writings. Referring to the works of Mexican intellectual José Vasconcelos and his notion of race mixture, Arellano asserted a claim to New Mexico's landscape that evokes a kinship with Mexicans and is based, in part, on indigenous rather than Spanish ancestry. He wrote:

> Though once we, *la raza cósmica* (The Cosmic Race), might have been an alien presence in this land—because of our Spanish fathers—we have now become as natural in this landscape as the piñon tree. Whether we (or Native Americans) acknowledge it or not, most of us have Native blood running through our veins. That communion with the landscape ties us to the enduring code of brotherhood just as the poet makes the landscape itself the carrier of memory. (Arellano 1997b, 32)

Arellano is an intellectual and author strongly influenced by the early works of Chicano literature and cofounder of a Chicano literary organization, the Academia de la Nueva Raza. (Arellano 1984, 1992, 1997a, 1997b; Parsons, Padilla, and Arellano 1999). In the wake of Oñate's dismemberment, Arellano sometimes sought to reframe the Oñate Center in both Chicano and Hispano terms. In an interview with a journalist for the *Santa Fe New Mexican*, he referred to the Oñate Monument and Visitors Center as an "Indo-Hispano cultural center in the heart of Hispano culture" (López 1998).

Options for the Foot

The statue's foot was soon replaced, and the police investigation is now closed, but Oñate's wound and the mystery that it aroused remains open. Indeed, the identity of the people who cut off the statue's foot is still unknown, and speculation proliferates. The event was even the topic of a much-discussed essay by infamous author and Navajo imposter Tim "Nasdijj" Barrus (Fleischer 2006; Lee 2001, 1; Nasdijj 2000, 140–56).[8] Perhaps because of such broad fascination with the incident, both New Mexican academics and some Española Valley residents questioned the perpetrators' connection to Native American communities. Some believe that the statue cutters were Anglo newcomers to the region. More specifically, Arellano suspects the foot cutting was done by Anglo environmentalists who were embroiled in a long and bitter conflict with Nuevomexicano land activists in Rio Arriba County (Arellano 1999).[9] Others, including Española Valley residents who have ties to Ohkay Owingeh, have told me that they believe the perpetrators were Native Americans. Some suspect the ritual Pueblo clowns who have long used humor and wit to playfully ridicule and chastise Nuevomexicanos and now Anglos.[10]

In the end, all we are left with are the three notes from the Friends of Acoma. These messages leave us with much to contemplate. In their message to the *Santa Fe Reporter*, they included a bulleted list of points they wished to make (*Santa Fe Reporter* 1998). Among these assertions, they stated that the Oñate Monument and Visitors Center was a waste of money and effort, but they also noted the center had done a good job of representing their act of vandalism. The note writers maintained that they had no sympathy for Nuevomexicanos' assertions that Anglo Americans unjustly took their land because Nuevomexicanos themselves took land from native peoples. They told the Roman Catholic Church that "God is not some white guy sitting in judgment of us all. It's about spirit, you dolts, spirit!" Finally, they stated that monuments should be created for the Spaniards who came to New Mexico as human beings rather than conquerors.

The note writers followed these points with a list of options for the captured foot's fate. Among the more self-explanatory answers were "cut it up and send it back to Spain" and "melt it into medallions." I find two other options suggested by the Friends of Acoma more powerful, though. In reference to the twenty-four men who lost their friends at Acoma, they stated, "The foot only has to come off 23 more times." They also asked, "Do you know where Starvation Peak is?" Here they are referring to a hill where, according to one version of the legend, a group of Spaniards retreated in a battle with native peoples. This story strangely parallels the events at Acoma.[11] Rather than attack the Spaniards' extremely defensible position, the native people simply camped below. Outsmarted, the Spaniards died of starvation on top of the mesa. Presumably, the foot would be left there to suffer a similar fate. Among the note writers' other options for the foot were to "make a nice new stamp" and "Popé gets a statue." The "new stamp" refers to the U.S. postal stamp issued to commemorate the cuartocentenario that featured a picture of Española's mission/convent—a re-creation of the Spanish church and mission located in Oñate's capital of San Gabriel. Po'pay refers to the Ohkay Owingeh religious leader who led the rebellion that ejected the Spanish colonial government from New Mexico during the years 1680–92 (Knaut 1995, 167–70). New Mexico's then governor estimated that 389 settlers and 21 Franciscan friars died as a result of the revolt (Knaut 1995, 14).

In addition to showcasing the wit of the Friends of Acoma, such options clearly deconstruct Oñate as an icon and reveal him as a far less powerful figure than he first appears. The Alamo is a master symbol emanating from a position of power that, at least through the 1950s, was tied to an ever more increasing and all-encompassing structure of Anglo-American domination. As such, the Alamo and exhortations to "remember the Alamo" held an almost absolute power to assert a world view and silence alternatives. In contrast, this New Mexican icon is almost exclusively honored at the limited locations of Nuevomexicano control and, I suspect, of little significance for New Mexican Anglos. In other words, he is a weak master symbol, if a master symbol at all, that cannot compete with the likes of the Alamo. Instead, the New Mexican icon emanates from a position of weakness—sometimes in protest against Anglo power and sometimes in capitulation to it. Therefore, I find it no surprise that whenever Oñate statues are proposed, a mixture of enthusiastic support, indifference, and ferocious opposition often meets them. Indeed, the Friends of Acoma wrote that they had to overcome an initial degree of indifference to the Oñate statue. In their note to the *Santa Fe Reporter*, they state that Oñate's foot "came off Dec. 29—a full week before anybody noticed." They added that nobody noticed the evidence left by a previous effort to sever the foot. Addressing Arellano personally, the note states, "Finally, to you who are so smug in your jobs at the Oñate center—this was our 2nd attempt. Had you looked at your beloved statue last spring you would have seen our effort."

At the beginning of this chapter and as proof of the widespread importance of Oñate, I stated that multiple locations, including Albuquerque and El Paso, planned to erect Oñate statues. There is more to this story, though. In Albuquerque, the statue was fiercely opposed, and a far less celebratory statue was unveiled in 2007 (Gonzales 2007; Hendricks 2009). The El Paso statue also met with stiff opposition, and the city council has agreed to change the statue's name from Oñate to simply "The Equestrian" (Blumenthal 2004; Leyva 2007).[12] Moreover, perhaps even more astounding is the fact that few of my students here at the University of New Mexico, which is based in Albuquerque, are aware of the Albuquerque, Española, or El Paso statues. Thus, Oñate cannot even command the attention or even recognition of the public. Furthermore, one of the Friends of Acoma's options for the foot came, at least partially, to pass.

Ohkay Owingeh's Po'pay received a statue (Archuleta 2007; Gisick 2005; The Architext of the Capitol 2009; Agoyo 2009). While, as far as I know, Oñate's foot was not melted down for the statue of Po'pay, the statue does speak to the specifics of rebellion against Spanish rule. Sculptor and Jémez Pueblo native Cliff Fragua depicted Po'pay as a traditional pueblo dweller, wearing a deerskin and holding a bear fetish in one hand. More important for this essay, he holds a knotted maguey fiber that was used to coordinate the uprising (Knaut 1995, 169–70). While Oñate must be content at the Oñate Monument and Visitors Center, Po'pay's statue will reside in a far more prestigious location. He is one of New Mexico's two statues housed at the National Statuary Hall in the nation's capitol building.

Oñate is not even safe in Española. In 2001 a group of young activists who called themselves La Verdad (The Truth) was given control of Española's annual fiesta and immediately set out to transform the festival's patriarchs, Oñate, and la reina, or queen. They took away Oñate's sword and armor, and, in acknowledgment of indigenous ancestry, they initially intended to rename the queen after Hernán Cortés's indigenous consort, La Malinche (Cypress 1991, 2; Esquibel 2006, 23–26; Paz 1985). In choosing the queen's new name, that year's fiesta council intended to rename her in honor of a woman their spokesperson described as "the mother of mestizos." Their choice was influenced by both Chicano valorizations of *mestizaje* and northern New Mexican traditions reflected in the matachines dance. In this dance, La Malinche is a young girl dressed in white who signifies the Virgin Mary's power and love (Rodríguez 1996; Romero 1993, 2006, 2007). La Verdad, however, did not realize that as the mistress of Cortés, she is seen as a symbol of the rape, conquest, and colonization of native peoples under Spain and the great betrayer of the Mexican nation (Esquibel 2006, 23; Paz 1985). They were also unaware of Chicana feminists' reclamation of La Malinche as both a strong woman unbounded by the patriarchal logic and the prototypical victim of Mexican and Chicano patriarchy (Alarcón 1989; Anzaldúa 1987, 44; Cypress 1991, 138–52; Del Castillo 1977; González 1991). In the ensuing controversy, they instead renamed her La Mestiza.

Remembering Oñate

While the National Statuary Hall's Po'pay, La Verdad's kinder and gentler Oñate, and La Mestiza are interesting icons, I prefer the Oñate Center's bronze statue and the space where his foot should have been.[13] In the dismembered icon, the complexities and contradictions of New Mexican Chicana/o identity are manifest and demand confrontation. Here, I refer to the insights of Michael Taussig cited in this essay's first lines. In *Defacement: Public Secrecy and the Labor of the Negative*, Taussig explores what happens when something sacred is defaced. He finds that defacement imbues the sacred with its power and works on objects the way jokes work on language, bringing out their inherent magic (Taussig 1999, 5). He writes:

> When the human body, a nation's flag, money, or a public statue is *defaced*, a strange surplus of negative energy is likely to be aroused from within the defaced thing itself. It is now in a state of *desecration*, the closest many of us are going to get to the sacred in the modern world. (Taussig 1999, 1)

In Taussig's view, defacement is most powerful when it reveals public secrets, "as is the case with most social knowledge, *knowing what not to know?*" (Taussig 1999, 2). For New Mexicans who identify exclusively with European ancestry and discourses of Spanish-American identity, so-called miscegenation and its embodiment evidenced in mestizo bodies and New Mexico's conquered and impoverished "Mexicans" are public secrets that must be denied. Of such secrets, Taussig writes, "Knowing it is essential to its power, equal to the denial" (Taussig 1999, 6). When the iconic representations of such discourses are broken open, however, its secrets spill out, making it more than the sum of its parts. The conquering conquistador on horseback is cut open and thus simultaneously embodies the brutally oppressed and gendered native as well as the Anglo-American conqueror. Taussig elaborates, "Defacement is like Enlightenment. It brings insides outside, unearthing knowledge, and revealing mystery. As it does this, however, as it spoliates and tears at tegument, it may also animate the thing defaced and the mystery revealed may become more mysterious . . ." (Taussig 1999, 3).

Recognizing the power of the dismembered statue, the Friends of Acoma hint at the possibility of reconciliation. According to their second note to the *Albuquerque Journal*, their quarrel is with Oñate and his supporters rather than people they refer to as "our Hispanic brothers and sisters," and they have no desire to "disrupt any of our communities." They wrote to the *Reporter*, "In respect to the foot, dialogue is dangerous, but we feel a response is the proper thing to do. It must be admitted that we are proud of our actions, not so much the action itself, but the resulting education it caused."

Near the time of the statue's dismemberment in 1998, one veteran activist from the battles in the northern part of the Rio Arriba County, María Varela, told me that her teenage daughter and her friends were approached by an Española organization that sought to make a film about Oñate. The film was intended to raise Nuevomexicano youths' self-esteem, but the daughter and her friends told the filmmakers that "they saw little or nothing in Oñate's life that was relevant to theirs. He was Spanish. They viewed themselves as Mexican." Furthermore, Varela invoked the specifically gendered violation of the colonial encounter in her alternative response to the foot-cutting crises:

> What several of us women thought the boys should have done
> was make a cast of the cut off foot, put it on a velvet pillow, made
> a horseback pilgrimage to Laguna and Acoma, and presented it to
> the elders with apologies. Then we realized that we were the ones

who should have done it, because it probably would have been accepted much better from the women, as the women represent the mestizo-izing of la raza in New Mexico. (María Varela, personal communication with author, 1999)

In their second note to the *Albuquerque Journal*, the Friends of Acoma suggest they might have accepted the gift of the foot on a velvet pillow. They wrote, "It would have been a brave thing to have left the foot off as someone suggested!"

Unimpressed by such arguments, Arellano states it was right to repair the footless statue. Rather than Native Americans, he saw Anglos in the space where Oñate's foot should have been. In the context of the late 1990s battle between Nuevomexicano land activists and largely Anglo-American environmental groups (Arellano 1999; Kosek 2006, 2004), Arellano specifically saw Anglo environmentalists undermining his Indo-Hispano land claims. He told a journalist from the *Santa Fe New Mexican*:

> What we are seeing now is that the Anglos are trying to revive the Black Legend. They are trying to create the schism between Native Americans and the Indo-Hispanos, so they can exploit it. . . . I know it wasn't done by Native Americans or Hispanos, it was done by some extreme environmental group. I think the environmentalists are the ones responsible because they don't want some of the things we are doing here at the Center in relation to the land grants and water rights, are things they are trying to appropriate for their agenda. . . . (López 1998)

In seeming response to such statements, the statue cutters wrote in their second note, "You were wrong about our heritage, we are Native Americans and native New Mexicans."

Indeed, in New Mexico—as in most other places—the dynamics of domination and subjugation continually haunt one another. This foot's amputation requires Nuevomexicanos to remember the complexities and ugliness of their own history as well as its beauty. In this way, the dismembered icon parallels the views of mestizaje articulated by literary

Juan Estevan Arellano shows the space left by the removal of Oñate's foot.
Photo by Jane Bernard, copyright Albuquerque Journal. *Reprinted by permission.*

and cultural critic Rafael Pérez-Torres. He writes, "The double-edged sword of mestizo subjectivity—subject in and subject to history—is marked on the body. The doubleness is within" (Pérez-Torres 2006, 35). It is this dual and seemingly contradictory nature that is both confounding and its power. When the Oñate icon was cut, this same doubleness was released. Talking to me, Arellano, a man who is proud to be descended from both "Basques and Apaches," seemed to open the door to such an ambivalent view:

> Oñate wasn't the best role model, but at least we admit we are humans, and we make mistakes. . . . I never heard anybody say that Oñate was God or make him into a saint. But he probably represented the best and worst in all human beings, and that is

probably why people say, "Well, let's have a statue about Oñate just to remind us who we are." (Arellano 1999)

In the space where his foot should have been, the wounds and pains of enslaved Native American ancestors beckon, the United States' colonized "Mexicans" haunt the heroic Spanish colonizer, and patriarchy evokes its oppressed and gendered opposition.

Such contested representation is instructive for Chicanos and people of Mexican origin anywhere in the United States. After all, on closer inspection, many Chicanos, Hispanics, Latinos, Mexican Americans, or whatever we call ourselves face contradictory and mixed histories. In Texas, California, Colorado, Washington state, and Oklahoma, I have seen multiple identities with differing politics similarly dialogue, argue, and compete against one another. The footless statue renders such contestation visible and strangely generative. Indeed, only in absolute dismemberment may don Juan de Oñate be fully remembered. "Y cada año celebramos nuestra herencia," as Ángel Espinoza sang in her "El Corrido de Don Juan de Oñate," "¡Viva la historia de ese gran señor!" In Taussig's words, a mystery has been reinvigorated, not dissipated, and the icon now has properties of an allegorical emblem, complete with its recent history of death. This desecration gives such dismembered icons the strange property of opening out (Taussig 1999, 253).

In the next chapter, I will explore a far more terrible act of violence, the murder of two valley teens by another valley teen as the two participated in one of the most powerful symbols of New Mexican culture. As the vandalized statue indicates, such dismemberment can be both beautiful and truly horrible.

CHAPTER TWO

Good Friday

The Life of Spirit is not the life that shrinks from death and
keeps itself untouched by devastation, but rather the life that
endures it and maintains itself in it. It wins its truth only when,
in utter dismemberment, it finds itself.

—Georg Wilhelm Friedrich Hegel, *Phenomenology of Spirit*

"I don't know. I just, I don't know what the hell was going
through my head."

—Herrera Interrogation

New Mexican folk Roman Catholicism places a special emphasis on
Holy Week, which commemorates the events surrounding Christ's
Passion, crucifixion, and resurrection on Easter Sunday (Steel 1978;
Carroll 2002). During this time, tens of thousands of mostly Latino New
Mexicans walk to Chimayó and its chapel, the Santuario de Chimayó.
The *santuario* has long been the destination of pilgrims seeking the
healing dirt found within its walls (Gandert et al. 2000; Howarth et al.
1999). Good Friday, in particular, marks the date of Christ's terrible
suffering on the cross and the height of the annual pilgrimage. The
tens of thousands who travel to Chimayó often walk great distances
themselves and find penance in the trip. For many, the pilgrimage has
come to symbolize New Mexican identity, tradition, and piety.

Early Good Friday morning in 2000, a young couple experienced
their own terrible suffering on their way to Chimayó, and two years
after the dismemberment of Oñate, the Española Valley achieved

renewed notoriety in the regional and national press. A nineteen-year-old valley youth named Carlos Herrera murdered the teenage couple, Ricky Martínez and Karen Castañón. These events would reverberate throughout the valley for years, and the murders cut open this sacred symbol of New Mexican identity and become an integral part of an allegorical retelling of the New Mexican experience.

Like the previous chapter's account of the statue's vandalism, this chapter's description of Herrera's murder of Martínez and Castañón relies primarily on the public representations and is therefore drawn from news media accounts, a documentary film, a transcript of Herrera's interrogation and confession to the police, and court testimony. In the final section of this chapter, I will also describe a related experience that comments on Christ's Passion, don Juan de Oñate, and New Mexican identity. Key to this understanding is the Roman Catholic notion of allegory. The murders, the Passion narrative, and the Oñate icon are articulated in a continuously linked series of multiple meanings that are believed to speak to a transcendent meaning: the Christian Passion and its themes of suffering and redemption. For Benjamin this transformation of things into signs is not exclusively an intellectual event, and it is both what allegory is and its content. The signs strike notes at the depths of one's being, regardless of whether they point to heaven, to an irretrievable past, or to the grave (Cowan 1981, 110). In the proliferation of stories that emerged from the murders, they become, in both literary and religious terms, a Passion narrative.

Sacred Geography

The story of the Passion and its ritual enactment have been especially elaborate and widespread in New Mexico since colonial times (Steel 1978; Carroll 2002). In *Pilgrimage to Chimayó,* University of New Mexico folklorist Enrique Lamadrid describes Chimayó's pilgrims in allegorical terms that reaffirm their place in tradition and geography in the annual pilgrimage. Lamadrid writes, "Voices rise in prayer, song, and conversation from the silent landscape" (Howarth et al. 1999, 9). Indeed, the New Mexican lay Roman Catholic order formally titled in English the Brotherhood of Our Father Jesus the Nazarene and popularly known as the Penitentes often spends the entire week commemorating Christ's suffering and resurrection (Briggs 1988; Carroll 2002; López Pulido 2000; Weigle 1976, 2007). Speaking to the importance of the dates of Holy Week in the Roman Catholic calendar and linking them to the specifics of the Chimayó pilgrimage, Lamadrid describes the road to Chimayó as spokes on a wheel whose sacred center is the earth itself and a crucified Christ. He states that the journey of the life of the Santo Niño de Atocha joins the people on their spiritual quest to find divinity within humanity. The Santo Niño is an image of the Christ Child as a pilgrim with a staff and cloak.

The Santuario de Chimayó. *Photo by author.*

The Passion. Christ painted on the side of a car at the
2001 Española car show at the Ohkay Casino in Ohkay
Owingeh Pueblo. *Photo by author.*

The Santuario on Good Friday. *Photo by author.*

Still, such stories are not complete descriptions of the Good Friday pilgrimage; I have visited the santuario many times and occasionally collected dirt for sick relatives and friends. Indeed, I hoped that this sacred dirt and my visits would help my father combat his health problems, and, despite his death in 2005, I believe they did. Similarly, I have walked in the Good Friday pilgrimage on three separate occasions, but I find Lamadrid's tales of spiritual communion to be only partially representative of my experiences. Absent from Lamadrid's narratives are the hypodermic needles over which I stepped each of the three times I walked to the santuario on Good Friday. Absent is the public knowledge that Chimayó is a central location in the valley's drug trafficking and the irate young man who stood behind my wife and me in 2002 as we waited to enter the santuario. When asked by an older woman whether he had been drinking, he told all within earshot that he would not change himself for anybody, including God. Below I will show that a more whole, if horrible, experience is evoked in events that blocked the pilgrimage one Good Friday.

The pilgrimage's destination is a picturesque adobe chapel that houses a crucifix dedicated to El Señor de Esquípulas (Our Lord of Esquípulas). This depiction of Christ is directly associated with the similarly syncretic cult of Our Lord of Esquípulas of Guatemala (DeLoach 1999, 55). Bernardo Abeyta is said to have discovered the crucifix buried in the sand at the present site of the chapel in Chimayó on Good Friday in 1810 (DeLoach 1999). From the Chimayó location where it was first found, the crucifix was taken to the large church in Santa Cruz but disappeared and was soon found again in its original location. After the crucifix disappeared from Santa Cruz and reappeared in Chimayó twice more, Abeyta petitioned the church to build a chapel at the site of the crucifix's discovery. The santuario was completed in 1816.

In the 1850s, Chimayó also became associated with the Santo Niño de Atocha. At that time, the Medina family built a small chapel devoted to the Santo Niño near the santuario. The Santo Niño is known as a miraculous healer and is the patron saint of children and captives, and the santuario's sacristy contains a Santo Niño *bulto*, or statue. Miraculous stories of Medina's discovery of the Santo Niño are similar to those about El Señor de Esquípulas. The Medina family still owns the chapel, which still receives pilgrims, but it no longer rivals the santuario in reputation, importance, or atmosphere.

Today, the santuario is best known for its healing dirt collected from the *pocito*, or small hole, located where Abeyta is said to have found the Señor de Esquípulas crucifix. Just as native peoples consume sacred earth at the shrine to El Señor de Esquípulas in Guatemala, in Chimayó the dirt is either rubbed on the body, eaten directly, or mixed with water and drunk. Crutches, eyeglasses, photographs, newspaper articles, and other mementos left by the healed decorate the sacristy.[1] This healing aspect of the site has a significance that reaches further back in time than the finding of El Señor de Esquípulas.

For the Tewa-speaking people of the Española Valley pueblos of Santa Clara and San Juan, Chimayó is one of the cardinal cosmological sites and the scene of a key event in their world's creation (DeLoach 1999, 76; Ortiz 1969, 19, 142). Indeed, the name of Chimayó is the Hispanization of a Tewa place name Tsi May Oh (DeLoach 1999, 76; Ortiz 1969, 142). According to DeLoach, *tzimmayo*, or "place where big stones stand," describes one prominent physical feature of the area, while *tsimajo* has been interpreted to mean "flaking stone of superior quality." DeLoach states that Tewa belief notes that during the time of the ancient ones, great geysers of hot water were located in Chimayó. When the Tewa war gods killed a giant, fire erupted and dried the healing springs at several locations, including Chimayó, into mud (DeLoach 1999, 2). Ohkay Owingeh native and anthropologist Alfonso Ortiz describes Tsi May Oh as one of the sacred *tsin*, or flat-topped hills, created by two of the six primal brothers called Towa é and explains that each of these hills is sacred because it is particularly dark and foreboding and has a cave and/or tunnels running through it (Ortiz 1969, 14, 19). The Towa é watch over the pueblos from these hills. The mud surrounding the sacred Indian shrines was thought to have healing qualities and to have been used in native rituals (DeLoach 1999, 2; Kay 1986, 17). Moreover, as stated in the previous chapter, the area's colonists intermarried with Native Americans from surrounding communities, and many are descendants from and related to the Pueblos who have visited the area since before the village of Chimayó's founding.

Good Friday

Shortly after five in the morning of April 21, 2000, Carlos Herrera drove past Ricky Martínez and Karen Castañón as the couple walked between Española and Chimayó near an area called La Puebla. On the road, Herrera shot and killed Martínez. He later killed Castañón in an arroyo north of Chimayó. Media accounts and court testimony made much of the fact that Herrera was both high on cocaine and drunk at the time of the murders.

The aftermath of Martínez's murder is captured remarkably by documentary filmmakers Joe Day and Manuel Machuca in the film *Rio Arriba: Tragedy and Hope* (2000). Protecting the crime scene, police created a detour through a field and hung blue and yellow vinyl tarps over the barbed-wire fences that separated the field from the road, but Martínez's lifeless form remained unavoidable as it lay in the pilgrims' intended path. Standing in the field that is the detour, Day and Machuca filmed pilgrims' reactions to the detour and the covered body. The pilgrims would ask the filmmakers why the road was blocked. When told of the drive-by murder of a young man, the pilgrims reacted with inarticulate shock: A middle-aged woman covered her mouth and said, "I don't know how somebody could do that." A man in his thirties paused as if digesting the information and then simply nodded his head.

Neither the regional nor national media missed the power of this story. Events surrounding the murders were followed closely by Española's *Rio Grande Sun*, the *Albuquerque Journal, Santa Fe New Mexican*, and Albuquerque's television stations such as CBS affiliate KRQE-TV 13 and NBC affiliate KOB-TV 4. The story also made headlines in the national media, including papers such as the *Los Angeles Times*, the *Houston Chronicle, Atlanta Journal and Constitution, Denver Post*, and the *Montreal Gazette*, among others.

The Passion of Ricky and Karen

Despite onlookers' first reactions of inarticulate shock, a group of community leaders, as well as the members of the murdered teens' families, almost immediately incorporated the deaths into the narrative of Christ's Passion. In this way, the murder of the two teenage pilgrims became allegories of the New Mexican experience. When Herrera shot Martínez and Castañón on the pilgrimage path to Chimayó, he cut open New Mexican identity. Archbishop and pilgrim Michael Sheehan, San Juan priest Fr. Paco Vallejos, and Ricky's father, Ray Martínez, quickly closed this wound with an allegory that reinforced tradition, piety, and the murdered teenagers' purity. In Father Vallejos's telling of the murders, a Passion play is acted out, and this carries a strong moral lesson addressed to the current struggles of his flock: on that Good Friday morning, Martínez and Castañón were the Lamb of God, and Herrera played the role of Christ's killer.

This work of discursive and selective reformulation of the events was already in progress at the murder scene and even before community leaders probably knew the identities of the victims. At the detour, Archbishop Sheehan told the filmmakers Day and Machuca, "The first Good Friday there was an incident too, Jesus dying on the cross, so we shouldn't be surprised that violence and the power of evil are part of our world" (*Rio Arriba: Tragedy and Hope* 2000). Sheehan immediately went about the work of assimilating the murders into his vision of Roman Catholic moral order:

> But despite [the reality of violence and power of evil], look at the many people, the thousands of people that honor God by their pilgrimage. Giving people an alternative to a life of drugs and alcohol. Giving them something good to do with their lives rather than to burn their lives up with sinful things. (*Rio Arriba: Tragedy and Hope* 2000)

In Sheehan's narrative, the two deaths are overcome by the power of the thousands of living who honor God.

This Roman Catholic narrative would only become further elaborated as the teenagers' identities became known. The victims, Martínez and Castañón, were portrayed by their families and media accounts as innocents. Indeed, very real evidence of their upstanding lives was abundant. Both were good students, and they attended Los

Alamos High School, where Martínez played basketball and Castañón was a cheerleader.[2] Newspaper reports stated that the young couple walked so early in the morning so that they could attend class that day. Martínez walked the pilgrimage in preparation for receiving the sacrament of confirmation later that year, and Castañón walked with the hope of healing a back injury she sustained while cheerleading. An Associated Press article stated:

> The slain boy's father, Ray Martinez, told the Associated Press that his son was a good student, active in sports and very religious.

> "He was a beautiful kid, now he's gone. I'm still in shock," he said while sitting in his son's bedroom at the family home in La Villita, northwest of Chimayó.

> The teen's room was adorned by sports jerseys, football helmets and photographs of Castañon. One photo showed the high school sweethearts kissing. The engraved wooden frame read, "this moment will last forever." (Baker 2000)

In an extraordinary coincidence, the murdered Martínez was set to play Jesus that evening in a Passion play at St. John the Baptist Parish in Ohkay Owingeh.

At the joint funeral mass at Ohkay Owingeh's San Juan parish, the teenagers' deaths became an allegorical interpretation for New Mexico's social problems. Fr. Paco Vallejos told his parishioners that the teenagers were with Jesus that Good Friday and "they were crucified with him. They felt our Lord's passion. They felt his death." Vallejos said the bullets that pierced their bodies and killed them were also the vials of crack cocaine and heroin consumed by northern New Mexicans. He said, "We called ourselves *la buena gente* (the good people). We learned to live together. Our culture grew, and our traditions grew. But lately, something has happened to la buena gente." He said, "It's sad to hear the reports of our Northern New Mexico . . . and how we've become more and more violent with one another." Vallejos described Chimayó as a holy place, a sanctuary, a place of refuge, a place of safety, and a place filled with God's love but said, "It's become one of the most violent places as well." Ricky's father made this narrative more personal. He told Karl Moffat of the *Rio Grande Sun*, "I have to believe the devil was out that morning," and, "Anybody who is cruising high on cocaine and whiskey on Good Friday looking to kill someone has got to have the devil in him" (Moffat 2000, 1). Ray Martínez told Moffat that the devil shot his son and Castañón and that God then took them away (Moffat 2000, 1).

There is another largely unheard story that resists articulation by these grand narratives. This story is told in a transcript of Herrera's interrogation by police. Interestingly, one aspect of this encounter is given the name of a sacrament, confession. In the specifics of the events that Herrera recounted, a more ordinary and ineffable story emerges, a narrative that is truer to that inarticulate moment when pilgrims discovered that their path was blocked by a corpse.

Interrogations and Confession

The winding, two-lane highway from Española would have been dark at five in the morning, and relatively few pilgrims would have yet ventured out on the road. Herrera, a nineteen-year-old dropout from Española Valley High School, had been up all night partying on cocaine, alcohol, and other drugs and was, as the teenagers walked, then driving back and forth between Española and Chimayó (Herrera Interrogation 2000). On his final pass through the area known as La Puebla, Herrera saw Martínez and Castañón. Herrera stopped his truck and fatally shot Martínez in the shoulder with a .22 rifle he carried in the vehicle.

Shortly after five in the morning another pilgrim, Fidel Maestas, found Martínez bleeding to death. Soon thereafter, a patrol officer came upon Maestas as he administered cardiopulmonary resuscitation to the teenager, but Martínez later died at the scene. Minutes earlier, as Martínez lay in the road, Herrera told Castañón to get in his truck. He drove with Castañón on the road to Chimayó and later up the arroyos to the north of the road from Española. After the pavement ended, Herrera told Castañón to get out of the pickup, and as she walked away, he shot her in the back of the shoulder. Autopsy reports state that

Martínez died of blood-loss injuries and Castañón died of blood loss and internal injuries caused by a small caliber wound in her left rear shoulder.

Two days after the murders on Easter Sunday, an arrest warrant was issued for Herrera. He was soon apprehended with the help of his stepfather, Leo Montoya, at the time an Española police lieutenant.[3] In the morning hours after his arrest, state police interrogated Herrera, seeking to gain his confession and an explanation for the murders. State police officers Randy Trujillo and Billy Martínez interviewed Herrera, and the transcripts of the interrogation show the two state troopers repeatedly attempting to extract a reason from Herrera for the killings. Trooper Trujillo told Herrera that they needed to find out "why did it happen" and asked Herrera whether he was a serial killer, he did this "all the time," he was "crazy," or the murders were a "one time deal" (Herrera Interrogation 2000). Trooper Martínez told Herrera that Ricky's family had already forgiven him but wanted to face him and ask him why. Herrera immediately admitted to the murders but could not supply a reason that satisfied the troopers. In a typical exchange Trooper Martínez asked, "Did you single them out or did they just get in your way?" and Herrera replied, "I don't know. I just, I don't know what the hell was going through my head" (Herrera Interrogation 2000).

Instead of supplying a reason, Herrera told the state troopers that he was up all night partying on cocaine and repeatedly said he was "flipping out" (Herrera Interrogation 2000). A defense witness and neuropsychologist, Thomas Thompson, testified at Herrera's sentencing that Herrera claimed to have consumed a half ounce of cocaine during the day previous to the murders and split a quarter ounce of cocaine with friends the night before the murders. Thompson also stated that Herrera said he drank several fifths of vodka and shared several cases of beer with friends.[4] He said he remembered driving his truck back and forth between the town of Española and Chimayó. He said, "I just remember driving and turning and turning around again and I seen them and that's all" (Herrera Interrogation 2000). He said he saw "some guy," and then when asked why he shot him, Herrera responded, he "probably just pointed the gun out the window for the dumbest fuckin' reason. I don't know why" (Herrera Interrogation 2000).

As Martínez lay dying in the street, Herrera told Castañón to get in his truck and she, inexplicably and according to Herrera, complied without resistance. Once in his truck, Herrera said she asked him if he planned to hurt her and complained of her cheerleading back injury. At first, Herrera said he did not plan to kill her and instead intended to leave her somewhere distant in order to give himself time to get away. As he drove to Chimayó and later up the arroyos to the north of State Road 76, though, he realized he had to finish what he started because "I figured if I let her go she was going to say shit" (Herrera Interrogation 2000). He told her to get out of the truck, and as she walked away, he shot her in the back with his only remaining bullet. He described what was going through his mind at the moment. "I didn't even look to see if she had fallen or anything. I just took off. I was fuckin' freaked" (Herrera Interrogation 2000).

After the completion of Herrera's interrogation, Herrera returned later that morning with a different story. Law enforcement and expert witnesses would later conclude this second explanation of the murder expressed Herrera's anger and frustration more than anything Martínez had done. In any case, the story would prove to be too horrible to believe. Herrera told the troopers that he killed Martínez over a drug debt (Herrera Interrogation 2000). He said that Martínez and a cousin of Martínez owed Herrera more than four hundred dollars for an ounce of cocaine and described the newspaper descriptions of Martínez as "bullshit." He said, "The way his parents are saying that they knew that he was a good kid and he never gave anybody shit. That's a lie. They don't know half the shit. Everybody was all making it sound like he was art . . . and everything. But I knew him" (Herrera Interrogation 2000). At Carlos Herrera's February 26, 2001, sentencing, Ray Martínez seemingly addressed these accusations. He told Santa Fe Judge Stephen Pfeffer, "My son was drug free, alcohol free. He never smoked cigarettes. He never drank coffee. The only alcohol he consumed was wine on Sunday for Communion." Herrera's defense team chose not to pursue Herrera's claim that Martínez owed Herrera a drug debt.[5] Herrera also later claimed that another individual participated in the murder, but his defense team also did not pursue this in his defense. In his police interrogation, Herrera simply insisted that he knew Martínez better than his parents did. He said, "I knew [Ricky Martínez] better than his mom and dad . . . I knew the shit he did because I partied with him" (Herrera Interrogation 2000).

I do not know if Herrera partied with Martínez. What I do know is that Herrera's narrative remains outside the allegory community leaders told. Nevertheless, for many, the Passion narrative retained its explanatory force. Indeed, as I will show below, this invocation of another dialectic of the Christ story—the purity of divinity and embodied humanity—this story gains its redemptive power.

Oñate's Passion

Just as Archbishop Sheehan, Fr. Paco Vallejos, and Ray Martínez found power in the story of Christ's crucifixion, I have heard other insurgent Passion plays—even ones that might serve to cast Herrera in redemptive terms. Here, I will move to another narrative that brings together the seemingly divergent strands of this chapter and the previous discussion of Oñate's foot. I also intend to show that locals too have conceptualized that more complex juxtaposition of positivity and negativity.

In the summer of 2004, I stood and watched the parade that marks the high point of Española's annual festival, La Fiesta de Española. This event is just one of the similar festivals in Taos and Las Vegas, New Mexico. Like these other festivals, Española's is attended almost entirely by area Latinos and, now, Mexican immigrants. These events are rarely promoted as tourist events, and tourists seem to stay away from them. To ensure a decent vantage point, I arrived several hours early and waited in the Big Rock Casino's parking lot on Riverside Drive. Soon a crowd of fellow parade-goers began to gather in the lot. A quick survey of the crowd confirmed that nearly everyone around me was Nuevomexicano, Mexican immigrant, or perhaps Native American from a nearby pueblo.[6] Many even set out lawn chairs, others sat in the back of pickups, and many carried coolers full of food and drink. For the several hours before the parade began, I sat in the back of a pickup with newfound friends and enjoyed beers with them. The pickup occupants were locals, men and women ranging from middle age to young children. The adults shared beers, covering them when police would pass by. The fiesta itself was delayed for more than an hour because of a motorcycle accident and a serious injury along the route.

When the parade finally began, I left the pickup truck and began to circulate among the crowd in an effort to find the best spot to see the parade and take photos. As usual, the parade entries included a large collection of politicians, area businesses, sheriffs' posses, and the festival royalty of nearby communities. Like every other year, Española's fiesta was presided over by a local man crowned Oñate and his consort, the fiesta queen.[7]

What made this fiesta unusual for me, though, was the final entry in the parade. As this float neared, I could hear the amplified, forceful, and staccato preaching of an evangelical preacher telling onlookers to return to Christ because only he could heal their community. The float consisted of a white truck with placards pulling a flatbed trailer. Signs on the side of the truck read "THE ESPAÑOLA CHRISTIAN CENTER" and "JESUS GAVE HIS LIFE FOR YOUR FREEDOM." The preacher, a Latino man with short black hair, wore a short-sleeved shirt and pleated pants and stood under a blue canopy on the black flatbed trailer. He held the microphone close to his mouth as he faced the spectators and preached to them in Chicano-inflected English. Festive green-silver tinsel fringed the side of the trailer, nearly touching the ground to hide the trailers wheels. Raised above the speakers that broadcast the preacher's voice rested a blue-gray casket that seems intended to evoke the valley's social problems. On a canopy over the preacher's head a sign read "JESUS SAVES FAMILIES • HEALS COMMUNITY • CHANGES CULTURE." On the end of the trailer, underneath, another sign read "THE ESPAÑOLA CHRISTIAN CENTER." Beneath two large speakers stood a man clearly intended to represent the crucified Christ, wearing a long black wig, false beard, flowing white robe, and white tennis shoes, his arms tied to a large wooden cross.

Still, what made this Christian group's parade entry most remarkable and pertinent to both this chapter and the previous one are the two figures that followed the float and brought home the preacher's message. In this parade entry, members of this evangelical church reconfigured Christ's narrative as told by community members and created a new

Oñate Bearing a Hypodermic Needle. A man dressed as a conquistador carries a giant hypodermic needle down Riverside Drive, Española 2004 Fiesta parade. *Photo by author.*

Oñate's Passion. Oñate is whipped by a woman dressed as the devil. Both are participants in the Española Christian Center's entry in the 2004 Española Fiesta parade. Their float was the last one in the parade. *Photo by author.*

powerful narrative of their own. In the manner of Christ bearing the weight of his cross to Calvary, the man carried a giant hypodermic needle made from what looked to be an extraordinarily large muffler. The bearer of the needle wore, in addition to khaki shorts and black Chuck Taylor basketball shoes, a conquistador's helmet and a medieval-style smock emblazoned with a gold lion, likely taken from the Spanish royal seal. In the parade's context, this man clearly represented the festival's patriarch and New Mexico's founding figure, don Juan de Oñate. Spurring the conquistador onward, a young woman dressed as a devil—she wore red makeup, plastic wings, horns, black clothes, and a cape—whipped the hypodermic-needle-bearing icon. Thus, Christ's suffering and crucifixion and New Mexico's founder were brought together in what can only be described as Oñate's Passion. In this retelling, drug use is the cross Nuevomexicanos must bear.

Descansos

In the course of the year following Martínez's and Castañón's murders, the victims' families and friends erected two crosses near the location of Martínez's murder and where Castañón was told to get in Herrera's truck. Similar memorials called descansos dot New Mexico's highways and mark the spots where loved one's souls left their bodies. Martínez's and Castañón's crosses are particularly large, remain well tended, and often hold mementos family and friends leave. In a more sordid update, Raymond Martínez, Ricky Martínez's father and the most public advocate for the innocence of the victims, was later sentenced to probation for statutory rape. Herrera pleaded guilty on July 26, 2000, in Santa Fe District Court to two counts of first-degree murder in order to avoid a death-sentence trial. The chief question of Herrera's February 26, 2002, sentencing was whether he would serve his life sentences consecutively or concurrently. As each term carries thirty years before Herrera is eligible for parole, Defense Attorney Buckles asked Judge Stephen Pfeffer to temper justice with mercy and sentence Herrera to concurrent sentences. After a parade of expert witnesses testified to an extraordinarily difficult life and neglect of Herrera at the

Descansos. Crosses on State Road 76 from Española
to Chimayó mark the place Ricky Martínez and
Karen Castañón encountered Carlos Herrera and
where Martínez died. *Photo by author.*

hands of his family and the schools, Herrera muttered almost inaudibly
into the microphone, "I would like to tell the Castañón family and the
Martínez family, I'm sorry and I'd like to tell my family, I'm sorry for
what I put them through. That's it." Pfeffer sentenced Herrera to serve
consecutive life sentences. He is now serving his time in prison and will
likely leave prison as an old man.

The next chapter explores the cross that Oñate bore, a cross of
heroin and other illicit drugs that evokes another horrible and liberating
power of the negative.

CHAPTER THREE

A Northern New Mexican "Fix"

"It's like the girls say, I need crack for my back,
tokes to joke . . . and *chiva* in my *vida*."

—Dolores Montoya, 2002[1]

I was not prepared for what Joey Jaramillo told me that afternoon in the winter of 2002.[2] I had spent much of the day sitting at a kitchen table with him and other drug users. Jaramillo, a New Mexican man in his mid-forties, elaborated a profound difference between the discourses that described the traditional culture of Latino northern New Mexico and his own experience. About a week before his interview Jaramillo had overdosed and stopped breathing twice. Nevertheless, that early afternoon, Jaramillo was high on both speed and cocaine and looked forward to using heroin. Not surprisingly, his mind seemed to race faster than his words. He said, "What happened to the life of simplicity, man? What happened to the life where our ancestors used to grow the wheat and share it with the Indians, man?" He continued, "Now it's the casinos, and everybody's wanting everybody else's money. It's a money thing. The devil's got his trip going, man." In an effort to draw some direct relationship between Jaramillo's drug use and the community transformation he described, I asked Jaramillo why he used drugs and if the high rates of drug use had some relationship to the valley's transformation. His comments disrupted my effort to find a causal explanation. He told me that he used drugs because he liked it. To my chagrin, when I pressed the point with additional questions, Jaramillo said, "You know what, brother? Believe nothing you hear and half of what you see. Okay? That's how I look at it around here."

In the late 1990s, a series of articles and reports in the regional and national media described with shock how Española's putatively idyllic and bucolic Rio Arriba County statistically had the highest rate of illicit drug overdoses of any county in New Mexico. New Mexico, in turn, was reported to have the highest rate of illicit drug overdoses of any state (Morgan and Morgan 2002, 172, 176, 184–85, 187–88). Española's drug problem also became the object of social science study and frequent citation, including an early version of this chapter (García 2006, 2007, 2008; Glendinning 2005; Kosek 2006; Singer 2008; Trujillo 2006; Willging, Trujillo, and La Luz 2003, 2004, 2005). In the course of my ethnographic research in Española, I found that the disjuncture between the traditional and contemporary worlds resonated with Española drug users' perceptions of their own lived experiences. This chapter draws on research done in 2002 during the course of a University of New Mexico drug-treatment study funded by the New Mexico Department of Health that was conceived in the wake of the media revelations.[3]

Following on Jaramillo's comments, I eschew attempts to attribute drug use to a specific societal "cause," and instead focus on a topic that, judging from current and former drug users' comments, has greater currency in their lived experience: what does drug use do for drug users? In pursuing this line of inquiry, I want to develop two distinct but overlapping arguments. The first follows Georg Wilhelm Friedrich Hegel's *Phenomenology of the Spirit* as well as current trends in illicit drug use research. Before all else, Hegel argued that human existence can be formed and maintained only within a biological reality that requires that desires be fulfilled (Hegel 1977; Kojève 1980). He argued that desire disquiets the person and moves him to action, and born of desire, action therefore tends to satisfy desire. Action does so by the negation, the destruction, or at least the transformation of the desired object. Such a view of drug use is supported by recent research focused on the innate pleasure as well as the wanting and seeking of illicit drugs that anthropologist Daniel Lende terms "incentive salience" (Blum et al. 1996; Di Chiara 1998; Pihl and Peterson 1995; Lende 2005; Robinson and Berridge 1993). In this vein, drug use is a visceral, embodied practice that confronts and momentarily negates, transforms, or displaces the drug users' multiple and proliferating desires.

It is also worthwhile to point out that I am not positing that drug use is resistance or counterhegemonic, although at some times and some places it may have these qualities. Rather, for some Española Valley residents, drug use momentarily transforms experience—an experience now largely lived within modernity and more specifically framed by the service-sector socioeconomic structure of northern New Mexico. My second argument unpacks the premise that culture is a cure for the problems that affect the community. I describe the reactions of several drug users—the subjects of these interpolations—demonstrating some of the ways in which they respond to these characterizations, ranging from grudging acceptance to disdain and disagreement.

Within a Quarter Mile of Here

Since the mid-nineties, the prevalence of drug use has come to symbolize the contradictions between discourses of tradition and a reputation for extreme social problems. This perception of widespread drug use has some reality on the ground. Heroin and cocaine use, as well as the abuse of prescription drugs, are widespread among the valley's Nuevomexicanos. The statistics themselves are shocking. As previously noted, according to figures presented to the Rio Arriba County Commission by New Mexico Department of Health epidemiologists, in 1995–97 Rio Arriba County had the highest rate of illicit drug overdose deaths in New Mexico—a rate more than three times the state average. In turn, New Mexico had the highest rate of illicit drug overdose deaths in the United States—a rate several times the national average (Halasan et al. 2001). Rio Arriba County has an overdose death rate more than ten times the national rate (Winn 2005, 41). Such rates translate into a terrible toll in human lives. Statewide, Office of the Medical Investigator data show an increase in overdose deaths from 121 to 307 in 2003 (Landen 2005, 7), and between 1995 and 2003 there were about three hundred overdoses in Santa Fe and Rio Arriba counties (Scharmen, Roth-Edwards, and Shah 2005, 7).[4] A Department of Health map clearly shows that nearly all Rio Arriba County overdoses occurred among residents living in the Española Valley. There was a similar death toll in the valley's Santa Fe County census tracts (Halasan et al. 2001).

Even more graphic is heroin user Lonnie Martínez's description of the availability of drugs near his home in the same government-subsided apartment complex where I interviewed Joey Jaramillo. Martínez said:

> Look at this small town. Look at this, within a quarter of a mile of here, a quarter mile, there's three crank labs, six people selling heroin, fourteen selling coke. Pot is just like going to the liquor store. Pharmaceutical drugs, Lortabs, Valiums, Percs, Xanax, the barbiturate family. It's just like going to the grocery store, putting a quarter in the machine, and pulling out bubble gum.

Jaramillo said, "It's everywhere. It's everywhere. It's everywhere . . . It's just all around me. I don't have to look for it."

At the turn of the millennium, the area's drug use also seemed to coincide with the popular perception of drug use as disproportionately common among Nuevomexicanos as opposed to other racial-ethnic groups. Observation in treatment programs and harm-reduction sites bore out that drug addiction was most common among Nuevomexicanos rather than among Native Americans, Anglos, or Mexican immigrants. This view is further supported by statistics provided by a needle-exchange program that operates in Española. Between October 2001 and March 2002, 631 "Hispanics" and only 7 "Anglos" participated in one such program. Their numbers do not differentiate between Nuevomexicanos and Mexican immigrants, but ethnographic evidence suggests few of the participants were immigrants. For instance, as I rode along on a needle-exchange trip, an exchange staffer, a Mexican immigrant who lives in Santa Fe, told me that he did not like Española because it was *puro cholo* (all cholo). The needle-exchange program cited no statistics for Native Americans, probably because virtually no Native Americans use its services.

Drug(s) of Choice

While media accounts usually focus on heroin use, area drug users consume a variety of drugs. Still, most picked among heroin (chiva), cocaine (usually smoked in crack form), or prescription drugs as their drugs of choice.[5] In Española, the most common form of heroin is the black tar or mud variety that is purchased in a black or brown, hard, or gummy form and is imported from Mexico. Relatively uncommon in the mid-1990s, crack cocaine seems to be the emerging preferred drug of choice among many younger users. Nearly all cocaine users smoked cocaine, although a few said they injected it or snorted. Most purchased cocaine powder and cooked, or transformed, it into a cocaine freebase or smokable form by heating it in water with baking soda. This method creates an impure form of cocaine freebase that is popularly known as crack. A few used the older and more dangerous form that employs ether and produces the purer form popularly known as freebase.[6] In conversation, some Española users who employed the baking soda method differentiated their cocaine freebase from crack as they viewed their home-cooked freebase as purer. Nevertheless, others failed to differentiate between home-cooked freebase and crack purchased in "ready-rock" form. Former drug user Lisa Chávez said, "I've noticed that it's like everywhere I go; everybody is smoking crack. Everybody."

In addition, many current and former drug users consumed prescription drugs, sometimes prescribed by their doctors or sometimes bought illicitly, often from the same dealers who sell heroin and cocaine. Among the prescription drugs informants used most commonly were opioids such as hyrocodone bitartrate with acetaminophen (Vicodin, Lorcet, Lortab), oxycodone with acetaminophen (Percocet), oxycodone with aspirin (Percodan), oxycodone hydrochloride (Oxycontin), tranquilizers such as benzodiazepine (Diazepam, Valium, Zentrab), barbiturates (Amobarbital or Secobarbital, Seconal, Tuinol), and alprazolam (Xanax). Interestingly, one woman's entrance into narcotic addiction was through methadone—a medically controlled substance two area programs distributed as a substitute for narcotics such as heroin. This woman had never been in a methadone program and purchased her methadone on the streets. Current and former drug users also reported a wide variety of illicit drugs such as cannabis (usually marijuana, although some cited hashish), mushrooms, peyote, opium (heroin), lysergic acid diethylamide (LSD), methamphetamine (including "speed," "crank," and "crystal"), and phencyclidine (PCP). Finally, most users also drank alcohol, and a minority described alcohol as either their drug of choice or a greater problem than substances such as hard drugs.

Most users and ex-users mixed a variety of drugs and alcohol, often in a manner that balanced or intensified their highs. For instance, many often combined the "up" high of cocaine with the "smoothing out" high of heroin in a single injection known as a speedball. Dolores Montoya remarked, "[I used] alcohol, oh baby, 24–7. Marijuana, 24–7. My pills, 24–7. My narcotics. Twenty-four–seven pretty much in everything, except the coke. That was when I had the money." Echoing Montoya's experience, Charlie Lucero stated:

> I drank alcohol, I smoked pot, heroin, and coke. And then the
> prescription pills; Valiums, Percocets, Xanax, Lorcets. There's these
> other pills that we'd call *colorados* (reds). They looked like a little
> bullet. We fixed those, too. Take 'em and what do you call 'em fender
> benders 'cause you'd get all fucked like you're a car or something. You
> know? Let's see, what else? I huffed gas. That's pretty much it.

Within the twenty-four-hour period preceding his interview, Joey Jaramillo told me he consumed half a gram of speed, a gram of coke and half a *gorra* of heroin.[7] Jaramillo said, "I don't have no drug of choice, bro. I just do this and that and all of it." The mixture of heroin, in particular, with this smorgasbord of other drugs is likely responsible for the area's extraordinarily high rate of fatal overdoses. For instance, Lucero reported overdosing several times when he took prescription drugs shortly before he injected heroin.

You Feel this Intense Rush

In Española drug users' accounts of their use, they show themselves to be actively manipulating these substances for desired results (Willging,

Trujillo, and La Luz 2003). This view of drug users is supported by now-venerable ethnographic tradition that views users as agents in addition to objects of these substances' addictive qualities. Since the 1960s, a number of ethnographers have rejected the essentialism of earlier psychological explanations of drug addiction that portrayed addicts as both passive and retreatist (Tracy and Acker 2004, 14–22). Now-classic texts such as Michael Agar's *Ripping and Running* (1973), Edward Preble and John Casey's "Taking Care of Business" (1969), and Norman Zinberg's *Drug, Set, and Setting* (1984) portray drug addicts as acting with purposeful energy. Terry Williams writes, "Many of those in the drug culture want to escape reality, but just as many—perhaps more—want to be absorbed into a meaningful way of life" (Williams 1993, 3). These ethnographic texts have also shown that, in addition to the physiological element of some drug addictions, many drug users are utilizing their drug use as a means to deal with difficult sociohistorical circumstances. For instance, in *The Vietnam War Drug User Returns*, Lee Robins showed that most heroin-addicted Vietnam veterans did not continue using heroin after they returned from the front to their home settings (Robins 1974). They instead used while facing the turmoil of Vietnam. More recently, in the monograph *In Search of Respect* (1995), Philippe Bourgois contextualizes the involvement of a number of Puerto Rican youths in the New York City crack market in a multigenerational history of poverty and underemployment. Bourgois and Jeff Schonberg's new book, *Righteous Dopefiend*, similarly explores indigent poverty and social exclusion among homeless heroin addicts in San Francisco in order to understand the relationship between intimate experiences and broad social forces (Bourgois and Schonberg 2009).

Marxist critic Walter Benjamin's experiments with hashish, opium, mescaline, and the opiate eucodal are chronicled in *On Hashish* (Benjamin 2006). His description of the "trance" or high he experienced in pre–World War II Marseilles, France, addresses this aspect of drug use. He said, "I was incapable of fearing future misfortune, future solitude, for hashish would always remain" (Benjamin 2006, 124). It should be of no surprise, then, when in 1940 he was turned back from the Spanish-French border and faced life and death in Nazi-occupied France, this Jewish intellectual committed suicide via morphine overdose. With this in mind, this chapter's exegesis returns to the notions of desire and negation.

Drug use is a visceral, embodied practice that confronts drug users' multiple and proliferating desires and provides a moment not entirely defined by sociomaterial contradictions or residents' own increasingly complex and internally differentiated subjectivities. This is not to say, however, that drug users are, like Benjamin, explicitly rethinking their place in the world. In Española, most describe getting high in terms of the momentary feeling of well-being their fix provides, the forgetting of life's troubles, the relief of physical pain, and, especially for heroin users, the relief from the physical sickness of withdrawal. *Malias*, as heroin withdrawal symptoms are called in northern New Mexico, may be described as extremely horrible flu symptoms. People suffering from withdrawals often describe themselves as "sick" and therefore require a "fix." Symptoms include, but are not limited to, diarrhea and vomiting.[8]

In their stories of drug use, users and ex-users reported, often wistfully, moments of intense pleasure no longer dominated by metaphorical and physical pain. When I asked a thirty-something Nuevomexicana named Irene Goodnight to describe the feeling that smoking cocaine provides, she said, "It takes away your problems for that five, ten seconds. You don't even care about your problems. You could care less about anything after that hit." Feliz Chacon described smoking crack:

> You feel this intense rush. Almost like you are lifted outside of
> yourself. You're just up in the clouds somewhere. You're way above
> yourself, and almost sounds nuts, almost spiritual feeling and like I
> say . . . this feeling of a total being, of you're with yourself. You're
> lifted to this place that you don't want to come down from.

Similarly, twenty-three-year-old Charlie Lucero told me how he felt pursuing his fix and then shooting up. In his description, his words fail, but the intense and distant look in his eyes indicated he knew well the feeling he could only partially articulate. He said:

You're just trying to score that fix, let's say all morning, you're just
stressing and stressing and sweating, anxious. You know? You're driving
up wherever you're going to score this stuff and you're just, it's just
every time, you know? It's just like a trip. I don't know. It's hard to say.
You get like this real like, your stomach cramps up and you just feel
like using the restroom and you're anxious, real anxious . . . to make it
and you're wanting to throw up and just feeling awful but you know
you're going to get your fix. Until, finally you're like in a rush and
boom you fix. And once you pull that syringe out you just, you're
like, you're the king. You know? Right away, you just start talking to
people and it's just completely different. It's like if you [pause] you
feel at home with everything or something. I don't know. You just
feel more powerful and more relaxed. You get that rush like pins and
needles. You know? Just like a nice cramp. I don't know. It's weird.
Through your whole body, you just get like a chill but it feels good.
You know? You just don't have no worries.

Finally, thirty-something Lisa Chávez described with fondness the first
time she used heroin:

We were sitting around the table and my girlfriend that was there,
my friend she was, she would snort it and the other two were
shooting it up. We were just sitting around the table drinking,
partying and when it got to me, [my boyfriend] told me, "Do you
want some? Try it." So I said okay. So we did it on a little tiny spoon.
I snorted and after a while I was throwing up like a dog. It makes
you throw up, but yet it made me feel good. I was just sitting there
and my eyes were shut and I could hear everybody. They were
standing there and talking and I know they kept saying, "Make sure
she's okay. Are you okay?" "Yeah I'm okay." But it was just peaceful.
I don't know. I was like, I was just calm, mellow and nothing hurt.
Everything was nice, just a good feeling and then I was, I stayed
with them for a while. We all stayed in there and he'd go in the
room and he'd be all "Here's your morning thing." He would go in
there in the bedroom and he'd already have it in a syringe and he
would squirt it up my nose and it was every day, every day.

For some, drug use not only blessed the users with a general feeling of well-being, it also removed the pain from injuries received in the course of wage labor, their daily activities, and sickness, sometimes exacerbated by inadequate medical care. Already a drug and alcohol user, construction worker Dolores Montoya became addicted to prescription pills because of preexisting health problems, work accidents, and allegedly incompetent health care. She said that in a work accident she crushed her ankle and was subsequently prescribed morphine for two weeks and painkillers such as Percocets. Current user Lisa Marie Martínez said she became addicted to heroin because it eased her pain from preexisting hepatitis C symptoms:

> I was real sick. Sick, sick and I couldn't even move or nothing. The medication wasn't helping me and one day my husband came and told [me], "I know what will help you. I don't want to give it to you but I know what will help you feel better." So I tried it and I didn't like it at first but then afterwards, I tried it again and then it just got to be every day of that. And it did take away the pain, you know? All your pain gone. It got took away.

In other words, in the minutes of a crack-cocaine rush and hours of a heroin high, the metaphorical pain of the users' daily lives and the specific physical pain of their injuries and illnesses were negated, transformed, or displaced.

Furthermore, as suggested by Charlie Lucero's description of shooting up, the psychobiological reactions of heroin and cocaine use are supplemented by the complex and embodied process of drug use. Both are profoundly visceral activities that require skilled preparation and result in intense psychophysical reactions that set them apart from other daily activities. Indeed, drug users and ex-users described drug consumption in almost ritualistic terms. Heroin injection practices, such as mainlining, in which a small amount of heroin is typically placed on a spoon, dissolved in water, and then heated, were often discussed in this way. Star Frésquez said:

I think I was addicted to the needle itself. You're addicted to
the ritual of putting it in a spoon, of lighting it and smelling and
picking it up and seeing the blood register and, you're like addicted
to that. I think I was more addicted to that than anything else, than
the actual high.

Similarly, Feets Ortiz's description of heroin use evokes his own intense
feelings and longing for the experience (Willging, Trujillo, and La Luz
2003). Despite his preference for mainlining, Ortiz told ethnographer
Azul La Luz that he turned to "skin popping" because he had "no
veins left." La Luz noted he had visible, open wounds and thick scar
tissue caused by abscesses. Ortiz described the delight of finding a vein
appropriate for injection. He said, "For a guy that don't have no veins,
sometimes I can find one." Ortiz then made a motion that mimicked
the act of sticking a needle in his arm. With growing excitement,
he continued, "And I see the blood, it's like a rush feeling that you
could . . . actually! No!" Ortiz closed his eyes and turned up his face
to the ceiling in pleasure. "You actually know it's going to go into
you!" His eyes still closed, tears coming down his face, he commented,
"Instead of something cutting you! I don't know." He finished wiping
his eyes; his shoulders slumped. "I done it to myself quite a bit of times,
you know" (Willging, Trujillo, and La Luz 2003, 31–32).

In a similarly complex process, cocaine is typically cooked in water
on a stove top with baking soda in a process that takes some skill and time.
In this way, cocaine freebase is "rocked up," or formed as a precipitate
in the cooking process. The process of smoking crack also includes its
own special smells ("burning plastic"), sounds (the "crackling" that is
the source of its name crack), and intense psychophysical reactions.
Feliz described smoking crack for the first time:

So she put this boulder about the size of a marble in it and I still
remember lighting and the sound it made. It's almost like a log in
a fire, this cracking noise and she said, "Inhale it and hold it as long
as you can." So being the pig that I am, I thought this was all mine,
this was for the three of us. So I lit it and I remember my lungs felt
like they were on fire and it smelled like burned plastic and I still

remember it. So I held it in and they're talking and I'm waiting for her to tell me to let it out. She just assumed I knew it and she is like "Let it out!" I let it out and immediately just got this head rush that was, I couldn't even describe it. And I immediately, I got sick, and thank God we were in the bathroom. I mean I just started to vomit and I heard people do that with heroin sometimes, but then I wanted that feeling again. About twenty minutes later, like I say, it was downhill from there, we did it again and then it was like it wasn't enough. I just wanted more and more and more and we stayed there at her house doing it.

Statements such as these suggest that in the act of drug use, people performed a labor set apart from other activities that had immediate and profound visceral impact.

In their stories of drug use, these people described contradictory and internally differentiated subject positions as wage earners, family members, participants in an underground and illicit economy, and drug users (Willging, Trujillo, and La Luz 2003). Women in particular described contradictions between their identities as mothers, romantic-sexual partners, and family members. Many related difficult economic and material and social relations as major stressors in their lives. Finally, some described physical and physiological pain that was often both the result and embodiment of these contradictions. In the act of their drug use, though, these feelings found a "fix," or momentarily negated, transformed, or displaced the metaphorical pain of life's struggles as well as the specific physical pain of injuries and illness. They re-created the work day, removed their labor from the complete control of their employers, transformed their desires, and achieved immediate and visceral rewards. Here again, Benjamin's statements on his hashish "trance" or high are instructive, if perhaps naive, when compared to the actual payback of harder addictions. He wrote:

When I recall that state I should like to believe that hashish persuades nature to permit us—for less egoistic purposes—that squandering of our own existence that we know in love. For if, when we love, our existence runs through nature's fingers like

golden coins that she cannot hold and lets fall to purchase new birth
thereby, she now throws us, without hoping or expecting anything,
in ample handfuls to existence. (Benjamin 2006, 126)

For Española's drug users, these desires were often basic needs such
as hunger and absence of pain. Others dealt with more complex
frustrations at their socioeconomic position in life, torn families, and
inability to maintain romantic love. Lonnie Martínez explained, "Oh
sí it's not that alcohol or heroin, it's not the high that gets me. It what
it does for me. It takes me out of the realities of society. I can create
my own world in my head and still live over here or wherever, but I'm
living in my own world. My own world."

Culture as Cure

Nevertheless, the question, "What does drug use do for drug users?" is
not the most widely asked question in professional and political debates
concerning drug and alcohol addiction in the valley. Rather, most are
looking for a "cause" of the valley's high rates of addiction, and many
find the answer within the loss of traditional culture. In particular, many
area leaders—a group now largely drawn from the region's emergent
middle class—appear to be attempting to (re)assert their vision of
tradition and community. They draw implicitly and explicitly on the
concept of culture to explain the conundrum of a perceived extreme
social malaise in a place defined by its strong cultural heritage and
conceptualize a growing cultural deficit, especially among the young,
and its material underpinnings as the cause of illicit drug use. In the
process, they reproduce a cultural logic that conceptualizes modernity
and culture in opposing terms.

In northern New Mexico, the trope of culture is particularly
powerful and loaded. As I have noted in previous chapters, in the United
States, few non–Native American populations of comparable size have
been the objects of such tremendous discursive production as northern
New Mexican Latinos, a group that here, in contrast to neighboring
communities, continues to constitute nearly all of the population. This

vision of continuity with a traditional culture is evident and lends support to the homegrown political movement. In Española's Rio Arriba County, community-based political mobilization efforts that seek to reassert and enforce Nuevomexicano rights to land and resources are long-standing and suffuse local political discourse. Moreover, Española's current inhabitants are situated within a complex historical matrix of already existing representations that transmit a concept of Nuevomexicano culture as a functioning holistic system of traditional beliefs tied to an agrarian economy. Not surprisingly, then, much popular community discourse reproduces and deploys the cultural logic of loss elaborated by land-grant activists.

This notion of culture loss fits with common interpretations of the etiology of drug and alcohol use and modalities for the treatment of addiction among Native Americans, other indigenous peoples, and Latinos (Brady 1995; Santiago-Irizarry 1996). Maggie Brady writes, "Drug and alcohol abuse, and ill-health too, are said by many indigenous people to have arisen from, or been exacerbated by, deprivation and the erosion of their cultural integrity as a result of colonization" (Brady 1995, 1489). Where the evangelicals in Española's 2004 fiesta parade asserted that Christ cures culture, here culture itself becomes the cure. Harry Montoya, the Santa Fe County commissioner who represents much of the southern part of the Greater Española Valley and director of a nonprofit called Hands Across Cultures, states:

> The whole emphasis of what we are trying to do is based on
> the concept that I've defined . . . and that is *la cultura cura*, the
> culture cures. Our belief is that a lot of what's happening in our
> communities here in northern New Mexico has to do somewhat
> with a loss of culture. (*Culture as a Cure/La Cultura Cura* 1997)

This framework often produces a definition of ethnicity, language habits, and culture presumed to constitute the identity categorized as an authentic lifeway. The referential contents of culture are identified as art, food, and tradition (Santiago-Irizarry 1996). In the same video where Montoya cited culture as the cure, he said:

The food, the music, I mean that is a beautiful thing of who we are as a people. The dance, the traditions we have within the Hispano and Indian cultures. The things we have done for thousands of years that have been passed from generation to generation. And we need to see those as curative factors, resilient factors in terms of this is who we are. (*Culture as a Cure/La Cultura Cura* 1997)

In such narratives, culture has become a reified object that you either have or you have lost. Finally, in the particular context of northern New Mexico, this definition of culture is often specifically tied to a traditional agricultural economy and the alienation of that economy's land base. This etiology of culture loss is often directly transposed onto the Española Valley by community leaders in their confrontation of the valley's problems. Montoya's organization offers educational services intended both to prevent substance abuse and promote cultural activities.

Members of the area's emergent middle class, as well as sympathetic Anglos, have increasingly taken up this rhetoric of culture loss. Community leaders' specific responses to these issues tend to take three forms: denial of the problem and assertion of the continuity of tradition; the assertion of cultural disintegration; or the advocating of a return to traditional culture. Richard Lucero, mayor of Española at the time, steered me clear of negative portrayals of the community to discussions of traditional culture, regional roots, and the community's impoverishment at the hands of external forces. State Sen. Richard Martínez went even further. At a traditional healing conference sponsored by a local treatment provider, Martínez attributed the area's reputation as a drug Mecca to sensationalist stories from the local newspaper, the *Rio Grande Sun*.

In contrast, comments by Anglo residents such as Bruce Richardson of the Chimayó Crime Prevention organization and Suellen Strale of the Chimayó Youth Conservation Corps, often represent the community as culturally bankrupt. For example, Strale stated in a front page article in the *Dallas Morning News*, "I suppose that there's no place like it on earth" and continued, "You live in this beautifully pure place and a low rider passes you slowly on the road and the driver pretends to shoot you. You look in his eyes and see pure evil" (Weyerman 2000).

More thoughtfully, a report Rio Arriba Department of Health and Human Services published attempted to account for and recapture drug use within the traditional culture paradigm. The study's author, Lauren Reichelt, county director of Health and Human Services, attributed the area's high rates of drug use to "culturally specific issues such as land loss and disintegration of Española's agricultural economy and related social institutions" (Reichelt 2001). She further recommended efforts to promote local culture and return traditional lands now in the hands of the Forest Service to village communities. Harry Montoya even more explicitly attributes substance abuse to colonialism and an accompanying Americanization that causes tremendous social and psychic pain. Interestingly, Santa Cruz parish priest Fr. Ron Carrillo is a driving force in Montoya's nonprofit organization, Hands Across Culture. Similarly, Montoya is a Eucharistic minister at Carrillo's parish. Further, Hands Across Cultures's efforts to reinvigorate traditional cultural forms seem to complement Carrillo's own vision for parish youth. Following this logic, social problems are characterized by culture's perceived absence and therefore a logical solution is to inoculate people with culture.

The attribution of the valley's high rates of drug use to social transformation and cultural dislocation is also found in other anthropological descriptions of area drug use. Jake Kosek's award-winning book about politics surrounding New Mexican forests relates such arguments in its preface and conclusion (2006).[9] Chellis Glendinning's popularly oriented book *Chiva: A Village Takes on the Global Heroin Trade* fully elaborates this conceptualization of drug use and community efforts to combat it (Glendinning 2005). Glendinning connects global problems to the suffering and intimate details of her life and the lives of people close to her. At the local level, however, her description of the area residents' mobilization elides the tremendous visionary and practical conflicts that sometimes tear the groups apart and often set participants against one another. Furthermore, when the Greater Española Valley is understood as a whole, Chimayó's partial success combating endemic drug use must be understood in the context of an increase in drug use in other valley communities and the valley's overall lack of decline in fatal overdoses.

Anthropologist Angela García and, based on García's analysis, the work of the influential ethnographer Merrill Singer cite specific causes for Española's drug epidemic in cultural change and land loss linked to the swindle of Spanish and Mexican land grants (García 2006, 2007; Singer 2008). Her 2008 *Cultural Anthropology* article "The Elegiac Addict: History, Chronicity, and the Melancholic Subject" loosens that connection and makes land loss one element of a broader focus on "historical loss" through one addict's story. She writes "My particular concern here is with how forms of historical loss, the embodied complexity of addiction, and local and biomedical logics of chronicity tragically coincided in Alma's life" (García 2008, 720). While García's description of Alma's tragic experience is both powerfully written and heart-breaking, it also suggests a weakness of her arguments (García 2006, 2007, 2008). Her primary evidence for historical loss, and especially land loss, as causal factors comes in the forms of quotes from a woman from the northern Rio Arriba County community of Tierra Amarilla, a rural collection of villages sixty-five miles north of the city of Española.[10]

This reasoning may be spun into a romantic narrative. Relying on García's newspaper article, Singer paints a fanciful image of Española's drug epidemic and the efforts of locals to fight it (2008, 216-20). In one remarkable sentence, Singer conflates the valley's struggle with the widely read John Nichols' novel *The Milagro Beanfield War*, the mid-twentieth century film *Salt of the Earth* about southern New Mexico miners, and the work of the internationally famous Anglo artist Georgia O'Keeffe. He writes, "While the book [*The Milagro Beanfield War*] is fiction, it effectively captures the lives and social struggles of the salt of the earth inhabitants of the picturesque Española Valley, a place known to many through the remarkable landscape paintings of Georgia O'Keeffe" (Singer 2008, 216). García's work aside, many area residents—a disproportionate number being members of Española's emerging middle class and Anglo immigrants—and some scholars attempt to quarantine the disruptive and ineffable negativity of drug use within the narratives of traditional culture. In the context of the complex and internally differentiated subjectivities described by drug users and their often precarious but thoroughly modern economic and social positions, the notion of cultural renewal becomes a panacea for social problems.

Let's Get Real

While some Española area users express anxiety about issues of culture, most are more concerned with everyday experiences such as making ends meet, physical pain, family troubles, romantic difficulties, and, especially for heroin and prescription drug addicts, the need to placate the physiological manifestations of addiction. Furthermore, I met numerous drug users who were highly engaged with the traditional aspects of their culture, some as Spanish-language musicians and matachines dancers. Indeed, some drug users were more engaged with supposed traditional culture than the community leaders who propose culture as the cure.

The logic that renders drug use the result of culture's absence does not recognize drug users as creative agents confronting complex social realities. This account refuses to situate both culture and drug users outside the mess and contradictory intersections of actual material life. Rather, drug users are modern subjects who address their world and drug use as a sort of solution to current social difficulties. In so doing, they undermine the tidy and nostalgic narratives of culture and culture's functionalist wholeness. This view of drug use as a critical engagement with socioeconomic problems is largely my interpretation of drug users' acts and statements. One drug user makes this argument explicit. Facing community leaders' assertions of tradition head on, Lonnie Martínez describes his drug use as a remaking of the world and a negation of the past. For him the contradictions between his experience and those community leaders envision may be part of what makes drug use so attractive to him in the first place. Martínez's dual aim at "the elders" and "society" that I will outline below becomes an intuitive grasping and aggressive play on Española's homegrown and emerging middle-class pretension.

Down a potholed road, past an Española supermarket, stands a newly rebuilt, multistoried, government-subsidized apartment building. Inside, on an early October afternoon, I sat on Lonnie Martínez's couch and chain-smoked cigarettes as he and a young woman found the correct spot to insert their respective hypodermic needles. As I sat and smoked, the woman, careful not to leave track marks in a visible spot, disappeared into the bathroom and perhaps stuck the needle between her toes or in some other hidden location. Martínez inserted the needle in his arm. Before his fix, Martínez and I matter-of-factly discussed money and health issues, but afterward he was in a much better mood and no longer talking business. He insisted that in shooting up he alleviated both the physical pain caused by the fresh beatings evidenced on his face and a lifelong lack of proper medical care. Perhaps even more important, he explained, "Why we do it? To me, it's just a medication, a product that I use in order to live the way I want, how I like to create and build what I want, if I want, where I want." Martínez said:

> Being in this part of the country, New Mexico, we relate to the elders, the traditions and that doesn't work no more. That's not what's happening no more. . . . You see the grandchildren selling an acre of land for two grams of heroin because they sign the signatures. You see the little old man over here across the street in the old age home. All they talk about, "Oh I had two hundred and forty acres of land" and they're telling the truth, and then you see their children that sold all their land asking for dimes and quarters to get their bag of heroin right down the block.

He continued, "I can't use grandpa to teach 'eeh *hijito* (my child) over here is how to use a needle to plow the land. [A young person] ain't got no fucking interest in plowing land. Put grandpa out to pasture. Let's get real." Nevertheless, the more frequent target of Martínez's criticism was directed at what he saw as mainstream society. Martínez said:

> They'd rather put me in a cave than have me in society. Little do they know we have our own society. They know, but they'd rather have us out of their society. They couldn't function to begin with. They're barely able to function in their own society. The other day my psych [psychologist] said, "Well that's crazy." I said, "Oh well everybody in the world's crazy in one way or the other." The only thing that divides is those of us that knows it, deals with it, work with it, accept it and are comfortable with it. But look at those that pilot planes, drive trains, educate our children, rolling and running our government that are crazy and don't even know it. My God,

why do they think we're going through what we're going through in the world today? You know?

After fixing, Martínez opened his apartment's front door, and friends and neighbors began to stop in, and some took beers from his refrigerator. An older woman offered swigs from a pint bottle. In pleasant anticipation, they discussed the food Martínez and several of the women had prepared earlier and that now simmered upstairs. In sum, Martínez told me that through heroin, cocaine, alcohol, prescription drugs, and other substances, he could create his own world while sitting in the physical surroundings of his government-subsidized apartment, and he could move on from the past. For a moment at least, in the act of using, Martínez felt good, and his problems were forgotten.

Bulletproof

I began this chapter by describing how Joey Jaramillo rejected a simple causal explanation for his addiction and the valley's high rate of addiction. Rather, Jaramillo insisted that he used because he "liked it." I posited that part of what he liked about drug use is that drug use is a visceral, embodied practice that overcomes the contradictions of their lives. In this transcendence, for many, emerges a tremendous feeling of power. Jaramillo said:

> I could shoot myself in the chest and who cares you know what I mean? That kind of stuff. Bulletproof . . . Man! Do you know what I mean? And I never ever got busted. Never in my whole life. No and I used to bring it in. I used to pick it off of planes. I've always had plenty. I've never held a job more than a couple of paychecks when I was really hurting. Get a couple of paychecks and that was it. I'd quit. Just like go to those rehabs somewhere. You know what I mean?

This creative power of drug use cannot be grasped by a culture-loss model. Rather, getting high is somehow regenerative as well as destructive, and Feliz Chacon, Lonnie Martínez, and Charlie Lucero are "fixing" the contradictions of an emerging Nuevomexicano condition. This regenerative power suggests why drug use is so widespread. Further anecdotal and state Department of Health statistics for Rio Arriba County indicate many valley residents are experiencing great pain and loss. In a recent study of 286 people arrested in Rio Arriba County, New Mexico State University public administration professor Russell Winn found very high rates of drug and alcohol use, and his preliminary results suggest widespread depression and traumatic experiences (Winn 2005, 41–46). Substance use has become participant in a synergetic death spiral that promises to relieve the pain it has simultaneously come to create. This synergy certainly plays a role in the following statistics: in Rio Arriba County, cirrhosis mortality death rates are more than four times the national average, homicide rates are more than twice the national average, and suicide rates are more than three times the national average. Motor vehicle death rates are nearly four times the national average (Halasan et al. 2001).

In this sense, drug use cannot be dismissed as merely social pathology. Consider that, for the moment following his fix, twenty-three-year-old Charlie Lucero experienced a profound, if illusory, reversal of fortune. Without drastically changing his life circumstances or returning to the land, he left behind the relatively downtrodden position of a working-class Española youth. Instead, Lucero felt great power, became a "king," and his worries were forgotten. Similarly, Jaramillo became, for a while, an important man who "held the bag," and Lisa Marie Martínez could forget her pain. Drawing on Walter Benjamin, we might say that this transcendence is experienced as a feeling that is beyond or prior to culture. Benjamin described it as thrown "in ample handfuls to existence."

In this context, drug use may be seen as motivated by a utopian impulse that seeks to render whole the fragmentation of drug users' daily lives. In shooting up, smoking crack, or popping pills, as if in some sublime, momentary, and horrible Hegelian overcoming, the most painful contradictions of late capitalism are confronted, negated, transformed, or displaced through symbolic violence. An Española Valley heroin addict named Michael Trujillo made this point in both poetic and terrible terms.[11] He said, "Electrified paralyzed look in my eyes. / Illusion, confusion without compromise. / Consolation, segregation, darkness and meditation. / Dying will I rise."[12] Another current user, whose father was murdered and whose mother died from cirrhosis of the liver, described his overdose experiences in terms that suggest a similar transcendence that simultaneously burrows into an embodied misery. He told La Luz:

> I got in the habit of playing Russian Roulette . . . Like when you fill up your syringe full of cocaine, say that much [holding his thumb and index fingers about two inches apart] and shoot in your neck, and you don't know if you're going to make it to the dark side or the light side . . . [I did it] for entertainment. I didn't have anything better to do. (Willging, Trujillo, and La Luz 2003, 51–52)

Joey Jaramillo also speaks of drugs and death:

> I've never wanted to quit. I've always liked it. I've always loved drugs. Even, even after a friend dies, what did we do? We'd . . . go throw a party. That's what we'd do. Instead of talking and watching the funeral cars come up the hill. We were already drinking and pounding and, already did it man. And that's the reason our friends die.

In a moment of reflection on his description of partying after the death of a friend, Joey Jaramillo said, in a manner that suggests both his anguish and the strength of drug use to momentarily overcome irreconcilable contradictions, "It makes no sense man. You know what I mean? It makes no fucking sense."

Martínez's personal description of intergenerational drug use and dissatisfaction with both tradition and modernity had resonance for some other addicts and seemed more generally applicable to the experience of other users. When asked why he used drugs, Joey Jaramillo said he enjoyed the high and feeling of power that "holding the bag," or controlling the drugs, supplied. He said, "I just liked it, you know?" Jaramillo concluded, "Everybody just likes it around here. That's all." On another occasion as I sat at a table with both Martínez and Jaramillo, Jaramillo said, "Yeah, it's a tradition, a generation man! It's tradition. That's right," and Martínez responded, "and it's a ritual of tradition for four generations."

CHAPTER FOUR

A Time for Bitterness

It seems we anthropologists have more difficulties in
entering into modernity than do the social groups we study.

—Néstor García Canclini, *Hybrid Cultures: Strategies for Entering
and Leaving Modernity*

One way of highlighting this is to lay bare what goes on in
anthropological fieldwork as a prolonged encounter with
others fraught with misunderstandings that actually open up
the world more than do understandings.

—Michael Taussig, *Walter Benjamin's Grave*

This chapter is a sympathetic critique of the work of a cohort of
anthropologists who conducted fieldwork in Española's Rio Arriba
County in the 1960s, 1970s, and 1980s. They did so in the wake of
the area residents' political mobilization in the Chicano-era land-
grant movement that sought to regain and enforce rights to land
and resources (Knowlton 1976; Swadesh 1968). It focuses first on the
ethnographic work of anthropologists Paul Kutsche, John R. Van Ness,
and Charles Briggs in the Rio Arriba County villages of Cañones
and Córdova and second on the largely overlooked work of Joseph
W. Whitecotton, Richard Stewart Ellis, and Alfredo Jiménez Núñez in
the semiurban Española Valley proper. In their ethnographic work, all
these anthropologists were confronted by Nuevomexicanos' complex
subjectivities and the ever-present negativity that seems to proliferate
in the efforts to describe New Mexican cultures. I also explore these
precursor works' implications for current ethnography.

Revealed in the juxtaposition of these diverse and sometimes contradictory ethnographic accounts of communities only miles apart are fundamentally different problematics or politics of scale. Like scale in cartography, for ethnographers and cultural critics scale refers to degrees on a conceptual continuum spanning from materiality on one end to abstraction on the other (McCarthy 2006, 24). Each of the various theoretical approaches followed by anthropologists discussed here, such as cultural ecology, Gramscian Marxism, ethnicity theory, and word systems approaches, suggests differing senses of scale and related methodologies.[1] Ultimately, the heart of this chapter is the argument that the village ethnographers' focus on residual culture forms ultimately "contained," in Fredric Jameson's sense of the term, the more complex, contradictory, and often negative identity formations (Jameson 1982). In the process, I will describe the unintended consequences of even the savviest and best-intentioned ethnography, offering a somewhat sympathetic critique, in recognition of the difficulties and fraught nature of representation. This chapter also takes seriously Taussig's assertion that misunderstandings may open up the world (Taussig 2006, viii).

Village Ethnography

As I have already suggested, the rural villages that surround the Española Valley occupy a special place in both the anthropological as well as popular imaginations. In the 1960s, 1970s, and 1980s, Paul Kutsche, John R. Van Ness, Charles Briggs, and others published a collective body of ethnographic literature. These anthropologists were concerned primarily with "culture" and conceptualized these communities as vital social organizations that utilize and adapt a traditional village culture as an organizing force for resisting broader economic and social transformations (Briggs 1988, 1986, 1981, 1980; Briggs and Van Ness 1987; Knowlton 1976, 1969, 1961; Kutsche 1983, 1979, 1976; Kutsche and Van Ness 1988; Quintana 1991; Van Ness 1979; Reich 1977; Swadesh 1974). As will become clear later, Kutsche, Van Ness, and especially Briggs viewed the villages as residual elements of an earlier socioeconomic order that remain active organizing principles for addressing current socioeconomic circumstances (Williams 1977, 121–27). It is also worthy of note that the intellectual genealogy of Paul Kutsche, Charles Briggs, and John R. Van Ness is even closer than it first appears. Both Briggs and Van Ness were undergraduate students of Kutsche at Colorado College in Colorado Springs. Additionally, Briggs is the grandson of University of New Mexico folklorist John Donald Robb, to whom Briggs's definitive work in New Mexico, *Competence in Performance: The Creativity of Tradition in Mexicano Verbal Art* (1988), is dedicated.

Both Kutsche and Briggs chose particularly "intact" villages that were almost exclusively inhabited by families tracing their occupancy back for many generations and containing clear geographic centers of adobe homes clustered around a historic Roman Catholic church. Kutsche stated that he selected Cañones with the goal of finding a small, isolated, subsistence village that would be a baseline to serve as a measure for change elsewhere (Kutsche and Van Ness 1988, 2). Cañones remains today a small and fairly remote village located in central Rio Arriba County and just beyond the borders of the Española Valley School District. In 1967, the time of Kutsche's first research stint in Cañones, the village consisted of thirty households and 173 people and was entirely Nuevomexicano. Briggs's field site, Córdova, is located in the southeast corner of Rio Arriba County, just within the Española Valley School District, and is nationally known for its *santero* wood-carving tradition (Briggs 1980). At the time of Briggs's fieldwork, the village consisted of 700 people, that population entirely Nuevomexicano with the exception of one Mexican immigrant, several Anglo-Americans who had married residents, and a few transient Anglo-American youth (Briggs 1986, 31). Despite both Briggs's and Kutsche's field sites' rural character, they and a substantial literature agree that the traditional village economy of subsistence agriculture was superseded long ago (Deutsch 1987; Forrest 1989, 1987; Hamon 1970; Weigle 1975; Williams 1985).

In addition to the physical setting, their ethnographic choices were shaped by a discursive field rife with tremendous and sometimes contradictory pressures. First, Kutsche and Briggs were confronted by a formidable body of previous anthropological and sociological Spanish American village literature that viewed village culture as dysfunctional and a barrier to villagers' positive adjustment to their assimilation into

The village of Córdova in November 2004. *Photo by author.*

The village of Cañones in November 2004. *Photo by author.*

the dominant society (Edmonson 1957; Kluckhohn and Strodtbeck 1961; Saunders 1954; Walter 1938). Kutsche described the previous social scientists as focused on the following negative qualities of village culture: atomistic social structure, factionalism, patron–peon economic and interpersonal relations, personalism, fatalism, "present-time-ism," inefficient land use, and unwillingness to be melted down in the great pot of assimilation (Kutsche 1979, 7). Even more aggressively, Briggs specifically criticized the same prior generation as uncomfortably close to providing an intellectual tool and raison d'être for maintenance of Anglo-American domination (Briggs 1981, 59).[2] Interestingly, Kutsche describes his generation of village ethnographers' divergence from their predecessors in terms of Robert Redfield and Oscar Lewis's paradigmatic disagreement over the cohesion–dysfunction in the Mexican village of Tepoztlán (Lewis 1951; Redfield 1930). In a chronological twist, Kutsche casts his generation of New Mexico village ethnographers in the role of the empathetic Redfield while their interlocutors, such as Edmonson, Kluckhohn, and Saunders, take the role of dysfunction-centric Lewis. As will become clearer later, I also suspect Kutsche saw his work in contrast to the work of his contemporaries working in Española proper.

Second, many researchers and, more important, many Nuevomexicanos consider the alienation of the Spanish- and Mexican-era land grants from villagers by the illegal and extralegal actions of government officials and land speculators as the chief cause of the destruction of the resource base for the area's traditional economy (Briggs and Van Ness 1987; Ebright 1994; Van Ness and Van Ness 1980; Westphall 1983). As a result, for many Nuevomexicanos, the loss of the land grants and the transformation of village sociocultural structure have come to symbolize the expropriation of Nuevomexicano labor and natural resources and the marginalization of the villages in the regional and national economy. University of New Mexico anthropologist Sylvia Rodríguez said, "Nuevomexicanos' sense of ethnic and cultural identity is tied explicitly to their land base and to the memory of a subsistence pattern, long superseded by the wage economy, which once embodied and now symbolizes that tie" (Rodríguez 1992, 110).

Third, simultaneously with the displacement of northern New Mexico's traditional subsistence agriculture economy, the region was incorporated into the national imagination as the antithesis of the rapidly urbanizing and industrializing East. For eastern intellectuals who witnessed the onslaught of the industrial revolution, northern New Mexico seemed an exotic, pristine world that assumed shape and meaning in contrast to the urban industrial world that they had escaped (Rodríguez 1994, 110). This discourse of nostalgia idealized "Indians" and occasionally also New Mexico's folkloric "Spanish" or "Mexican" peasants (Dilworth 1996; Gutiérrez 2002; Martin 1998; Mullin 2001; Reed 2005; Rodríguez 1998, 1994, 1989; Weigle and Fiore 1994; Wilson 1997). Soon Santa Fe, twenty-five miles south of Española, and Taos, forty miles to the north, were transformed into art colonies and, later, centers of tourism and recreation.

The village ethnographers' writings cannot be understood without their contextualization within a discursive landscape permeated by a precursor social science literature, land-movement politics, and Anglo modernist longing. Kutsche and Van Ness, in particular, and sometimes also Briggs, draw on cultural ecology to assert the adaptive (positive) status of the village's traditional socioeconomic system. Moreover, this cohort of anthropologists entered the field during the peak years of both the political activism that sought the return of Mexican- and Spanish-era land grants to grant heirs and their communities and increased Anglo-American immigration (Nabokov 1969; Swadesh 1968; Tijerina 2000, 1978). Indeed, Nuevomexicanos' smoldering anger and frustration exploded in 1967 when land activists "raided" Rio Arriba County's courthouse in Tierra Amarilla.[3] Also in 1967, at Kutsche and Van Ness's field site, Cañones, the residents' fight against their elementary school's closure and then the busing of their children down unsafe roads played a role in the state governor's race (Kutsche and Van Ness 1988, 153–97). In the following discussion of Kutsche's, Van Ness's, and Briggs's work, I will show that these anthropologists threw their lot in with the villagers' positive vision of their communities and against the negativity or disorganization previous social science literature had described. In addition, I suspect that, although unknowingly, their choices reflected their own modernist longing. Ultimately, they reshaped village ethnography with a vision that focused on the continued relevance of residual cultural forms and village society.

Informed by their larger oeuvres, my analysis now turns to their most weighty and mature ethnographic descriptions of their respective field sites: Kutsche and Van Ness's monograph *Cañones: Values, Crisis, and Survival in a Northern New Mexico Village* (Kutsche and Van Ness 1988) and Briggs's theoretically ambitious and most important statement on Nuevomexicano ethnography, *Competence in Performance: The Creativity of Tradition in Mexicano Verbal Art* (Briggs 1988).

In the style of the classic ethnographic monograph, Kutsche and Van Ness found cultural patterns, institutions, and quasi institutions that ordered and shaped all aspects of village life in Cañones. The ethnographic heart of the book described the village as a cultural-ecological adaptation to the surrounding environment. They wrote, "We also try to show that Spanish-Mexican land tenure, law and custom, as well as systems of land utilization, fit the microbasins of northern New Mexico particularly well" (1988 2). Chapters 1 through 7 included in-depth descriptions of the community's history, material and economic life, social institutions, beliefs, and the rituals of daily life. Still, in the final chapters, Kutsche and Van Ness moved beyond the classic monograph model and left the use of the ethnographic present behind. Rather, they concretely narrated in historical time the community's unification in the face of the 1967 closing of their elementary school and the busing of children down dangerous roads to the faraway village of Coyote.

Kutsche and Van Ness argued that despite the village's economic dependence on a broader system of production, most Cañoneros continued to see themselves as rancheros, even though only twelve of thirty households owned cattle, and only five of those households had more than ten head (Kutsche and Van Ness 1988, 44–45). Kutsche and Van Ness believed this perception fit the "self-image of the Hispano as *caballero* (which means both *horseman* and *gentleman*), an unbroken tradition since the Reconquest of the Iberian Peninsula in the late middle ages" (Kutsche and Van Ness 1988, 45). Nevertheless, they noted the economic base for this self-identification has been largely disrupted. They wrote, "That is the ideal. The reality for many is that they have no grazing permits and thus are effectively landless. The discrepancy between ideal and real drives a number of Cañoneros away from home for long periods of time, or forces them to emigrate entirely" (Kutsche and Van Ness 1988, 45).

Despite these socioeconomic contradictions, Kutsche and Van Ness's description and ethnographic evidence documented the unifying institutions and was an argument for the reality of village cohesion. In the monograph's final paragraph, they summed up their conceptualization of village culture as a vital and adaptive force. "Cañones changes within the Hispanic tradition, not away from it. It takes the materials of its change from any sources that give promise of enhancing its survival, and uses them to weave freshly every day the fabric of the village" (Kutsche and Van Ness 1988, 222). Kutsche and Van Ness wrote, "One of our goals is to present our description of Cañones in such a way that the strengths of Hispanic culture under stress are as clear as the tensed muscles of a boxer" (1988, 3–4). Ultimately, this vision of village culture as an ideal adaptation to the communities' sociomaterial circumstances supported land politics. Within this vision, village communities were perfectly suited to their environment before the sociocultural and economic disruption produced by the alienation of their land base.

While Kutsche and Van Ness's goals were primarily ethnographic, Briggs's *Competence in Performance* was more ambitious, befitting a work that would be Briggs's major statement concerning his New Mexico research. Indeed, Briggs wrote the preface to this book from the site of his current research, Venezuela (Briggs 1988, xix; Briggs and Mantini-Briggs 2003). In *Competence and Performance*'s introduction, Briggs positioned that book as a synthesis and step forward in the cutting-edge debates of the time concerning ethnopoetics and performance theory, and in the body of the text he catalogued his long-term research into the elders' verbal art genres that collectively make up the elders' "talk of bygone days." In particular, the text of *Competence in Performance* includes chapters on historical discourse, proverbs, scriptural allusions, jests, anecdotes and humorous tales, legends and treasure tales, and, finally, hymns and prayers. As will be demonstrated below, Briggs's text includes some of the functionalist elements of Kutsche and Van Ness's cultural-ecology approach. For example, he sometimes sought to document the adaptive (positive) aspects of village culture in opposition to the negative depictions of earlier, sociological, depictions of village communities. Briggs's work also, however, often sought to express a realist description of social relations that lacked the normative approach of Kutsche and Van Ness. In this vein and of greatest interest to me are the final pages of *Competence and Performance*, where Briggs described elders' "talk of bygone days" within a western Marxist framework. It is here he made some of his most impassioned and strongest statements about Córdova (Briggs 1988, 358–76).

These final pages are among the first places Briggs explicitly valorized the elders' verbal art genres as counterhegemonic, as resistance against Anglo-American domination and industrial capitalism. In particular, he argued the earlier Nuevomexicano social order's view of production as social and spiritual as well as material provided an excellent organizing principle for a counterhegemony because it contrasted profoundly with the dominant view of production. Briggs wrote, "The Mexicano conception of production is doubly alien to us, both in its emphasis on non-industrial (primarily agricultural, pastoral, and 'handicraft' production) and its refusal to isolate the purely material components from the production process" (Briggs 1988, 366). He stated that land expropriation deprived most of Córdova's residents of the right to articulate a counterhegemonic position through their labor, and, therefore the view of production and social life that was articulated by the elders might simply have become archaic, treated as a way of life that was the object of romantic evocation but lacked relevance to the present. By virtue of its incorporation into the elders' verbal art, however, their residual view of production reinterpreted the past in keeping with its relevance to the present and future.

In accordance with the notion of counterhegemony, Briggs stated the elders' goal was to enhance their juniors' awareness of the dangers posed by the dominant hegemony to the political, economic, and cultural survival of Nuevomexicanos (1988, 366). The centrality of the pedagogical aspects of the elders' verbal art to Briggs's thesis was described in a scenario in the first paragraphs of *Competence in Performance*'s introduction. Briggs wrote:

> Imagine that a number of individuals are sitting in a kitchen,
> crossing a field, or driving to town. Their talk is unfocused,
> touching on recent events or tasks to be accomplished. When
> one of the participants, an older person, begins to speak, the tone

shifts. Her voice rises suddenly then falls. Her eyes become fixed
on a younger person, her grandson, who has just spoken, and
he responds in kind. Her words break the hold of the here and
now, drawing the group through the window of the community's
past. . . . She continues more slowly now, with a relaxed and even
tone; the family members laugh or smile, and their gazes become
unfocused. As she finishes speaking, most murmur words of assent.
The grandson is the last to respond, nodding and replying, *sí, es
cierto* "yes, it's true." (Briggs 1988, 1)

In this way, Briggs reconceptualized the village elders as linguistic gue-
rillas deploying verbal performances and discursive representations to
fight the destruction of their communities and the onslaught of the dominant culture. Moreover, through the introduction of Gramsci, Briggs
followed the then-most-current trends in cultural studies (Hall 1986,
1996). In that field, the introduction of Gramsci displaced Marxism's
totalizing, grand narratives with a more careful effort to address the
things that Marxist theory could not answer about the modern world
(Hall 1996, 280–81). In the place of often blunt and imprecise Marxist
assertions of broad social and historical causes for individual problems,
Gramscian analysis provided for more nuanced, supple understandings
of the specificity of social experience that continues to fuel much of
cultural studies.

While Briggs's and Kutsche's work sought to focus on the position
in both popular and cultural terms, neither denied the existence of
individualistic, atomistic, or factionalistic aspects of village social
structure that previous ethnographers had documented. But where
the negatively valued structures and other evidence of un- or disorganization existed, Kutsche attributed them to outside domination
rather than inherent characteristics of village culture (Kutsche 1979,
10). Similarly, in his dissertation Briggs deftly turned the tables on those
who attributed oppressive patron–peon relations to traditional Latino
culture. He argued the balance of Nuevomexicano cultural structure
along the hierarchical/egalitarian axis was upset by industrial capitalism
and Anglo-American individualism, and therefore the grossest excesses
of unmitigated hierarchy in village society were not the result of

traditional New Mexican culture but Anglo-American domination. The village ethnographers left the evidence of un- or disorganization largely unexamined, however. I suspect that in the face of the previous anthropological focus on these negatively valued structures, they chose to refocus their work on the positively valued structures that had been overlooked. In this manner, they stood in allegiance with the villagers' ongoing political-economic struggle to retain control of their village communities and (re)assert their rights over their traditional land and resource base.

Indeed, both Kutsche's and Briggs's empathy for the people they studied is palpable in their writing. Kutsche explicitly stated with a note of sadness that it took him several years after the end of his intensive fieldwork in 1968 to accept the fact that he would never be "Hispano" (Kutsche and Van Ness 1988, xii). Furthermore, his empathy for Cañones had a strong quality of romance. After adult Cañoneros began to accept him in their homes; after the teenagers began to take delight in teaching him dirty words and how to drink Cañones style; and after the children found him a source of amusement on demand, he "began to discover that Cañones did not have a culture of 'rural poverty,' but one of powerful grace, style, beauty, richness, and amazingly open and warm human relations" (Kutsche and Van Ness 1988, xii). He stated he "was seduced by these qualities, which are largely absent from Germanic and New England patterns" (Kutsche and Van Ness 1988, xii).

Briggs's text suggests more subtle, but perhaps even more intense, identification. In an interesting caveat to his chapter outlining the social history of Córdova, Briggs described himself in the early days of his fieldwork as a sociolinguistic child, and this identification inserted him in a position analogous to the grandson who muttered "*sí, es cierto.*" By the time he conducted his doctoral fieldwork six years later, though, he wrote:

> After several years of such involvement [in community life] and
> much additional work on *la plática de los viejitos de antes*, elders
> became aware of my knowledge of the subject; this prompted some
> individuals to believe that I was in fact twenty to thirty years older

than I was at the time, a perception that surprised and somewhat disconcerted me. (1988, 52)

In other words, the older, dissertation-writing Briggs had learned well and became, at least in terms of cultural knowledge, the equivalent of a middle-aged Córdovan.

In sum, Kutsche and Briggs recast village culture as a current, albeit residual, adaptation to those communities' sociocultural circumstances. In so doing they dismantled the previous ethnographic descriptions of the villages as dysfunctional by showing how village culture functions as an adaptation against the destructive forces of the dominant society and that previous ethnographers ignored equally salient and positive aspects of village culture. In particular, Kutsche described village culture as a vital cultural-ecological adaptation that continued to provide the guiding force in villagers' lives, while Briggs conceptualized the Córdova elders' talk of bygone days as a counterhegemony that resisted that community's ongoing domination. Briggs, like Stuart Hall only a few years before, incorporated through Gramsci a Marxist problematic that spoke to general theory and cultural-historical specificity. Still, as will become clear in the next section of this chapter, even Briggs's more nuanced vision left out other emergent sociocultural realities with profound ramifications for the ongoing understanding of Nuevomexicano culture. For that ethnography we must leave the "frying pan" of the rural villages for the "fire" of the semiurban Española Valley proper. In the context of previous ethnographic views of village cultures, their work was critical and stands in alliance with the villagers' own idealization of village culture.

Española Ethnography

In her article "Cultural Studies and the Politics of Scale," Anna McCarthy (2006) broadens and deepens Stuart Hall's thesis in "Cultural Studies: Two Paradigms" (1980) to address the more general methodological problem of the establishment of valid conditions for empirical generalization. This insight is helpful for understanding the differences between village and Española ethnography. This notion of "scale" moves beyond the mathematical application of quantified and exact relations of proportion to the more general expression of relations between physical specificity and theoretical generality or degrees of a conceptual continuum spanning from materiality on one end to abstraction on the other (McCarthy 2006, 24). Such issues have broad-ranging implications for the fields of anthropology and cultural studies and the problematics of the ethnographic enterprise. In the case of New Mexico, issues of scale and the very object of ethnographic analysis shift differ. While the village ethnographers, especially Kutsche and Van Ness, were primarily interested in residual culture and cultural experience, University of Oklahoma anthropologist Joseph W. Whitecotton and his student, R. Stewart Ellis, as well as University of Chicago graduate student Alfredo Jiménez Núñez, a Spaniard, focused on the community's transformation.

As I have already noted, the town of Española first rose to prominence in the late nineteenth century as a stop on the Denver and Rio Grande Railway and was itself the engine of economic and social transformation that would engulf the valley and surrounding communities. Not surprisingly, anthropologists working in Española in the 1960s, 1970s, and 1980s produced a different sort of literature than those working in the villages. Whitecotton, Ellis, and Jiménez Núñez were more interested in broader or macrosocial models, and their texts tend to be more sweeping and often view social phenomena as local manifestations of social structural issues. In a detailed study of previous ethnographic works (including, among others, Calkins 1935, 1937; Hurt 1941; Johansen 1948; Saunders 1954; Moore 1947; Waggoner 1941; Walter 1938), Whitecotton's student Gerry Williams described the destruction of the villages' land base as just one of a number of processes that impoverished Nuevomexicanos. Among those processes he included the creation of a capitalist economy, shifts in the nature of production, the establishment of a new political order, and finally, a restructuring of land rights and ownership patterns. He stated that each of these contributed, in varying degrees, to the creation of a population that could be described as living in poverty and, in many ways, representing the lowest level of the American socioeconomic system (Williams 1985, 262). For Whitecotton, Ellis, and Jiménez Núñez, culture is one variable within a broader social analysis. In particular, Whitecotton and Ellis described the valley's incorporation into the world economic system (Ellis 1980; Whitecotton 1996, 1976, 1970), while Jiménez Núñez tested theories of acculturation and structural assimilation in the course of producing the only scholarly book focused on Española, *Los Hispanos de Nuevo México* (Jiménez Núñez, 1974).

Both Whitecotton and Jiménez Núñez chose to base their work in the Española Valley because that location promised to illustrate broader economic and transformative processes. Whitecotton ran a field school in the Española area during the summers of 1969, 1970, and 1971 (Joseph W. personal communication with author, 2003) and stated in his 1970 article, "The Social History of a New Mexican Region," that he chose the Española area rather than a remote or isolated location because he was less interested in the identification of residual culture traits than "Spanish-Americans'" involvement with the larger society (1970, 2). Jiménez Núñez similarly choose Española as the site of his graduate fieldwork in 1964–65 because Española had a large and diverse Latino population that therefore offered an excellent opportunity for the analysis of contact between Nuevomexicano culture and the larger American society, Española appeared to be a good place for the study of Nuevomexicanos' adaptations in the context of their direct contact with Anglos, and Española offered the possibility of showing how Anglos react in contact with an "ethnic minority" that within the area constitutes a clear numerical majority (Jiménez Núñez 1974, 16–17).

Whitecotton and Ellis's interest in a location like Española was promoted by their theoretical interest in world systems theory as developed by Immanuel Wallerstein (1979, 1974). Accordingly, they viewed northern New Mexico as a peripheral region serving national centers first in Spain, then in Mexico, and finally, in the United States. Ellis wrote, "[The Española Valley community of] Santa Cruz, like so many villages and small towns in marginal regions around the world, has become enmeshed within a complex national and even world, political and economic system over which it has very little objective control" (Ellis 1980, 198). According to this model, modernization of the peripheral and semiperipheral regions like northern New Mexico

The city of Española's historic Main Street. *Photo by author.*

Ohkay Owingeh's Ohkay Casino. The casino and hotel are located just north of Española. *Photo by author.*

is accompanied by the persistence of elites who utilized noncorporate means for organizing power inputs in the region. Ellis argued that the concept of dependent modernization is extremely useful in understanding the seemingly traditional or transitional features of the social structure in New Mexico. His dissertation details how from the founding of Santa Cruz in 1695 until the time of his research, the history of that Española Valley community consisted of adaptation to a succession of events and circumstances emanating from some broader context.

Jiménez Núñez's primary theoretical interest was acculturation and structural assimilation as the processes by which minority groups adapt to and supposedly become part of the dominant society. Like many theorists who use these concepts, Jiménez Núñez seemed to conceptualize ethnicity in primordial terms of culture as the causal source of ethnic-group formation. Accordingly, he was interested in documenting the replacement of Nuevomexicano cultural traits with Anglo traits and the eventual melting of Nuevomexicanos into the dominant society. In particular, he sought to test the relationship between the supposedly primary step of minority group acculturation and the following step of assimilation into the structure of the dominant group. Still, perhaps of greatest importance to our discussion are the specific findings of his measures of the supposed acculturation and structural assimilation of Española's residents.

In an effort to measure the retention or abandonment of Nuevomexicano culture, Jiménez Núñez conducted a survey of three hundred students in area high schools and junior high schools.[4] Jiménez Núñez believed that language retention was an index of Nuevomexicanos' fidelity to their culture. He therefore designed his survey to discover, on the one hand, the retention of Spanish and rejection of English, or, on the other, the students' adoption of English and abandonment of Spanish. Jiménez Núñez found the dominant language of the students' grandparents was Spanish, the parents' generation occupied an intermediate position but still favored the use of Spanish in the home, and English clearly dominated with the students themselves (Jiménez Núñez 1974, 127–28). Jiménez Núñez also found that more students, especially students from the city of Española and the immediately surrounding communities, reported themselves to be more comfortable in English than Spanish (Jiménez Núñez 1974, 130). With a similar goal of discovering the Nuevomexicanos' structural assimilation, Jiménez Núñez also asked the same students the ethnic affiliation of their three best friends (Jiménez Núñez 1974, 154) and analyzed marriage data to find the number of mixed marriages (Jiménez Núñez 1974, 157–58). He found that most Nuevomexicano students' best friends were also Nuevomexicanos and a rate of intermarriage below 10 percent.[5] He concluded that while Nuevomexicanos were acculturating, they were not assimilating into the structure of the dominant group (Jiménez Núñez 1974, 213).

Whitecotton and Ellis conceptualized acculturation in more complex terms than Jiménez Núñez. In particular, they argued that dominated groups such as Nuevomexicanos not only adapt to cultural structures and forms emanating from metropolitan centers, but they also actively adapt features of metropolitan style to the regional patterns. Ellis wrote:

> Thus northern New Mexico has Kentucky Fried Chicken, Dairy Queen, Tastee Freeze and McDonald's. But each of these mass influences has been adapted to some extent to regional food tastes: Colonel Sander's sells rolled chicken tacos, Dairy Queen and Tastee Freeze sell green chile hamburgers, tamales, and tacos, and McDonald's sells little cups of green chile to put on your Big Mac. (Ellis 1980, 200)

While conceptualizing cups of green chile for your fast-food hamburger as emergent cultural forms may at first seem facile, Ellis and Whitecotton saw these cultural adaptations as specific tangible examples similar to more widespread changes that ameliorate the impact of institutional arrangements on local and regional society. Within a world systems framework, he thus anticipates the work of Arlene Dávila and Valle and Torres concerning Mexican food. They have more recently demonstrated there are multifarious sources, including the marketing divisions of major corporations as well as local/ethnic desires, for these adaptations (Dávila 2001, 2004; Valle and Torres 2000). In this vein, Ellis's dissertation convincingly described the ways in which Santa Cruz both adapted to and adapted local representations of broader sociocultural structures like the Roman Catholic Church, education, livelihood, and politics over the past three centuries.

Whitecotton goes further than his student Ellis. As early as 1976, he was already envisioning a more complex theorization of Nuevomexicano ethnicity in situational terms that reflected his internalization of Fredrik Barth's notion of ethnic boundaries as processual and adaptive (Barth 1969). Along these lines, Whitecotton argued that society should be understood in terms of group situations, with power as central, and as an ever-moving process and from situation to situation, and context to context (Whitecotton 1976, 132). Whitecotton expanded this notion of ethnicity in a 1996 article that compared ethnic groups in the Española Valley to those in his other major field site, Oaxaca, Mexico. Here, Whitecotton described the ongoing reconstitution and even intensification of Nuevomexicano identity as a creative act resulting from these communities' incorporation into the modern capitalist world system. He specifically described this emergent ethnicity as "invented," "created," and situational and rejected primordial notions of ethnicity as exclusively based on bundles of cultural traits that have been passed down from preceding generations.

Sylvia Rodríguez, informed by Michael Hannan's theorization of ethnic boundaries in modern states, described ethnic identity formation in Taos and in the northern Rio Arriba community of Tierra Amarilla in similar terms (Hannan 1979; Rodríguez 1992). In her work, Rodríguez shows how a dynamic and dialectical relationship among a variety of local, regional, and national influences shaped the Nuevomexicano ethnopolitical mobilization that emerged in the 1960s, 1970s, and 1980s. More specifically, she argues, following Hannan, ethnic identity formation is constituted in a dialectical process where opposition in the periphery, resulting from penetration by the core, becomes organizationally isomorphic with the core. She writes:

> Local level oppositional organization accordingly grows larger and more complex, in order to meet the external onslaught effectively. Hence the widely observed emergence or increasing salience of large-scale ethnic identities, at a stage at which an earlier generation

of theorists would have expected assimilation to be near complete.
(Rodríguez 1992, 105)

Building on Barth's work, later theorists have differentiated "ethnicity" from "race." Michael Omi and Howard Winant define race as a concept that signifies and symbolizes social conflicts and interests by referring to different types of human bodies (Omi and Winant 1994, 55). Their concept of race emphasizes the fact that race, unlike ethnicity, is specifically defined by certain phenotypic characteristics such as skin color, hair, and body shape—in popular language, to be labeled white, Black, red, yellow, or brown—and entails a flattening of diversity groups so that, for example, Japanese Americans and Hmong immigrants are all Asians.

These notions of race often better fit how Nuevomexicano identity is experienced on the ground than do notions of ethnicity. Jake Kosek has also found that some Nuevomexicano land activists utilize discourses of race and class (Kosek 2006). I suspect that Whitecotton would be sympathetic to this argument, as might other intellectuals who apply ethnicity theory to New Mexico. Whitecotton stated in his 1996 article that the reconstructed Nuevomexicano identity he saw in land activism was based on a language of more universalistic ethnic characteristics than more traditional community-based identities. Whitecotton believed these more universalistic characteristics could be easily subsumed under a Chicano or Latino ethnic movement (Whitecotton 1996, 19). Such work suggests, in practice, an internally differentiated and complex subject position. Whitecotton wrote:

> The Chicano lowrider on the streets of Española, like his middle-
> class politician counterpart, faces in two directions. He can look
> to his Hispano land-based community identity. He also can look
> toward a much broader horizon and consider himself to be a
> member of an enormous group that has tremendous potential
> political and economic clout. (Whitecotton 1996, 19)

Such a statement still rings true. Despite the failure of federal and state governments to address longstanding grievances as the land-grant question, the power of the northern New Mexico's largely Democratic voting bloc was well demonstrated in the 2008 Hispanic elections.

The trips of Democratic presidential nominee Barack Obama (September 2008) and former presidential candidate Hillary Clinton (August 2008) to Española demonstrate Española's significance on Whitecotton's broader horizon. These national leaders journeyed to the relatively small town so as to mobilize Hispanics in an effort deemed crucial to the 2008 presidential election. Obama's massive Española rally in particular caught national attention and demonstrated his efforts to reach out to Hispanics and their enthusiasm for him. Moreover, Obama and Clinton's efforts seemed well founded, and they achieved results. According to *New York Times* exit polls that followed the 2008 elections, Rio Arriba County voters favored Obama 74 percent to Republican presidential candidate John McCain's 24 percent. In New Mexico overall, Hispanics voted overwhelmingly for Obama and were key to his victory in the state.[6] Interestingly, these same polls showed that New Mexico's "Whites" voted for McCain at a rate even higher than they voted for George Bush in 2004, suggesting a deepening ethnic/racial divide along party lines in state politics.

More than a decade earlier, in Taos, Rodríguez similarly noted that many people who were engaged in localized northern New Mexican forms of ethnopolitical mobilization, such as ritual revivals of dance forms like the matachines, also participated in "Chicano innovations" such as Danza Azteca, lowriders, and local celebrations of Cinco de Mayo (Rodríguez 1992, 106). Clearly, these forms of "ethnic" mobilization also fit well within Omi and Winant's conceptualization of race and race conflict in the United States. Moreover, in the paragraph following Whitecotton's comments concerning the Chicano or Latino ethnic movement, he wrote that the older Chicano movement and more recent Hispanic or Latino ethnicities are similar to other "core ethnicities" such as that associated with the label Black or African American (Whitecotton 1996, 19).

Further, this conceptualization of identity as complex and situational allows Whitecotton to consider different and potentially disturbing cultural forms that remain outside the purview of Kutsche, Van Ness, or Briggs's work. Here negativity proliferates. Whitecotton states that during the course of his field school in 1969, 1970, and 1971, his students lived in a tenement where most of the barracks residents were Latinos who were struggling to get by (Joseph W. Whitecotton, personal communication with author, 2003). In the course of her summer research, field school student Janice Harrison studied the tenement and found many residents exhibited characteristics of the social problems associated with urbanization (Joseph W. Whitecotton, personal communication with author, 2003; Whitecotton 1970). He cited heavy drinking patterns, lack of employment and hopes of getting employment, brittle marriages, and the formation of matrifocal families.

In this context of Whitecotton and Ellis's complex conceptualization of Nuevomexicano ethnic/racial identity/assignment, I here return to Jiménez Núñez's conclusions concerning Nuevomexicanos' accelerating acculturation and lack of structural assimilation. Jiménez Núñez found that the American political system or the failure to include Nuevomexicano concerns in the political system is partly responsible for the slow acculturation of Nuevomexicanos and many of the practical problems derived from the "cultural abyss" that separates Nuevomexicanos and Anglos. In light of Española's significance in Democratic, state, and national politics, such assertions can only be supported with a measure of agreement. Jiménez Núñez also stated that Nuevomexicanos have been very resistant to change because of their extreme traditional orientation that has reduced their capacity and flexibility to realize new adaptations (Jiménez Núñez 1974, 210). In the case of Española, the influence of Anglos has produced changes in the mentality of the Nuevomexicano population, causing a reduction of their conservatism and the degree of faithfulness to their culture (Jiménez Núñez 1974, 132). He stated that in Española these changes have reached the point where, for some, English has been converted into a status symbol.

After reading Whitecotton's description of the reconstitution and intensification of Nuevomexicano identity, I now understand Jiménez Núñez to describe a lack of retention of residual cultural traits such as the Spanish language and an agropastoral economy. I would consider any reduction to be contingent and situational. It is interesting that José Limón describes a similar transformation in south Texas. In contrast with the almost all-encompassing ethnic world of his parents' generation, Limón found the young people of the 1970s, 1980s, and 1990s experienced a kind of daily intercultural making-do, a social pastiche of everyday life, a growing depthlessness (Limón 1994, 112–13). The applicability of this view was further supported by my experiences teaching a course at Northern New Mexico College in the summer of 2008. Although the students were fiercely proud of their home communities, none of the students knew the specifics of Chicano-era civil rights leader Reies López Tijerina, and many did not recognize his name. Further, none spoke enough Spanish to understand the Spanish language exchanges in the predominately English-language film *Real Women Have Curves* (Cardoso 2002). Returning to the Briggs's scenario of a family sitting at a kitchen table, one wonders how many of these students would or could have mumbled "*sí, es cierto.*"

The general replacement of Spanish with English among the younger generations is a particularly apt illustration of the actual complexity of such culture change. Writing with a normative view of education and language, New Mexico education scholar George I. Sánchez wrote in an account first published in 1940 that New Mexico's education system did not develop students' home language, Spanish, and that many of these students left school without a command of English. Deploying a prescriptive notion of "correct" language that does not recognize the value or poetics of vernacular speech, Sánchez stated that these youths left school "without mastery of a language" (1940, 79). In the present decade, although most Española youth are more comfortable in English than Spanish, many remain sociolinguistically marked by a sort of English that is denigrated by the dominant society and results in low scores on standardized tests.[7] Again, this linguistic condition mirrors Limón's south Texas, where the schools do not teach youth the middle-class English skills necessary for social achievement, yet teach enough to contribute to the displacement of Spanish (Limón 1994, 112). In sum, Jiménez Núñez's work illustrated that Española residents are changing, but many remain sociolinguistically marked as different from the dominant society's ideal. Furthermore, the parallels with south Texas suggest this is a wider condition common to many other Chicano locations.

In contrast to Jiménez Núñez's conclusions concerning acculturation, his statements regarding structural assimilation require little
qualification and still ring true. Jiménez Núñez believed that after
finishing school, Nuevomexicanos and Anglos rarely visited each others'
homes or maintained friendships based on personal circumstances. He
suspected members of the two groups only interacted in workplaces,
some businesses, and public places and always in a limited way. He
stated, "Los obstáculos que impiden una mayor o más profunda
interacción son muchos y, generalmente, funcionan en doble sentido."
(The obstacles that impede a greater and more profound interaction
are many and generally function in a double sense.) He continued, "El
complejo constituido por la suma de todos los prejuicios dirigidos por
un grupo contra el otro y desarrollado a lo largo de la historia es una
causa muy importante de la evitación mutual" (A complex constituted
in the sum of all the prejudice directed by one group against the other
and developed in a long history is one very important cause of the
mutual avoidance) (Jiménez Núñez 1974, 156).

Negativity

In sum, a review of Whitecotton's, Ellis's, and Jiménez Núñez's work
allows us to conceptualize a Nuevomexicano identity that is both
emergent and residual, both positive and negative. Jiménez Núñez's
work in particular tells us that despite the dismantling of Nuevomexicanos' traditional economic base and their ongoing cultural transformation, they are not being structurally assimilated into the dominant
society. In other words, a new and emergent sort of Nuevomexicano
identity is being rearticulated and here to stay. This at least partly
negative articulation is situational and constituted from a complex and
internally differentiated subject position, which, I would also add, is
unpredictable, potentially messy, and not the stuff of tourist brochures
or anthropological seduction. Moreover, I suspect current Española-
Nuevomexicano subjectivities and their expressions may not exist as
a counterhegemony or in opposition to the dominant society. Instead,
we must also look for an emergent, proliferating negativity that now

also lives, at least some of the time, within the cracks and fissures of the hegemonic itself.

In this vein, Kutsche's language of romance with village culture is absent from Whitecotton's and Ellis's writings, while Jiménez Núñez himself is explicitly ambivalent. Indeed, Jiménez Núñez in particular was repelled by Española's modernity and Americanness. In comparison to the close-knit community and accompanying geography of the Andalusian villages in his homeland, Española seemed fractured into individual pieces, and therefore, he initially thought, difficult to study. He wrote:

> Una población sumamente dispersa, aislada en sus grandes casas tradicionales, en las modernas y típicas casas americanas de doble puerta con tela metálica que no deja entrar ni los mosquitos, o en los grandes trailers o remolques que agrupados en número variable reproducen la imagen del tradicional campamento de nómadas, no ofrece la situación más favorable para un estudio de comunidad y de relaciones interétnicas. Desde el primer día puedo observar que en almacenes, supermercados, cafeterías para consumir desde el coche, etc., impera la típica prisa americana. La gente acude a estos lugares simplemente como un fin: adquirir las provisiones para una semana, tomar un refrigero sin bajar del coche si es posible, y volver a casa a continuar su camino. Debo confesar que esta situación ha sido para mí en un principio un motivo de grave preocupación tanto por las dificultades prácticas que podría suponer en mi investigación, como por esa extraña sensación de encontrarnos con un lugar que a pesar de su flamante título de ciudad, está tan lejos de nuestro concepto y nuestra experiencia de pueblo, de comunidad, de lugares accesibles donde la gente se ve, se detiene a charlar en plena calle o se sienta a la puerta de sus casas para ver pasar a los demás mientras se charla con los vecinos. Nada de esto es posible en Española, como no lo es en muchas otras comunidades de qualquier parte del mundo, pero a mí esto no me consuela y, por otra parte, no es fácil evitar la comparación con el mundo que no es familiar. (1974, 73–74)

A highly dispersed population—isolated in its big traditional houses, in the modern and typically American houses with second doors made of metal screens that do not let even mosquitoes enter, or in the big trailers or that are grouped in various numbers producing the image of the traditional camps of nomads—did not offer the most favorable situation for a study of community and interethnic relations. From the first day, I could observe that in the grocery stores, supermarkets, cafes for eating in your car, etc., dominate the typical American rush. The people come to those places simply for one end: to acquire the provisions for the week, to eat without getting out of the car if possible, and going home to continue on their way. I should confess that at the beginning this situation had become for me a cause of grave worry, as much for the practical difficulties that could be assumed in my study as for the strange sensation of finding ourselves in a place that, despite the splendid title of the city, is very far from our [Spanish] concept and our experience of town, of community, of accessible places where the people are seen, stop and talk in the street, or sit in the door of their houses to see others pass while chatting with the neighbors. None of that is possible in Española, as it is not in many other communities of whatever part of the world. That did not console me, however. For the other part, it is not easy to avoid the comparison with the world that is familiar to us.
(My translation)

In this way, even though the Briggs's and Kutsche's villages are geographically close to the Española Valley, Jiménez Núñez's Española appears worlds apart from the communities the village ethnographers describe. For the Spanish anthropologist, what set Española apart was the community's highly dispersed population, modernity, and Americanness.

Village Ethnography Revisited

The preceding juxtaposition of village and Española Valley ethnography shows that the Española ethnographers conceptualized Nuevomexicano identity as complex and situationally contingent—a vision that allows for negativity. In contrast, the village ethnographers conceptualized Nuevomexicano identity in terms of residual cultural forms or a village sociocultural tradition—a vision that only speaks in positive terms. Still, Kutsche and Briggs did not argue that these positive forms of identity were the only legitimate expressions of Nuevomexicano ethnicity. Nor did they deny that Nuevomexicanos' subject position, especially in places like Española, might be too complex to be defined by an agricultural-pastoral past. For practical purposes, their ethnographic focus on village values, institutions, and folkloric genres in practice instead constructed Nuevomexicano identity in solely positive and residual terms. In contrast, by virtue of their ethnographic location in the semiurban valley, the Española ethnographers produced work that had to present, if in a nascent and unarticulated form, a more complex concept of Nuevomexicano subjectivity.

What makes the village ethnographers' elision of negativity more remarkable is that their own works did not fully contain such expressions. In terms of Kutsche and Van Ness's work, the negativity may be glimpsed in some of the cultural phenomena they describe but fail to address in depth. For instance, they struggled to contain the ethnographic evidence of the Cañones residents' drinking, travel, and sowing oats within the age and apparently male category of "*joven*," (Kutsche and Van Ness 1988, 120–21). In so doing, they contained the wildness of these "disintegrative beliefs" within an implicitly sanctioned age category for blowing off steam. "For the young Cañonero, this is the period of memorable drinking bouts, of extreme and fairly open sexual boasting, of sudden death in automobile accidents" (Kutsche and Van Ness 1988, 121). Nevertheless, in a telling caveat that preserved their field site's cohesion but implied another reality, Kutsche and Van Ness acknowledged that in other villages the disruptiveness of *los jóvenes* cannot always be contained. In a likely reference to the nearby village of Coyote that has long been known for its toughness, Kutsche and Van Ness wrote that, "Some other villages of northern New Mexico, particularly those on highways, suffer from gangs of their own aimless jóvenes who rob and beat other villagers" (Kutsche and Van Ness 1988, 121). Moreover, Kutsche and Van Ness's classic monograph-style discernment of cultural patterns suppressed the complexities of individuals' own subjectivities. For instance, they wrote, but without elaboration, that even in Cañones this period can also "be a time of bitterness, and some landless jóvenes turn to the Chicano movement for identity" (1988, 121).

Meanwhile Briggs's theorization of the elders' verbal art as counter-hegemonic necessarily posited the presence of a broader hegemony that is locked in a battle for the hearts and minds of Córdova residents. Briggs wrote, "Performers do not focus simply on the way that others, Mexicanos or Americanos, have internalized the dominant hegemony—the performers also point their fingers at themselves and their communities" (Briggs 1988, 368). For instance, he cited the example of an elders' attribution of a group of treasure hunters' failure to find the elusive wealth of nineteenth-century *rico* Pedro Córdova to one hunter's expression of his desire to profit. In other words, the treasure that originated in an earlier socioeconomic order would not be revealed to a person who expressed the hegemonic desire to amass individual wealth in commodities (Briggs 1988, 368). Briggs expanded these treasure stories and their analysis in his last book focused on New Mexico (Briggs and Romero 1990).

The most significant gap in Briggs's work is the near-complete absence of younger generations. This is particularly notable because, as Briggs describes it, a primary purpose of the verbal art is its pedagogical value for the young. In my reading of *Competence in Performance*, younger people only emerged as entities in their own right in one sentence in the entire book. In the first paragraph in chapter 2, Briggs described the experience that a generic "you" would see driving into Córdova for the first time. Among the things the hypothetical visitor would see is "a group of young men with longish hair and polished old cars [who] will probably be studying you closely" (Briggs 1988, 25). Yet, nowhere in his text did Briggs describe what they might have been discussing before the stranger's arrival. Nevertheless, Briggs must have seen the importance of these issues. While Briggs never published ethnographic work focused on younger people, at the beginning of his career he delivered a paper with the tantalizing title, "A Functional Analysis of Youth Gangs in a Spanish-American Village of North-Central New Mexico," as part of a Spanish and Mexican Land Grants in the Southwest Symposium at the Rocky Mountain Social Science Association Meetings in El Paso (Briggs 1974).

Briggs's exclusive focus on the elders' art in his published work elided the question of how younger people or even less linguistically skilled older people may experience the social transformations he describes so eloquently. Two decades after the publication of *Competence in Performance*, and after the passing away of perhaps most of Briggs's elders and the passing into middle age of the "young men with longish hair," this question becomes even more poignant.

Unintended Consequences

When Kutsche, Van Ness, and Briggs arrived in Cañones and Córdova, they entered a discursive field fraught with contradictory pressures, including a hostile social science literature, Nuevomexicano land politics, and Anglo modernist longing for New Mexico as exotic and pristine. Representing the latter two tendencies, these three village ethnographers threw their lot in with the villagers and reshaped village ethnography as the antithesis of their disorganization-centric precursors. When their ethnography is juxtaposed with the writings of their Española contemporaries, however, the de facto containment of Nuevomexicanos' proliferating and increasingly complex subject position(s) is brought into high relief as an unintended consequence of their empathetic ethnography.

Today we may add two additional components to the discursive field. First, just as the village ethnographers were confronted by their dysfunction-centric precursors, we now operate in a discursive landscape under the influence of the village ethnographers' preoccupation with the positive, residual cultural forms. This is, again, brought into high relief when the impact of the village ethnographies is compared to that of the Española ethnographies.[8] Most of the ethnographic research in the valley in the 1990s continued to concentrate on folkloric traditions or specific traditional arts (Lucero and Baizerman 1999; Romero 2007, 2006, 1993; Usner 2001, 1996). Furthermore, researchers who work in the Española area and otherwise demonstrate exhaustive bibliographies fail to demonstrate knowledge of the Española ethnographers' work or cite them.[9] For instance, in the early 1990s, Brenda Jo Bright and Brenda Romero wrote dissertations focused on lowriding and the matachines dance, respectively, in Española Valley communities. Both Bright and Romero cited Briggs, and Romero cited Kutsche and Van Ness, but neither cited the Española ethnographers (Bright 1998, 1994; Romero 1993).[10] Moreover, the American Encounters exhibit at the Smithsonian Institution described the Española Valley village of Chimayó in a manner seemingly copied directly from the pages of Kutsche's or Van Ness's work and implicitly cited Briggs's dissertation "Our Strength is the Land." The curators wrote, "Chimayó's people struggle to retain their unique character and values. Residents have their share of problems common to every American community: from drunk driving to domestic violence. But they find strength in their land, their culture, and their association with each other" (Morrison et al. 1992, 60).

In the present decade, two additional ethnographers of note have written lengthy ethnographic accounts with direct bearing on our discussion: geographer Jake Kosek and medical anthropologist Angela García. Kosek's award-winning book *Understories: The Political Life of Forests in Northern New Mexico* (2006) focuses on life in the neighboring village of Truchas and the struggles of villagers to enforce and obtain rights to natural resources often located on alienated ancestral lands. As mentioned in the previous chapter, medical anthropologist García's article "The Elegiac Addict" and her dissertation focus on the so-called drug epidemic in Española proper (2007, 2008). Kosek cites only the village ethnographers, Kutsche, Van Ness, and Briggs (Briggs and Van Ness 1987; Kutsche and Van Ness 1981). In terms of previous anthropological work done in Española or adjacent communities, García's article only cites Rodriguez and her dissertation cites Rodríguez, and our Department of Health study (Rodríguez 1987; Willging, Trujillo, and La Luz 2004).

Notably absent from both Jake Kosek's and Angela García's works are not only the Española ethnographers, but also citations of Briggs's work on folklore and aesthetics and even Briggs's Gramscian-influenced final work *Competence in Performance*. I suspect that both Kosek and García would find much relevance in this precursor's work that would directly

Locals enjoy the Chimayó Pride festival at Chimayó Elementary
in 2004. *Photo by author.*

speak to their emphasis on area residents' nostalgia for an idealized past.
For instance, in his analysis of Rio Arriba land-grant activism, Kosek
finds that Nuevomexicanos are assigned qualities of tradition that make
the reality of their modernity a contradiction (Kosek 2006, 140). This
presents land-grant activists a particular problem in that their appeals
are appreciated by the broader public only when delivered within a
discourse of tradition. In contrast, their arguments often are ignored
when couched in a fully modern discourse of race and class struggle.
Activists must then cede crucial parts of their own struggles in order
to achieve public approval and a measure of success in the achievement
of their goals.

Returning to the particular dialogue that has been the subject of this
chapter, I wonder how a more serious engagement of negativity would
have reshaped the village ethnographers' already careful description
and analysis. What would Kutsche and Van Ness have found if they
had taken more care to explore the "time for bitterness" that pushed
some marginal Cañones youth toward the Chicano movement? How
would Briggs's ethnographic description and theorizing have changed

if he had spent more time describing the linguistic play—or lack of it—of the "young men with longish hair"? Moreover, Briggs is a scholar with keen insight into material culture. Why did he not explore the profoundly playful implications of their "polished old cars"? If the village ethnographies had taken these sorts of questions more seriously, I suspect that their descriptions of their field sites would share much more with the Española Valley communities of Whitecotton, Ellis, and Jiménez Núñez. I suspect too that such a strategy would have lead to a richer if more fraught vision of both the Española Valley and northern New Mexico. How would an appreciation of the libratory as well as destructive power of negativity have transformed their work?

Just as ethnographers have confronted the riddle of Española's transformation, one valley artist struggled with similar issues. In the first decades of the twentieth century, embroiderer Policarpio Valencia stitched these themes into bedspread-size works of art that continue to inspire fascination. Where ethnographers have often failed, local artists have sometimes succeeded.

CHAPTER FIVE

Appearances Teach

You are going to have to operate your analysis of meaning without the solace of closure . . . to find the fragments, to decipher their assembly and see how you can make a surgical cut into them, assembling and reassembling the means and instruments of cultural production. It is this that inaugurates the modern era.

—Stuart Hall, *On Postmodernism and Articulation: An Interview with Stuart Hall*

If subversion lies in negativity, one early twentieth-century artist, the embroiderer Policarpio Valencia, insightfully evokes this same power in his confounding body of work. Valencia was born in the Española Valley village of Santo Niño, and his life (1856–1934) spanned the decade following the American annexation of the Southwest to the beginning of the Great Depression. In his old age, he created monumental and extraordinary embroideries unlike any others known in northern New Mexico.

Despite its now worn and faded state, his work remains striking and fascinating, inviting the viewer into the often-swirling texts to touch the figures seemingly haphazardly stitched onto their bedspread-size surfaces. One must strain and move around the embroidery to read the irregular text in his most abstract pieces. Within this new and radical form, Valencia simultaneously referenced traditional genres such as folk sayings and hymns as well as the area's traditional pastoral lifeways.

I suspect that Valencia would be pleased by my exploration of his art. Allegory and pedagogy appear to have been his goals, and sometimes the embroideries seem to be a riddle the viewer must unravel. In one embroidery, he states in colloquial New Mexican Spanish, "El que no parese ser. Y el que parese ser no es. Las aparencias enseñan. En eso se da entender" (That which is does not seem to. And that which seems to be is. Appearances teach. In that they give understanding) (Museum of Spanish Colonial Art [MOSCA] SCAS L.54.40). In another embroidery, Valencia first directs us to examine, read, and enjoy his work, "No para llebar la conbersacion bea el numero lo ay el prencipio de su naracion y adicionales sin numero, escritos con palabras interesantes" (Not to change the conversation, see the number [of animals] that are at the beginning of this story and numberless others written with interesting words) (Museum of International Folk Art [MOIFA] MNM A 9.54.28.M). He next tells us that his embroideries have something to teach us and goads us, in the form of a joke, to read more deeply. He stitched, "No las letras en este cuadro son tanbien de dar lecion a todo aquel las lean de rondon, a esto los causera risa, pero despues de la risa sie les lean de rondan, a etos los causera risa, pero despues de la ris sie les llaman su attencion, beran es cosas mas isa" (Note that the letters in the picture also give a lesson to all who read them around about. These will be made to laugh but after the laughs have caught their attention they will see more things here) (MOIFA MNM A 9.54.28.M).

In the effort to explore these "more things" and thereby answer the riddle his work poses, this essay reconnects Valencia's embroidery with his social milieu and suggests that Valencia's best work powerfully and simultaneously represents modernity and its implicit contradictions through two mutually haunting forms. Valencia was a Nuevomexicano who lived in a northern New Mexican community undergoing rapid and often impoverishing change. In his embroidery, Valencia (re)worked and transformed the contradictory experiences embodied by the valley's traditional center in Santa Cruz and the emerging economic center in Española. This chapter will explore the specificity of residual and emergent sociocultural forms manifested in Valencia's work and finally the implications of their juxtaposition. It will also examine the "folkloric" paradigms that earlier critics have brought to bear on these works as well as their parallels to critical modernism and twentieth-century Roman Catholic theology. Ultimately, I conclude that Valencia is a modern subject and his embroidery is the allegorical working through of modernity's contradictions. The source of these works' great and mesmerizing power is the dialectical shock such contradictions evoke.

Embroidering Santa Cruz and Española

Unable to assign Valencia's work to established genres, museum curators and textile experts Charlene Cerny and Christine Mather describe Valencia's embroideries as a personal statement or artistic vision and as "isolates" that "are clearly out of the mainstream and for which there is no easy explanation" (Cerny and Mather 1994, 144–45). I, by contrast, am not surprised by Valencia's innovation, as his artwork epitomizes a form of modernist contradiction evident in the landscape that surrounds his Española Valley home. Today, Valencia's former property is just off the road that now serves as the highway between the larger communities of Santa Fe and Taos. Valencia's particular village, Santo Niño, is a barrio within the boundaries of the city of Española and located just off of Española's central artery, Riverside Drive. Moreover, while Santo Niño continues to exist as a neighborhood in the expanded city of Española, the location of Valencia's residence is now considered to be part of the Española barrio, Riverside—a neighborhood named for the thoroughfare that runs through it and roughly parallel to the Rio Grande. In 2002 Valencia's descendants, including his grandson Paul Valencia, continued to live on Policarpio Valencia's former property (Valencia 2002), and this area of the Española Valley remains overwhelmingly Nuevomexicano. During Valencia's lifetime, Santo Niño was a somewhat isolated small village largely inhabited by the people descended from families who settled there during the Spanish and Mexican eras and was dominated by the area's ecclesiastical center in the bordering village of Santa Cruz (Ellis 1980). By the late 1880s, however, the shadow that Santa Cruz cast over Santo Niño was already joined by that of the growing railroad town and emerging commercial center. The city of Española was then located just across the Rio Grande.

Latin American anthropologist Néstor García Canclini contends that modernist aesthetics often arise at sites that are the complex conjunctures of different historical temporalities (García Canclini 1995, 2005). Of modernism's emergence in Latin America, García Canclini writes that "this *multitemporal heterogeneity* of modern culture is a consequence of a history in which modernization rarely operated through the substitution of the traditional and ancient. There were ruptures provoked by industrial development and urbanization that, although they occurred later after those of Europe were more accelerated" (García Canclini 1995, 47). In an independent but related analysis, literary scholar Marianne DeKoven describes critical modernism as an aesthetic practice that represents fragmentation but at the same time yearns for wholeness and synthesis (DeKoven 2004, 16). Within such textual and artistic practices, oppositions to modernity rise and push for audibility and visibility (DeKoven 2004, 14). In New Mexico in the early twentieth century, as in Latin America in the late twentieth century, people confronted divergent social views of livelihood and their modes of production and simultaneously, a still usable past, an undetermined present, and an unforeseeable future. This chapter demonstrates that Valencia's synergetic juxtaposition expresses an emerging Nuevomexicano structure of feeling.

The Embroidery

Valencia probably created the ten identified examples of his work in the decade preceding his death in 1934. In two of them, Valencia inscribed the years of their creation, 1925 and 1926 (MOIFA MNM B 89/13, MOIFA MNM A 5.54.3). His embroidery has received a strange combination of notoriety and obscurity: over the past sixty years a cadre of folklorists, textile experts, and museum curators has taken an interest in Valencia's work, although no one seems certain how to explain the confounding embroideries' seemingly unpredictable form. Today, six of his pieces are located in the collections of Santa Fe's Museum of International Folk Art, three in Santa Fe's Museum of Spanish Colonial Art, and one in the Fred Harvey Collections of the Heard Museum in Phoenix, Arizona. Famed Museum of New Mexico curator E. Boyd

Policarpio Valencia Embroidery, MOIFA A 9.54.28.M. Santa Cruz, New Mexico. Wool, cotton, cotton string. 117 cm by 155 cm. Embroidery in cotton string dyed various colors and white. The embroidery's ground is a patchwork of fabric patches including odd clothes. Bequest Henry Cady Wells to School of American Research, 1954, Museum of New Mexico, Museum of International Folk Art (DCA), Santa Fe, New Mexico. *Photo by Blair Clark.*

maintained a file of materials related to Valencia's embroideries and was instrumental in the purchase of several embroideries for the Spanish Colonial Arts Society in Santa Fe.[1]

His embroideries include a curious mixture of conformity to and divergence from traditional Nuevomexicano colcha embroidery. The colors of Valencia's materials have faded, but it is clear he used a variety of hues: orange, red, yellow, purple, blue, brown, and white (Barrett 2000, 154). Valencia employed the buttonhole stitch that was the staple of regional tradition long practiced in northern New

Mexico (although he employed industrially produced four-ply cotton rug warp as thread) and patched fabrics often constituted in part by traditional materials such as handwoven blankets in the Rio Grande style. The importance of this simple stitch cannot be overemphasized in conceptualizing the embroideries' creation, as multiple layers of stitches completely cover the ground cloth. Such stitching must have required great repetition. Valencia's grandson told me he remembered his grandfather embroidering late into the night (Valencia 2002). These works also innovated in a manner the sometimes resembles collage. Most of Valencia's stitchery is worked on pieced and patched clothing or household textiles. After he patched together enough materials for a base, he would cover the surface with a solid layer of stitches. If there was a hole or missing corner, he would fill the empty space with needle lace, which is done the same way as a buttonhole stitch but without piercing the cloth. Finally, he would stitch another layer of design: plants, animals, or text. In his most playful pieces, multiple layers of stitches completely cover the ground cloth in an obsessive working and reworking of the surface (Barrett 2000, 154). Turning his embroideries upside down to examine their base often reveals patchwork of traditional or industrial materials or both, such as faded blue denim or old handwoven blankets, that in turn complement the embroidery surfaces' industrially produced cotton string.

The single most analytical exploration of his work was done by textile expert Irene Emery (1953). She established both the authorship of the embroideries and proved they were twentieth-century works rather than much older, as previously suspected. Still, nearly all these scholars, outside of their clear appreciation of the embroideries' form, have attempted to understand these works according to their positive and seemingly traditional content rather than in terms of their confounding, indefinable form. In the following section, I survey the efforts of intellectuals to unravel the elements of Valencia's work that fit within established genres.

A More Genuine Culture

In the postwar period, two locations within the United States became centers for intellectuals who sought a more genuine culture in the geography of the United States than the supposed cultural morass of mainstream or middle America they rejected (Stocking 1989a, 217–18). New York's Greenwich Village arose as the metropolitan center for disaffected intellectuals who played a key role in the development of critical modernism. Other intellectuals and freethinkers who would figure more prominently in New Mexico's social history possessed primitivist tendencies and crossed the supposed cultural desert of middle America to found artists' colonies in Santa Fe and Taos. In the northern New Mexican landscape, they found a modernist oasis of seemingly primitive cultures. In *Culture in the Marketplace*, anthropologist Molly Mullin describes how these intellectuals were drawn to New Mexico as a world with distinctive local identities, histories, and aesthetic traditions (Mullin 2001). As George Stocking writes:

> Against a backdrop of arid ochre scarps and arching crystal
> skies, the crisp adobe lines of Spanish churches and Indian
> pueblos—artifacts of cultural traditions more deeply rooted than
> colonial New England—provided the setting for a resonantly
> exotic cultural life in the present. (Stocking 1989a, 219)

Among the discoveries of these art colonists, folklorists, and anthropologists were the weaving and the santero wood-carving traditions (Briggs 1980; Lucero 1986; Lucero and Baizerman 1999).

The reemergence of both the santero and Chimayó weaving traditions as both high and curio art was centered in nearby villages: Córdova and Chimayó. Two texts, Helen R. Lucero and Suzanne Baizerman's *Chimayó Weaving: The Transformation of a Tradition* and Charles Briggs's *The Wood Carvers of Córdova, New Mexico: The Social Dimensions of an Artistic "Revival,"* illustrate a profound contrast between Valencia's work and the genres of weaving and wood carving (Briggs 1980; Lucero and Baizerman 1999). Both texts describe Santa Fe and Taos intellectuals' efforts to re-create traditional craft economies as part of the larger national and international arts and crafts revival movement that flourished after the First World War. Briggs describes the shaping of the emergence of the village of Córdova's particular style of unpainted, wood-chip carving style in the context of the Anglo-American elite's tastes and patronage. Lucero and Baizerman elaborate a more complex push-pull exchange between middlebrow blanket dealers and highbrow and supposedly "enlightened" Anglos who sought to promote their vision of traditional craft production.[2] Within this framework, the wood carvings of Cordovan santeros were celebrated while Chimayó-style weavings were sometimes denigrated as less authentic. Nevertheless, both genres reflect the desire of tourists and collectors alike to purchase the handiwork of Nuevomexicano folk artisans.

Embroidering Continuity

Like the wood carvings and weavings, Valencia's work was understood by regional folk-art experts, often living in Santa Fe, as an affirmation of a Nuevomexicano way of life organized around a system of subsistence agriculture, related social structure, and Roman Catholic folk beliefs. Similarly, in perhaps the most complex description of Valencia's work, Museum of New Mexico curators Charlene Cerny and Christine Mather described Valencia as a man living in the rural poverty of Santa Cruz, New Mexico, or more specifically, Santo Niño (Cerny and Mather 1994, 144–46). They stated that "small though Santa Cruz is, it boasts an elegant, large adobe church built in the eighteenth century with altar decorations imported from Mexico as well as altar screens made in the nineteenth century by New Mexican santeros." They continue, "It is a church of great age and beauty, which one can easily imagine would dominate and fill the lives of the villagers. And so it seems with Policarpio Valencia" (Cerny and Mather 1994, 144).

Elements of Valencia's work may be understood as an affirmation of a way of life that inscribes a religious and traditional moral order. This aspect of Valencia's art would fit within Raymond Williams's notion of residual cultural forms: "The residual, by definition, has been effectively formed in the past, but it is still active in the cultural process, not only and often not at all as an element of the past, but as an effective element of the present." Several other of Raymond Williams's comments in this section of Marxism and Literature are pertinent to our discussion. Among them is the following statement: "The idea of rural community is predominantly residual, but is in some limited respects alternative or oppositional to urban industrial capitalism, though for the most part it is incorporated, as idealization or fantasy, or as an exotic—residential or escape—leisure function of the dominant order itself" (Williams 1977, 122).

Aspects of Valencia's biography suggest that much of his subjectivity was formed in a social order of a prior, primarily agricultural, folk Roman Catholic, and Nuevomexicano New Mexico. E. Boyd purchased three Valencia embroideries for the Spanish Colonial Arts Society from Santa Cruz native Tomás Valdez with the stipulation that Valdez write down everything he knew about Valencia. Valdez's description of Valencia's life describes his parents, Ijinio Valencia and María Antonia Montoya, as typical people of Spanish origin. "They cultivated the land as farmers. . . . Their son Policarpio followed the same trade" (Policarpio Valencia Folder n.d.). Moreover, Valdez reported that Valencia was the mayordomo, or ditch boss, of the acequia, or community irrigation ditch, and he also owned a traditional-style flour mill powered by the acequia's waters. In other words, Valencia was a participant in the traditional village economy of small-scale subsistence agriculture. According to Valencia's grandson, Paul Valencia, Policarpio Valencia was also a member of the Roman Catholic lay brotherhood called the Trinitarios that remains active in Santa Cruz even today (Valencia 2002). Valencia, therefore, was also a full participant in the folk Roman Catholicism that traditionally permeated all aspects of northern New Mexican life. Another element of Valdez's biography suggests that Valencia was a verbal virtuoso in the traditional verbal art genres richly described by anthropologist Charles Briggs in nearby Córdova. "People from all around sought his advice," Valdez stated. "He held the attention of all who would come and chat with him. His wise sayings or maxims were frequent in his conversation" (Policarpio Valencia Folder n.d.).

The religious aspect of Valencia's work may be understood in the context of New Mexican and Franciscan Roman Catholicism. Perhaps Valencia's most notable local precursor in this regard may be

Policarpio Valencia Embroidery, MOSCA L5.54.38. Santa Cruz,
New Mexico. Cotton. 77 cm by 22 cm. Collections of the Spanish
Colonial Arts Society, Incorporated. Museum of Spanish Colonial
Arts, Santa Fe, New Mexico. *Photo by Blair Clark.*

the eighteenth-century Santa Cruz poet Miguel de Quintana (Lomelí and Colahan 2006). Francisco Lomelí and Clark Colahan convincingly demonstrate that Quintana's supposedly heretical writings were not blasphemous when taken in the context of New Mexican and Franciscan Roman Catholicism. Like Quintana's work, Valencia's embroidery constantly dialogues a transcendent God who must be understood in order to fully grasp our reality. For instance, in one embroidery, Valencia stitched next to a series of animals, "Adajio que dies, no es el lion como lo pintan, mas que lo aga un buen pintor, el que lo pinto primero le puso has su color y asi es y sera" (There is an adage that says, the lion is not as he is painted even if he is painted by a good painter. He who painted it first did so even to the color and so it is and shall be) (MOIFA MNM A.9.54.28). Similarly, Quintana's poetry always speaks to a higher, transcendent truth that gives significance to his travails, including his confrontation with the Inquisition and its agents in New Mexico.[3]

Interestingly, Valencia's most critically discussed piece was both the easiest for folklorists and curators to understand through established genres and one of his least visually complex. The text of this piece was transcribed and published in its entirety in "E. Boyd's Working Notes on Policarpio Valencia and his Alabado Embroidery" (Weigle, Larcombe, and Larcombe 1983). In a note to Boyd, New Mexico folklorist Rubén Cobos stated that this embroidery consists of a New Mexican alabado, or hymn, that serves as the performer's *despedimiento*, or farewell, to his family, friends, and the world in general (Policarpio Valencia Folder n.d.; Rael 1951). Despedimientos were sung at traditional wakes for the dead. Cobos's description of the text as an alabado is attached to a transcription of Valencia's text in standard Spanish.[4] Cobos states that despedimientos such as this one affirm the laws of Roman Catholicism and remind the listener that, on the day of judgment, even a word said in jest will merit due punishment (Policarpio Valencia Folder n.d.).

In another piece, Valencia lists the animals of the world but also pays attention to the animals commonly used or hunted in northern New Mexico. He also lists the tools of traditional agriculture, as if ordering and inscribing the traditional mode of production into the embroidery's cloth. Valencia wrote in the colloquial Spanish of his community, itself a signifier of a traditional and rural culture:

Policarpio Valencia Embroidery, MOIFA B 89–13. Santa Cruz, New Mexico. 1925. Cotton. 139 cm by 164 cm. Museum of International Folk Art (DCA), Santa Fe, New Mexico. *Photo by Blair Clark.*

abril 2 del año de 1925 comense a poner hilo blanco en esta covija en la cual berá ud sierta colecion de animales de los cuales ya barios son raros en esta epoca y otros esisten aora en uso domestico pero llo he figurado ayi animales para recuerdo que prestaron serbisio al hombre anteriormente fueron el sibolo el caballo el buro la mula y el bueye y la borega y cabra el sibolo con su carne surtia la nasion el buro la mula con carga en el espinaso cambiando objetos comerciales de distancia muy larga y por sieras caminaban y manejados tratados mal con garote y el buy jalando primero con un palo atado a los cuernos era llugo dos prendian al llugo y les picaban con un topil era una bara puntiada el hombre en el caballo con su balor y una lansa en su mano asia uso del sibolo y la borega y la cabra con su pelo y cuero vestian a sus amos y con su carne leche se alimenta la nasion.

April 2 of the year 1925 I began to weave white wool thread in this blanket [bed cover] on which you [will] see a certain collection of animals among which various ones are rare in these here times and others still exist for domestic use, but I have sketched here [these] animals [beasts] to be remembered [for service to man]. Those that served mankind in times past were the buffalo, the horse, the ass, the mule, and the ox, and the sheep and goat; the buffalo with its flesh sustained [supplied] the people, the donkey and mule beasts of burden carrying loads on their backs exchanging commercial goods over great distances and mountains, traveling [slowly] and treated [manhandled] brutally with club, and the ox pulling with a [heavy] stick tied to his horns. This was a yoke: two oxen were bound to the yoke and they poked [stuck] them with a sharp pointed red [long pole]. The man on horseback with valor and his lance in his hand made use of the buffalo, sheep, and goat, whose hides and skins were skillfully used to dress their masters. Their flesh and milk feed the people.

Basing the views on Valencia texts such as this one, several earlier accounts of Valencia's work and life focus their speculation almost exclusively on his supposed status as a traditional New Mexican villager. Interestingly, an unsigned early description of several of the Valencia pieces, probably written by New Mexico material culture scholar Hestor Jones sometime before 1953, misdated Valencia's work.[5] The report's author mistook a nine for a seven in the above quoted statement ("abril 2 del año de 1925 comense a poner hilo blanco en esta covija") and believed the embroideries were created in 1725. The report's author stated that he or she was unable to find out the origin of the embroideries' design. Instead, the author continued to elaborate the isolated and typically "folk" nature of social groups that included their likely embroiderer:

They come from people who are farmers and cattle and sheep owners, who are poor in money but comfortable and content in their one-story adobe or wood houses; very religious and enjoying very much their local fiestas and their dances; with little desire for possessions or for change or speed. They are quick in their passions and live very close to the soil. (Policarpio Valencia Folder n.d.)

Later critics lacked the condescending quality of this early report, but they retained the author's focus on a folk tradition.

In her paper delivered at the 2000 meetings of the Textile Society of America, Annin Barrett similarly focused on the traditional folkloric aspects of the work and Valencia's isolated and traditional milieu. She described the Española Valley's deep roots dating to Spanish colonization, the strong influence of the Roman Catholic Church in general, and the specific regional influence of the Franciscan friars and Catholic lay brotherhood popularly known as the Penitentes. The Penitentes themselves are a common object of folkloric fascination and are much studied by folklorists and anthropologists (Briggs 1988; López Pulido 2000; Weigle 1976). According to Barrett:

Policarpio Valencia may well have been a Penitente since during his lifetime most prominent members of New Mexico Spanish communities belonged to the Brotherhood, and Santa Cruz de la Cañada was a center of Penitente activity. Whether or not he actually was one, there existed a general cultural aesthetic that valued self-denial and religious devotion. They coexisted with the frontier traits of self-sufficiency, reinventing traditions from the "old" country, and a keen awareness of death. (Barrett 2000, 153)

The point of my exegesis is not to quibble over the fact that Valencia was a Trinitario rather than a Penitente. Rather, the point is that earlier critics have focused almost entirely on aspects of Valencia's work that are easiest to assimilate into traditional folk paradigms and genres, a view supported by much of the text of Valencia's work. As we already know, though, this narrative only tells half the story. Indeed, in the transgressive form of Valencia's embroidery, the conceptualization of his embroideries as the pure affirmation of tradition unravels into something more ineffable and complex.

Embroidering Transformation

I now return to the other prominent avenue of modernist critique that was also emerging in the twentieth century. For many alienated intellectuals, New York's Greenwich Village served as a locus of heterodox ideas, new aesthetic modes, and alternative life-styles (Stocking 1989a; Stocking 1989b, 3–9). On the global stage, modernist art works presented a "both/and" that imagines an alternative to hierarchical dualism. In Europe, painters such as Cézanne, Matisse, Picasso, and Wyndham Lewis transformed and developed a diverse modernist aesthetics. For textual evidence of this modernist style, see Conrad, Eliot, and Proust. In Greenwich Village, continental artists such as Marcel Duchamp and Francis Picabia created a new art axis that placed New York at a central location in the art world. A chief characteristic of this intellectual milieu was an aesthetic form that valorized a radical inconsistency and self-contradiction (DeKoven 1992, 2004). In the following section, I show that this critical modernism more accurately describes Valencia's work than do the inadequate efforts of earlier critics to understand Valencia's oeuvre within the established folk genres that were at least partly defined by the needs of modernist intellectuals' paradoxically primitivist desires.

Interestingly, it is only through the exhibition of his artwork in New York that one of Valencia's contemporaries, the woodcarver Patrociño Barela, was able to cross the boundaries between folk artist and modernist (Gonzales and Witt 1996, 225).[6] Barela received attention and was briefly celebrated for his supposedly naive modernism by the New York modern art community when his work was exhibited as part of the Depression-era New Mexico Federal Art Project. Moreover, New Mexico is not the only place that so-called "primitives" would create modern art. In the article "A Picture of Black and White," Alison Ravenscroft makes observations about modernism in another (post) colonial location, Australia, that are relevant to our discussion of New Mexico (Ravenscroft 2003). Drawing on the work of DeKoven, she states that the modernist text is written in the context of the subjective experience of epochal change, where past, present, and imagined future are in tension (Ravenscroft 2003, 239–40). Here the imagined future is both desired and dreaded, and the experience of the subject is poised between temporalities. Such texts are constitutively and irreducibly ambiguous in their very form. Two or more meanings are held together but not fused. Rather, both meanings persist and refuse synthesis.

Like Australia and García Canclini's Latin America, the social geography that surrounded Valencia was far more complicated than critics such as E. Boyd suggested. By the second decade of the twentieth century, New Mexico in general was facing a demographic shift that was transforming Nuevomexicanos into a minority within New Mexico. The area of northern New Mexico within a sixty-mile radius of Española, in particular, was experiencing the influx of Anglos often interested in the region's Native American and, to a lesser extent, Latino populations. At this time, the Española Valley was converted into a reservoir of cheap labor for the region's burgeoning economy and, simultaneously, a stronghold of the remnants of northern New Mexican political power and Nuevomexicano demographic dominance.[7] Moreover, the social and economic forces centered in the railroad town and commercial center of the city of Española had already began to compete and even eclipse the power that Cerny and Mather saw in Santa Cruz's "large adobe church." Based on data gathered in 1935, the Tewa Basin Study described the Española area as already enmeshed in a wider market economy and stated that, by the First World War, wages had replaced agriculture as most residents' primary source of livelihood (Weigle 1975, 35).

Three intertwined area developments became the local engines of social and economic change: the railroad town and commercial center of Española; the Española-based sheep empire of businessman Frank Bond; and the mid-twenties establishment of an irrigation district. The Tewa Basin Study's authors compared the local sheep-raising system to sharecropping in the Deep South. This system ultimately concentrated nearly all the area's pastoral wealth in Bond's hands. Finally, the formation of the irrigation district was a source of great anxiety and economic hardship. Beginning in 1926, the irrigation district initiated a process of taxation and debt that ruined many farmers. These economic conditions resulted in residents' ever-increasing impoverishment. The Tewa Basin Study states:

> It is only since the forming of the irrigation district that radical
> change has overtaken the town [the Santa Cruz complex of villages],
> and this has probably taken place without the full realization of the
> inhabitants, and to their huge discomfort. Because of its location at
> the head of the irrigation district, where the lands are of a magnitude
> to appeal to Anglo farmers, Santa Cruz has had the most direct
> contact with the newcomers. There the fear of land loss is most
> common, and every conversation brings it up. (Weigle 1975, 68)

The study specifically described Santa Cruz's houses as old, dilapidated, overcrowded, and "with evidence of squalor." Perhaps most ominously, the study states that many of the schoolchildren were underweight and suffering from malnutrition (Weigle 1975, 78).

Valencia himself appears to have been a participant in the transformation this new economic and social order wrought. Whereas Tomás Valdez cast Valencia's parents as farmers "of typical Spanish blood," Valdez described Valencia himself as a merchant of sorts (Policarpio Valencia Folder n.d.). As a young man, Valencia would take farm produce to Santa Fe, where he would trade with a merchant "by the name of Mr Solomon Weist, with whom he became very intimate." Then, with a load of merchandise, mostly salt, he would proceed to Taos and do business there. Valdez states that Valencia became attached to his family and therefore curtailed his commercial trips. Still, one wonders if the increasing penetrations of the railroad and Anglo business into northern New Mexico did not play a role in the eventual cessation of this money-earning strategy. Finally, as a longtime mayordomo of the Acequia de las Herreras that passed near his home, Valencia must have been intimately aware of the economic dislocation developing within the irrigation district beginning in the mid-1920s. In those final years of his life, Valencia was elected to the position of justice of the peace. Valencia's prominent roles in the community and commerce suggest that he was an active agent who manipulated the social geography that lay before him, and he must have been fully aware of his community's social circumstances.

In the context of his community's transformation and increasing fragmentation, Valencia's embroidery took on a form that was likely never seen before and reflected an emerging tension that even Valencia could only fully articulate in his endlessly repeated buttonhole stitch. Furthermore, his work certainly did not fit comfortably within the traditional colcha style of embroidery long common in northern New Mexico.

Folklore literature, popular memory, and current practice tell us that colcha embroidery was a women's craft. According to Museum of New Mexico curator Nora Fisher, there were two types of New Mexican colcha embroidery: wool-on-wool colcha and wool-on-cotton colcha (Fisher 1979). In the first and older form, a handwoven, hand-spun, plain-weave woolen ground is covered with buttonhole-stitch embroidery. In the second, and mostly U.S.-era, form, a cotton ground is covered with wool colcha motifs. Fisher states that for the most part, wool-on-wool colcha embroideries are characterized by elaborate curvilinear floral patterns. This wool-on-cotton style is made up of a design embroidered in wool on a background of plain white cloth, usually cotton. She states that almost all wool-on-cotton pieces are framed by an outer floral border. The introduction of an animal motif is frequent, and a number of these embroideries have a central motif or a small circular motif placed at the very center of the textile.

Valencia's innovative form defies earlier critics' assimilation of his work into folk genres and simultaneously accounts for its attractiveness. Writing in the early 1950s, textile expert Irene Emery commented on three of his works. She was clearly fascinated and puzzled by the embroiderer's combination of innovation and his apparent lack of technical proficiency. Not yet knowing much about the embroiderer, she said, "The animal figures in two of the pieces suggest a pastoral life. The materials used all indicate a definite lack of affluence, [and] the size of the pieces, the actual weight and bulkiness, as well as the magnitude of the task involved, suggest an adult and determined approach" (Emery 1953, 36).[8] Emery described the form of Valencia's embroideries precisely in great detail:

The colors of the string of this embroidery seem to have been white, gray-blue (which originally may have been a deeper blue), red (now faded to a rosy shade), and orange. There are also a few apparently random bits of grayed brown and lemony yellow. With the exception of the rectangular space in the upper center, which seems to be somewhat padded with wool yarn held down by embroidery stitching of no discernible design, the face of the piece gives the impression of having some sort of plan and intention in the arrangement of color blocks. But what the intention may have been is puzzling to the extreme. (Emery 1953, 38)

Describing a similar piece, Emery states:

The design, in its present state, is quite incomprehensible. There is lettering across either end and some suggestions of a border design. A few small roughly drawn and executed animal figures are discernable in line with the lettering and also down the sides. There may be other forms that could have been recognized before the colors faded. There is a hint of patchwork effect, but for the most part, seeking an idea behind the work is rather like tracing out forms on a stained plaster wall—you can see practically anything if you look for it hard enough. One form which did not appear at all in the first piece described comes to seem almost the theme of this one. It is a small circle worked round and round so that the embroidery produces something like the effect of crochet. (Emery 1953, 42)

Moreover, both Emery's article and the conference paper by textile expert Annin Barrett—as well as materials collected by E. Boyd—suggest their awe upon viewing the embroideries as well as their inability to assimilate Valencia's work (Barrett 2000; Emery 1953). Despite the fact that Boyd was a prime mover in both the categorization of New Mexico folk genres and the popularization of "Spanish Colonial Arts" for Anglo collectors, she never explicitly published any work on Valencia's embroideries. Meanwhile, Emery described one Valencia embroidery as "unlikely" and "even unbelievable" (Emery 1953, 42).

Unable to assimilate Valencia's embroideries into established genres, Cerny and Mather describe them as a personal statement or artistic vision and as "isolates" that "are clearly out of the mainstream and for which there is no easy explanation" (Cerny and Mather 1994, 144–45). I contend, however, that the transgressive elements of Valencia's works are better understood as "emergent" or perhaps "pre-emergent," in Raymond Williams's sense of these terms. For Williams, such forms are in the process of their constitution in ongoing social relations and often are active and pressing but not yet fully articulated and cannot be confidently named (Williams 1977, 121–27). One suspects their form would appear incomprehensible to those expert in traditional genres but living in other sociocultural milieus and therefore not subject to the pressures of the same emergent and pre-emergent forms in their daily experience. This may explain why, in 2002, as a museum volunteer unrolled one of Valencia's embroideries for me to view, she speculated that the embroiderer might have been mentally ill.

Rather than insanity, I would suggest that, just like the social landscape that surrounded Valencia's home, Valencia's embroideries embody dialectical tension. In particular, a transgressive style is manifest in a collage of industrial and traditional materials and an aesthetic that seems to defy design. In contrast, the text of his messages often asserts a world vision defined in an earlier and distinctly Nuevomexicano order typified by Valencia's folk Roman Catholicism and the villages' traditional agropastoral organization. In this way, Valencia invokes the most traditional of New Mexican folk genres such as the alabado and folk sayings. In other words, Valencia's work manifests both halves of the dialectic evident in the New Mexican experience. In this sense, on one horizon, Valencia's work exhibits something akin to critical modernism. Valencia deploys two narratives that simultaneously conflict and strangely move in concert. Indeed, his embroideries' transgressive form has fueled the interests of generations of experts. Meanwhile, the assertion of traditional moral order provided those same critics a handle onto which they could hold.

In Valencia's most dynamic work, narratives of tradition and modernity chatter and swirl with equal ferocity and verve. While still unable to articulate this aspect of Valencia's vision, Cerny and Mather's

Policarpio Valencia Embroidery, MOSCA L 5.1954.40. This embroidery measures 122 cm by 133 cm. The piece is worked with white string or string dyed red and light blue. The design is almost solid animals with letters meandering between in all directions. Collections of the Spanish Colonial Arts Society, Incorporated. Museum of Spanish Colonial Arts, Santa Fe, New Mexico. *Photo by Blair Clark.*

enjoyment of Valencia's playful, unpredictable form is palpable, and here, one suspects, arises their actual admiration of his work. They write that there is nothing structured about the Valencia embroideries and marvel at how the lines of Spanish words come in at various angles and how animal forms may punctuate a line. "The play of the visual and the literary woven together," they state,

successfully imparts not only great visual stimulation but a sense
that an unanswered riddle is about to be solved. The answer of
the riddle seems to depend not only upon an understanding of
the words embroidered in cheap household string, but also upon
their relationship with the other forms of the textile: The animals
and the larger shapes emerge as patches. Animals and words move
together as the viewer distances himself from the textile. Valencia's
textiles require active involvement from the viewer. There is
a compulsion to circle the textile, to go around and round it,
viewing it from every angle in an effort to get at its inner meaning.
(Cerny and Mather 1994, 146)

I posit that the riddle these embroideries pose is that of an internally
differentiated subjectivity that both splits and merges and harmonizes
and argues among itself. The dialectical tension of these two narratives
seems to be the source of these works' confounding power.

This synergetic juxtaposition expresses an emerging structure of
feeling that reflects the social pressures of Nuevomexicano modernity.
Such structures are the affective elements of consciousness and
relationships, such as characteristics of impulse, restraint, and tone, that
cannot be simply reduced to a signifier. The notion of a structure of
feeling is not intended to be an impermeable category that has only a
causal relationship with fixed forms; rather, it is thought as feeling and
feeling as thought (Williams 1977, 132). During moments where the
interlocking and tension between structures of feeling and the formal
system of signs is explicit, we are still within the dimension of relatively
fixed form; at other moments, however, an explicit articulation of tension
may not come or may never come. At these moments, the relation between
the already articulated and the affective elements of consciousness are
complex. Valencia, a creative subject firmly engaged in the world around
him, would have felt such pressures. Moreover, this positing of a tension
and interlocking brings the theory of culture into the space between the
signifier and meaning (Stewart 1996, 5). As Williams writes:

There are experiences to which the fixed forms do not speak at all,
which indeed they do not recognize. There are mixed experiences,

where the available meaning would convert part to all, or all to part. And even where form and response can be found to agree, without apparent difficulty, there can be qualifications, reservations, indications elsewhere: what the agreement seemed to settle but still sounding elsewhere. (Williams 1977, 130)

Such tension may manifest as an unease, a stress, a displacement, or a latency. "It is a kind of feeling and thinking," Williams writes, "which is indeed social and material, but each in an embryonic phase before it can become fully articulate and defined exchange" (Williams 1977, 131). We may describe the form of Valencia's embroideries as emergent and expressive of not yet fully articulated structures of feeling.

The articulation of contradiction and unity in complexity and difference parallels a key element of modern structures of feeling then emergent. For Stuart Hall, this aesthetics of articulation refers to the complex set of historical practices by which we struggle to produce identity or structural unity out of and on top of complexity and distinct elements. Such articulation is a historical phenomenon that may then be rearticulated in different ways. Articulation is, therefore, a linkage, which is not necessary, determined, absolute, and essential for all time.[9] For those who idealize traditional genres seemingly untouched by Anglo-American culture and industrial society, this juxtaposition appears at a traditional genre's contamination by foreign elements. In her most influential work, *Popular Arts of Spanish New Mexico*, E. Boyd states that in the twentieth century New Mexican colcha work declined in quality of design and color because of Anglo economic, social, and cultural penetration. She writes, "The decline of fine embroidery and good design and color in the colcha ... coincided with the introduction of new materials and techniques by the so-called Anglo newcomers" (Boyd 1974, 214). She complains of the introduction of Saxony and Germantown yarn, aniline dyes, new breeds of sheep that produced inferior wool, as well as design elements borrowed from trade yardage, wallpaper, and oilcloth. Specifically, she describes three disappointing pieces that may be the same Valencia embroideries Irene Emery described. Boyd writes:

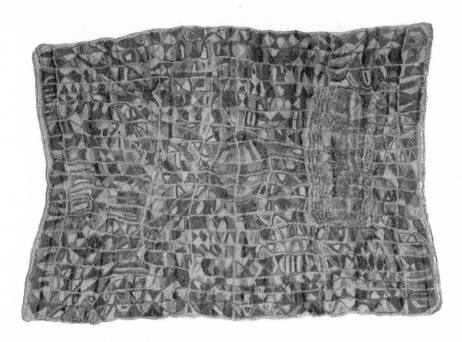

Policarpio Valencia Embroidery, MOIFA A 5.54.3. Wool, cotton 150 cm by 104 cm. Gift of the Historical Society of New Mexico. Museum of International Folk Art (DCA), Santa Fe, New Mexico. *Photo by Blair Clark.*

Three other specimens made use of salvaged materials. The first has a support pieced from scraps of a Rio Grande blanket, and is crudely stitched all over with colored squares. The others are also of multicolored check or tile designs worked on flour sacks. All three of these are coarse and asymmetrical in design, but exhibit the true colcha stitch. (Boyd 1974, 214)

It is interesting that if Boyd is here describing Valencia's work, her disappointment contrasts with the evidence of fascination that may be found in the Policarpio Valencia Folder in the E. Boyd Collection of the New Mexico State Records Center and Archives (Policarpio Valencia Folder n.d.). In this folder are multiple sheets of notebook paper that show clear efforts and great time spent to decipher Valencia's handiwork.

Articulating Transformation

In contrast with Boyd's thesis of decline, I offer a more generous reading of Valencia's work. In form and content, Valencia's embroidery is the allegorical working through of the contradictions that transformed and reconstituted northern New Mexican experience over the course of Valencia's lifetime. This work presents cultural form in process or, in other terms, the articulation of cultural formation, and dialectical shock is Valencia's pedagogical tool. The power of such shock is eloquently described in Fredric Jameson's description of a passage from Theodor W. Adorno's *Philosophie de neuen Musik* (Homer 1998, 18). "For a fleeting instant," Jameson writes,

> we catch a glimpse of a unified world, of a universe in which discontinuous realities are nonetheless somehow implicated with each other and intertwined, no matter how remote they may at first have seemed; in which the reign of chance briefly refocuses into a network of cross relationships wherever the eye can reach, contingency temporarily transmuted into necessity. (Jameson 1971, 8)

For Valencia, however, this reconstitution may owe more to an aesthetic system far older than Adorno's or Jameson's: the Roman Catholic notion of mystery.

Influential Roman Catholic theologians from Augustine to Thomas Aquinas argue that the internal truth of the mysteries of Christian faith can never be demonstrated, but miracles and prophecies show that faith is not without support or credibility within the created and visible reality (McBrien 1980, 41–42). In other words, God is knowable through history but also always remains hidden. In the twentieth century, grappling with many of the same historical issues that faced Valencia, Roman Catholic theologians explored such mysterious aspects of God's supposed power in an effort to re-create a sort of Christianity for a century of crises, poverty, war, and increased secularism. Following in the wake of influential Roman Catholic theologian Karl Rahner, such diverse theologians as Gustavo Gutiérrez, Johannes Metz, and David

Tracy each developed increasingly negative theologies. Within this framework, God is to be approached in those concrete experiences that somehow represent God's seeming failure. According to the theologians, this God is the "underside" God, the "fool" God, the "irrational" God, the "malformed" God (Martínez 2001, 247). Such a God calls for a reinterpretation of history and reality on the basis of its vanquished, dead, and repressed others (Martínez 2001, 242). Gaspar Martínez writes:

> This journey into the mystery of God starts with a historical
> diagnosis. The three theologies [of Gutiérrez, Metz, and Tracy] make
> three moves. First, they approach history from the repressed memory
> and actuality of its failures, catastrophes, and inner ambiguities,
> namely, from the memory of suffering in Metz, from the "underside
> of history" in Gutiérrez, and from the radical ambiguities of history
> and traditions in Tracy. Second, they denounce and discard the
> modern, Western reading of history as evolutionary progress, this is to
> say, as an ideology that, although modeled after concrete instrumental
> reason, presents itself as the measure of reason, right, and civilization
> and imposes its views, interests, and history on the others. Third, they
> call for a reinterpretation of history and of reality on the basis of its
> "underside," its vanquished and dead, and all its repressed "others."
> (Martínez 2001, 242)

Martínez writes, "The God of the grand narrative, the 'positive' God, is suddenly being shattered and replaced by the weak, 'negative' God who is disclosed just through 'fragments'" (Martínez 2001, 251). Gaspar Martínez describes this turn as a journey of intensification down the *via negatonis* toward the mystery of God and a progressive theological self-emptying (Martínez 2001, 228). In this model, God's apparent powerlessness is simultaneously proof of his power. In other words, people's seemingly contradictory experiences are finally reunited in an ultimate horizon defined by an all-encompassing God. Indeed, a powerful example of this seemingly contradictory mystery is the bloody, humiliated, and horribly human Christ crucified who is simultaneously divine and an expression of God's love.[10]

There is much evidence for other, less academic rearticulations of religion and faith. According to Stuart Hall, Rastafarians in Jamaica transformed biblical language into a new discursive formation. He states that "they had to turn the text upside down, to get a meaning which fit their experience. But in turning the text upside down, they remade themselves" (Hall 1996, 55). Is it then a surprise that Policarpio Valencia could have been responding to twentieth-century pressures through a similar conversation with God, albeit stitched in household string?

In Valencia's riddles, something similar seems to momentarily coalesce. As Emery insightfully stated, "To seek an idea behind the work is rather like tracing out forms on a stained plaster wall—you can see practically anything if you look for it hard enough" (Emery 1953, 42). In a world that seemed to be spinning out of control and defied containment within traditional patterns of thought—where God seemed absent—Valencia's embroideries are an allegorical working through that (re)inscribed God's power. In other words, in human pain and God's apparent absence are the redemptive power of Christ's Resurrection and proof of God's love. In this sense, Christ's death and Resurrection can be understood as Hegel's negation of the negation. Valencia stitched "Adajio que dies, no es el lion como lo pintan, mas que lo aga un buen pintor, el que lo pinto primero le puso has su color y asi es y sera" (There is an adage that says, the lion is not as he is painted even if he is painted by a good painter. He who painted it first did so even to the color and so it is and shall be) (MOIFA MNM A.9.54.28). Still, just as many have found solace in the contemplation of Christ's wounds, this *aufhebung*, or sublation, resists a simple closure. Rather, in dialectical shock, both positive and negative are present here, and therein resides a sort of modernist power.

Thus, as I viewed his embroideries now housed at the MOIFA and those housed at the MOSCA, I imagined Valencia in the twilight of his life, sitting in his Española Valley home, obsessively repeating the buttonhole stitch into the night, and somehow making sense of a world that no longer appeared as he knew it was. On the night I imagine, he embroidered the text that asserted God's transcendent power:

Isa y no allan contradiction pero quedan conbensidos que les dan
buena lecion y a d(e) bera. Tanbien beran escriptos muy debertidos
y de muy bien contenido. El que las lla no hay duda que quedar
a conbensido. No del mundo figurabola dejarlo siempre rodar
como abenido rodando que el tiempo se llegara. (MOIFA MNM
A.9.54.28)

There being no contradiction they will be convinced that they give
good lessons as to be seen. Also are seen very diverting writings of
very good contents. There is no doubt that he who heeds these will
be convinced. The world, spinning like a ball, turns as it has revolved
since time began. (MOIFA MNM A.9.54.28)

Nevertheless, despite Valencia's almost heroic assertion of continuity, his
analysis, like ours, must work through fragments and operate without
the solace of closure.

In Valencia's denial of contradiction, his work is simultaneously
its expression. In so doing, he describes a world and potential form
of critique that would be recognizable to both Marxist critics and
twentieth-century Roman Catholic theologians. In their new book,
Resolana: Emerging Chicano Dialogues on Community and Globalization
(2009), Chicano scholars Miguel Montiel, Tomás Atencio, and E. A.
"Tony" Mares chose to reference, as Valencia did nearly a century
earlier, the adage that the lion is not as he is painted. Addressing
the same issue of appearances as did their precursor, they titled their
book's introduction "No Siempre Es el León Como Lo Pintan." Mares
explained the significance of the saying or *dicho*:

Literally "The lion is not always the way he is painted," it implies
that the real lion is worse. Or, as we might say in English, "Things
are not always what they appear to be." Or, "If at your table there's
a lion or two, they might eat you if they're able to." Or, "Bring a
hungry lion home, and he might dine on you alone." Or, "Better
for you that the lion is a painting on the wall than that he's actually
here." Need I say more? (Montiel, Atencio, and Mares 2009, xiv)

In another embroidery that speaks of animals and our human world, Valencia warns, "Como peses en el mar el grande se come al chico y es una guera mundial. Otros ensisten tambien, enquerer que hayba igualidad . . . eso es un negada" (Like fish in the sea, the big one eats the little one and (there is) a world war. Others insist too in wanting that there should be equality . . . that is a negation) (MNM 5.54.3). A message, hidden on another embroidery's underlying reverse addresses the viewer:

SY ESTA PrENdA SE PerDIrE COMO
SUELE SUSEDIER★ SUPLICO AL QUE LO ALLA
DeYuemela, fE cAbO FUEra de★★★
Uñas largas ole coto en endimiento
Suplico que recuerde el setimo manadmiento. Es todo
Policarpio Valencia
(MOSCA L.5.54.38, transcription by Enrique Lamadrid)

If this treasure should be lost, as
It is wont to happen, I entreat the one who finds
It he must give it back to me, and if he should be
Long of fingernails and short of understanding
I beg of him to be mindful of the Seventh commandment. That is all.
Policarpio Valencia———ta [?]
[?]Cr-s New Mexico
(Translation by Fray Angélico Chávez in Emery 1953, 39–40)

Experiencing the fragmentation and poverty of a capitalist-dominated modernity—a world where malnutrition is common and land loss is on the tip of everyone's tongue—Valencia appeals to the viewer to keep God's law, "Thou shall not steal."

Just as Valencia confronted the riddle of his community's transformation, continuity, and negation, in the 1970s, fiction writer, poet, and essayist Jim Sagel struggled with similar themes in his literary efforts.

CHAPTER SIX

Cuando Hablan los Enamorados

Conversan como si estuvieran cambiando regalos,
cada palabra un obsequio de luz.[1]

—Jim Sagel, "Corozonazos: Poemas por Jim Sagel"

They converse as if they were exchanging gifts,
each word a gift of light.

—My translation

In the spring of 2002, artist Teresa Archuleta and I spent days going
through the more than eighty boxes of papers her husband, author Jim
Sagel, left behind when he died.[2] One afternoon, our discussion veered
to issues of marriage. As a lesson to me—I had not yet been married
a year—she offered to show me the love poems and notes of daily life
that Sagel had written during their twenty-eight years together. She led
·me to her living-room closet, where she asked me to reach for the small
cardboard box on the top shelf and place it on the coffee table. As we sat
on her living-room couch, she lifted three bundles from the box. Each
was wrapped in the torn white cloth of Archuleta's wedding dress. Sagel,
an Anglo-American from Colorado, moved to northern New Mexico's
Española Valley as a young adult and chose to live with Archuleta until
the last days of his life. In New Mexico, Sagel became one of the state's
preeminent writers and was particularly well known for his short stories,
poems, and essays filled with local color. Perhaps more significant he
displayed virtuosity in New Mexican Spanish in his texts.

Throughout Sagel's writings, the author uses multiple narratives that simultaneously conflict and strangely move in concert and exemplify notions of critical modernism. Marianne DeKoven describes critical modernism as an aesthetic practice that represents fragmentation but at the same time yearns for wholeness and synthesis (DeKoven 2004, 16). Within such textual and artistic practices, oppositions to modernity rise and push for audibility and visibility (DeKoven 2004, 14). The result is a powerful tension of domination and subversion where dominant modern forms are the aesthetic, cultural, and technological credo but are also profoundly distrusted as chaotic and destructive. Throughout Sagel's work, one sees a repetition of oppositions that he saw in the landscape that surrounded his New Mexico home: Anglo versus Nuevomexicano, masculine versus feminine, and connection versus alienation. In New Mexico's landscape, Sagel described moments in which such oppositions hold each other in dialectical tension, others where they harmonize and clash. I suspect that Sagel's simultaneous focus on pain and beauty expressed his own visceral, embodied experiences. As a sufferer of depression since childhood, Sagel had experienced periods of great productivity and periods of incapacity. A few years after Sagel and Archuleta were married, Sagel was hospitalized twice for his mental condition. In 1978, he was diagnosed with depression and received intensive drug therapy and eighteen electroshock treatments (Archuleta 2009).[3]

Despite Sagel's struggles, his literary production was immense in the two decades preceding his 1998 death. He published four collections of short stories, seven collections of poetry, two nonfiction books, three children's books, and one play. In particular, two literary awards served to bookend his career: Sagel's reputation was established when he was awarded the 1981 Premio Casa de las Américas for his short-story collection *Tunomás Honey,* and his life ended shortly after winning the 1997 Premio Literario Ciudad de San Sebastián for his play *Doña Refugio y su comadre.* He was also a columnist for the *Albuquerque Journal*'s Santa Fe bureau, *New Mexico Magazine,* and published in other regional, national, and international publications. He spent much of his time teaching at the University of New Mexico at Los Alamos and Northern New Mexico Community College. Included in the papers that I saw at Archuleta's Española home were at least one unpublished novel and numerous other manuscripts.

In the context of this body of work, this chapter explores Sagel and Archuleta's relationship as part of his wider New Mexico romance.[4] During their last years together, the couple had grown distant, as Sagel's depression grew increasingly self-destructive and the critical tension between the author's ambivalent visions broke into open opposition and discord. Shortly before Sagel's 1998 suicide, he asked Archuleta for a divorce. In pain and anger, she tore up her wedding dress. Decades of his poetic accounts of their promise to each other as well as the notes of daily life were carefully wrapped and stored in the shreds of a romance that ended tragically. This essay marks a second effort to unpack that box—a box that contains the remnants of both a love affair and a creative partnership. Nevertheless, I also view their romance in wider, more abstract terms.

But You Know What? It's Humanity

Sagel moved to northern New Mexico in search of salve for his alienation and the personal demons that left him dissatisfied with his life. The son of an eastern Colorado farming family of Prussian descent, Sagel grew up in the rural farming community of Fort Morgan. In the late 1960s, Sagel received an undergraduate degree in English from the University of Colorado at Boulder. He first visited New Mexico in 1969 and moved to the Española Valley in 1970. Sagel's decision to come to New Mexico was based in part on a close friend's recently established residence in the northern New Mexican village of Nambé and receipt of a fellowship to enter graduate school at the University of New Mexico.

As a popular writer, Sagel is perhaps best known for his celebration of the traditional culture of New Mexico's Latino elders. This aspect is particularly well illustrated by the essay collections *Dancing to Pay the Light Bill* and *Straight from the Heart*, coauthored with Jack Parsons (Sagel 1992; Parsons and Sagel 1990). His best work in my estimation, however, also uses a complex and ambivalent analysis of younger Nuevomexicanos who live in a hybrid culture. These works include the short-story collections *Tunomás Honey, Sabelotodo entiendelonada*, and *El santo queso/ The Holy Cheese* (Sagel 1983, 1988, 1990). For Sagel, this ambivalence divided culturally whole *viejitos* from younger generations, which were characterized by a distance from the Spanish language and Nuevomexicano culture as well as disproportionate rates of addiction and violence. For this Anglo-American who first came to northern New Mexico as a young adult, both thematic concentrations required a profound ability to understand the issues of the community that surrounded him. Rather than a bucolic premodern landscape, Sagel saw a landscape rife with social inequality. Reflecting on Española's difficulties, Archuleta commented that Sagel loved Española's complexities. She stated:

> He liked the fact that this was an area that was fraught with
> problems. It was real. . . . People put down Española, but you know
> what we are? We don't have the money to hide the problems that
> maybe Santa Fe does. We can't gentrify. It's right in your face and it's
> ugly sometimes and it's discouraging and you just want to scream.
> But you know what? It's humanity. (Archuleta 2002b)

You Must Get Out

Sagel initially found a seemingly more unified way of life in the part of the Española Valley located just off the highway and away from the gaze of passing motorists. Here lie the hearts of the centuries-old villages with their predominately adobe architecture, such as Santa Cruz's old adobe church, as well as the site of the Archuleta property in the area called La Angostura that would eventually become the site of Jim and Teresa's home. In the introduction to "Rebuilt," the collection of poems that was his thesis for a master's degree in English from the University of New Mexico, Sagel described his attempt to address the frustration and sense of powerlessness from the "intimate level of personal relationships to society's guilt over its ecological suicide" (Sagel 1976, iv). He writes:

The sense of magic and the supernatural which runs through the folktales of both the Spanish and Indians of northern New Mexico forms the basis for these poems. The material is not simply lifted from the sources but it is altered to shape "rebuilt" images that attempt to cope with the unreality of the late twentieth century. (Sagel 1976, iv)

Perhaps the poem "It all begins when you draw lines" from his thesis best describes this sense of alienation and suggests the proposed solution he would find in the culture of New Mexico's elders. He warns of the pending disaster of mainstream society; "the artifice will rain down on everyone here," he affirms, and "you must get out" (Sagel 1976, 6).

Sagel was not the first writer to find his or her subject in the New Mexican landscape. Indeed, Nuevomexicanos have produced a long list of literature focused on their experience. In the second half of the twentieth century, Nuevomexicano literature joined a burgeoning national Chicana/o literature, and many New Mexicans rose to prominence, including Fray Angélico Chávez, Sabine Ulibarrí, Rudolfo Anaya, Juan Estevan Arellano, Orlando Romero, E. A. Mares, Denise Chávez, and Levi Romero. At the time of Sagel's 1970 move to the Española Valley, northern New Mexico was experiencing another influx of disaffected Anglo-Americans, hippies (Keltz 2000). Like the artists who came before them, these people sought the answers of modern life through reclaiming a more "authentic" past. The continuity of the countercultures of these two periods is perhaps best epitomized by Dennis Hopper's ownership of Mabel Dodge Luhan's former Taos home. Moreover, as Iris Keltz has shown in a book aptly titled *Scrapbook of a Taos Hippie: Tribal Tales from the Heart of a Cultural Revolution*, the hippies of the 1960s and 1970s often found inspiration in so-called "tribal" ways of living.

The most popular Anglo-American writer concerned with Latino New Mexicans, John Nichols, arrived in New Mexico in this same period. His novel *The Milagro Beanfield War* (1974) achieved national acclaim and eventually became a film directed by Robert Redford (*The Milagro Beanfield War* 1988).[5] In contrast to Sagel, Nichols sometimes positions himself as a writer only incidentally concerned with New Mexicans. In Kevin McIlvoy's interview, "A Dialogue: Rudolfo Anaya / John Nichols," John Nichols stated that *The Milagro Beanfield War* was universal, and he already knew 85 to 90 percent of what the novel was about before he moved to Taos (McIlvoy 1998, 75). While few criticize Sagel's literary-oriented work as lacking a feel for New Mexican culture, I have heard people state that John Nichols's characters sometimes do not act or talk like northern New Mexicans. Nichols uses his claim to being a universal writer to disarm such criticism in his interview with McIlvoy. He states:

> One of the questions that people would often ask me and I keep trying to defeat is this—is people come up to me and say, "How could you know so much about our culture?"—this is often Spanish-speaking Chicano people—"if you only lived here for two and a half years?" There's other Chicanos that say, "Nichols don't know nothing, or he's full of shit, or he don't know nothing about Chicano culture." (McIlvoy 1998, 75)

Rather than address the needs of a specific community such as Taos, he states that he seeks to be "a little molecule in the cultural part of the revolutionary movement which will one day terminate the capitalist control of the people and the economy and the culture" (McIlvoy 1998, 74). In sharp contrast with Nichols, Sagel always remained chiefly focused on Nuevomexicanos, and he finds his inspiration in the words spoken around his home. Enrique Lamadrid, Sagel's colleague and friend, detailed these aspects of his work in an obituary for him (Lamadrid 1998). Lamadrid wrote, "His finely tuned ethnographic ear captured the nuance and the complex subtleties of folk sayings and folk humor. His inspiration was the voice of others. He often said that his true talent was transcription, writing down what he heard all around him."

Linda y Rara Brujería

Upon his arrival in New Mexico, Sagel's longing to "get out" would soon find an expressive focus in his love for an Española woman, Teresa Archuleta. Shortly after his move, the twenty-two-year-old Sagel began substitute teaching at Española High School, where he met Archuleta, then an eighteen-year-old high school student. She was the youngest sibling in a close-knit family of six sisters and three brothers. Archuleta's father, Jacobo Archuleta, was a carpenter, and, at the time of Teresa Archuleta's birth, her mother, Matilde Archuleta, cleaned dorm rooms in Los Alamos. Both Archuleta and Sagel described an immediate and intense love for the other. Sagel would later write of this encounter in his unpublished manuscript titled "Bisbee" (Sagel n.d.a). He wrote, "Our eyes collided for an instant and everyone else in B-Hall vanished" (Sagel n.d.a, 5).

Like most other Nuevomexicanos in the Española Valley, the Archuletas were descendants of people living in New Mexico before the American annexation of the Southwest following the Mexican-American War. Jacobo and Matilde Archuleta, along with some of their other children, moved to Española in the early 1940s from the remote northern village of Coyote. Several more children, including Teresa, were born in Española in the coming years. By the time she met Sagel, however, Archuleta was already exhibiting bohemian tendencies that set her apart from most other Española youth. Indeed, in an era when divisions between locals and hippies were sharply drawn, Teresa was known as Sunflower by her high school friends, and upon graduation, she planned to move to Greenwich Village to become a poet. Moreover, Teresa had already suffered profoundly life-altering experiences. At the age of sixteen, she fought a yearlong, near-fatal bout with what was then diagnosed as hepatitis and more recently as Budd-Chiari syndrome. During that time, she was in a coma for six weeks and received the last rites twice. Her illness resulted in the health problems that would plague her for the rest of her life. In short, Archuleta was both an Española native and a person who sought an escape of her own.

Sagel and Archuleta found love in each other and simultaneously the answers to the forces that threatened to stifle them. For Sagel, an Anglo outsider with hippie tendencies, his marriage to Archuleta would provide his entry to the Nuevomexicano world that he loved. As in any good romance, however, Archuleta would return Sagel's gaze. At the same instant that Sagel's love for Archuleta paralleled his love for her New Mexican ancestry, Archuleta wanted to escape the oppressive elements of her position as a Nuevomexicana. In *On the Make Again*, Sagel included a poem with seeming reference to Archuleta:

¿Cómo que me pescaste
con una sóla mirada?
¡Qué ojos tan fuertes
que me hechizaron con su linda y rara
brujería! (Sagel 1990, 60)

How did you catch me
with only one look?
What strong eyes
bewitched with their beautiful and strange
magic!
(My translation)

Archuleta and Sagel eloped only a month before she was to graduate from high school and a scant two weeks after their first conversation. They took a trip together to Mexico's Pacific coast and subsequently moved in together.[6] In his short unpublished essay "Bisbee," Sagel wrote of the first days of their union:

> There we lay as one body in a single sleeping bag as the Pacific lapped at our toes and cosigned our lifetime loan on the sand. The papers we drew up were the poems we wrote down with our eyes. And the letters—not letters home, for that was where we already were, but letters across time, cartas a nuestro niño, the baby we believed we had conceived under the comet that continued to glow over our heads. Our dinner was hard beans, cooked over a driftwood fire in the black clay pot your great-grandmother made in the previous century. (Sagel n.d.a)

Thus began a romance that would provide them both with inspiration for decades to come.

In the 1970s and 1980s, Archuleta emerged as one of the central figures in the renaissance of Río Grande–style weaving.[7] Archuleta's maternal ancestors were weavers, and she grew up surrounded by weavings, but she did not learn to weave until the 1970s when she studied under the tutelage of the famed weaver doña Agueda Martínez

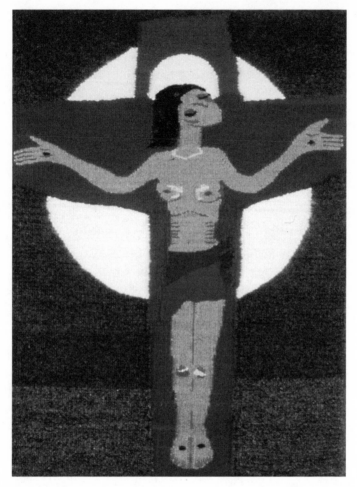

"Crista." This weaving by Teresa Archuleta depicts a woman on a cross.
The tapestry measures 24 inches by 24½ inches. The wool weft includes
handspun wool vegetal dyed with black walnut hulls, cota, dahlia
flowers, indigo, and mountain mahogany bark.

and Martínez's student, Ruth Vigil. Archuleta spent most of the 1970s
studying diverse weaving styles, and she found her voice by exploring
the traditional Río Grande weaving style and method. Nevertheless,
she soon became bored by the limited traditional motifs and patterns
and began to push the limits of the genre with high-art aspirations

and innovations inspired by the environment, her experiences, and her own poetry. Throughout the 1970s and 1980s, she developed a weaving style that both paid homage to the conventions of the genre and innovated with new sensibilities in color and design. By 1990, with the possible exception of Chimayó weaver Irvin Trujillo, Archuleta was the most sought-after New Mexican Latina/o weaver. Her mature style is perhaps best illustrated by her weaving "Too Many Paths and None Cross Yours," which combines desert colors, blue accents, and mountain symbols in a lyrical style inspired by her poetry. In this period she maintained an alternative expression that seems to echo a critical modernist aesthetic as well. This edge is already evident in some of her earlier experimental works. For instance, in a scathing feminist critique, Archuleta wove a woman with no mouth nailed to a cross in the manner of Christ. She titled the 1978 piece "Crista."

Sagel's love for Teresa Archuleta would open the doors for another relationship that would profoundly shape his life. After Jacobo Archuleta overcame the fact that the young stranger had eloped with his daughter, the two men's relationship blossomed into one resembling that of a father and son. In our interviews, Archuleta described her father's love for the young man. In return, Sagel saw the strength and self-reliance he envisioned as characteristic of New Mexico's elders. While participating in the dominant regional economy through his work in Los Alamos, Jacobo Archuleta retained his foothold in the older, small-scale agricultural economy. Throughout his life, he maintained a small ranch near Coyote as well as several Española-area landholdings, which he farmed using both a tractor and a horse-drawn plow. Both Teresa Archuleta and her father would become particularly influential in Sagel's life. Indeed, in a University of New Mexico at Los Alamos convocation speech titled "My Real Education," delivered in the year before his death, Sagel described Jacobo Archuleta's mentorship—and not his years at the University of Colorado at Boulder or in graduate school at the University of New Mexico—as the source of his true education (1997c). Sagel said that among the lessons Jacobo Archuleta taught him were respect, the ability to adapt, a connection to the land, humor, and a sense of one's place in history. Most important, though, Sagel stated that his father-in-law taught him that "*los hombres no se rajan*—A real man never gives up" (Sagel 1997c, 3). Still, Sagel's admiration for Jacobo Archuleta—and, in part, Archuleta's masculine strength—must be understood as a product of both the old man's qualities and Sagel's desire for something realer than the fragmented world he saw in mainstream society.

Teresa Archuleta describes a more complex vision of her father. With Sagel, Archuleta shares admiration, and she depicts their relationship with great warmth. She attributes her strength and assertiveness to her father. She states, "It was my father who taught me to stand up and say what I needed and respect myself and to excel in that way" (Archuleta 2002a). Still, some of her statements suggest a darker side to his strength—a side visited on her siblings rather than Archuleta herself. "My father was the Law," she states:

> My father was one strong son of a bitch that you did not dare,
> excuse my language, fuck around with. You know? I would not
> have dared disobey my father but I did it because I loved and
> respected him. I think some of my older brothers and sisters feared
> him because he was harsh. (Archuleta 2002a)

Sagel saw Jacobo Archuleta's strength expressed in the wider ways of northern New Mexico's elders.

Sagel's vision has been most popularly described in the essays collected in *Dancing to Pay the Light Bill* (Sagel 1992).[8] With admiration and with an optimism often absent from other works, Sagel writes that a sense of history permeates the everyday life of even the most assimilated Nuevomexicano. He writes, "Memories are long in this place where oral tradition is still alive in the stories swapped at the local post office and passed down through the generations over the kitchen table" (Sagel 1992, ix). The personal element of Sagel's admiration for the older generation is perhaps better shown in many of his more serious literary works. The first poem, "Cuando el zacate crecía silvestre en los llanos," from his unpublished manuscript "Corazonazos" describes both Sagel's relationship with his father-in-law as well as his hunger for wholeness (Sagel n.d.b):

Dejo la fiesta para dirigirme a una milpa de alfalfa cortada.
Yo vendo unos ojos negros
la voz de la cantora retumba a lo lejos,
pero no estoy dispuesto a comprar.
Todo lo que quiero hacer es oler la fragante tristeza
de la alfalfa cortada,
el olor al final del verano que me lleva en la memoria
a un agosto hace veinte años
cuando el zacate ondulaba en el viento
como un maremoto amarillo
y encerramos mil *biles* bajo un sol abrasador—
usted, el viejo poderoso,
y yo, el escolar con una pipa en la boca.
Esa noche, mientras que usted afilaba su navaja
a la luz de una lámpara de aceite
y me platicaba de los tiempos
cuando el zacate crecía silvestre en los llanos,
me hundí en un sueño prehistórico.
En la mañana, me dolían todos los músculos del cuerpo
menos el corazón.
Al hacer café con el agua del riachuelo
y freír papas en una sartén negra,
usted despertó en mí un apetito tan profundo
que yo necesitaba dos lenguas sólo para expresarlo.
Al fin entendí lo que sacaría mi hambre. (Sagel n.d.b, 3–4)

An English version of "Cuando el zacate crecía en los llanos" under the title "When the Zacate Grew Wild in the Llanos" is included in Sagel's English collection of poetry *Unexpected Turn*. The English text roughly parallels the Spanish version.

Leaving the fiesta, I walked through a field of freshly cut alfalfa.
Yo vendo unos ojos negros, the singer's voice reverberates in a distant
box: "Black eyes for sale," but I'm not buying. All I want to do is
smell the brittle fragrance of the cut hay, the end of the summer
smell of the last cut that takes me twenty Augusts back to a time

when the timothy hay undulated like a yellow tidal wave in the
wind and we stacked a thousand bales under the sweltering sun,
and I—powerful *viejo* and college refugee.

That evening as you sharpened your pocketknife in the glow of
a kerosene lamp and told talks in the tongue of your *abuelos* of
the days when the *zacate* grew wild in the *llanos*, I collapsed into
a primitive sleep on a dusty *colchón*. When I awoke the following
morning, you were already boiling fresh coffee in the water you
had carried up from the stream.

As you fried eggs and potatoes over the wood fire, I felt an appetite
grow so big inside me, I needed two languages to express it. *Al fin
sabía lo que era el hambre.* At last I had found what I was hungering
for. (Sagel 1997d, 4)

This was how, according to Sagel, Jacobo Archuleta taught him that
for which he hungered.

Sagel transformed his admiration for Jacobo Archuleta into a larger
vision of transcendence that he saw as the strength of the Nuevomexicano
world view. In a passage in his speech "My Real Education," describing
his admiration for his father-in-law, Sagel writes:

It is a way of being that is simultaneously independent and
connected to family, community and the natural world. It's a
sense of self-reliance that relies on the enigma of faith. It's the
quintessentially New Mexican way of living with one's feet
planted in two cultures and two times. (Sagel 1997c, 2)

In this way, Sagel's greatest admiration and hope is in his description of
earlier generations. He offers a vision of an explicitly masculine strength
to confront the pain of modernity.

The Cultural Dynamics of Spanglish

Sagel's collection of essays *Dancing to Pay the Light Bill* also fiercely defends younger generations' hybrid and seemingly more fragmented way of being (Sagel 1992). His essays "¿Cómo se dice 'Big Mac' en español?: The Cultural Dynamics of 'Spanglish'" and "Lowdown Laughs: The Española Joke" are particularly topical and defend area residents in the face of regional discourses that often disparage them. Many of his more literary-focused works are analyses of the complexities, ironies, and contributions of social and cultural transformation. For example, *Tunomás Honey*, *Doña Refugio y su comadre*, *El santo queso*, and *Sabelotodo entiendelonada* explore, often with black humor, the hurt of social transformation (Sagel 1983, 1997b, 1988).

This aspect of Sagel's writing is most clearly represented by his short story "El Americano," from *Tunomás Honey* (Sagel 1983). This story focuses on a single character, Darryl Francis Galván, who embodies social transformation through his transgressive tendencies. Darryl was born feet first, enjoyed wearing his mother's shoes, and suffered a number of humiliations that resulted from his own ineptitude and the ridicule of his family and community members. For instance, he overturns a truck while he helps his grandfather and uncle bale hay and speaks mangled Spanish to the amusement of his extended family. For his efforts, Darryl is nicknamed El Americano.

The central issue narrated in Sagel's story is the push and pull between Darryl and his rural relatives, a tension that is indicative of Darryl's circumstances in the wider world. Sagel wrote, "el Darryl se preguntó por qué estaba aquí, cómo podía ser pariente de esta criatura embolada charlando sin cesar en mexicano, y por qué pasaba una gran parte de su vida sintiéndose perdida" (Darryl retreated inside his head and wondered. Why in the hell was he here anyway? How in the world could he possibly be related to this drunken creature chattering away in Spanish? And why . . . why did he have to spend such a large part of his life feeling lost?) (Sagel 1983, 28, 29). Darryl's father cannot stand his son's predilection for books, education, and, in general, feminization. He sends Darryl to live on a ranch with his more rural relatives in order to harvest hay and, more important, teach Darryl to be a real man. The ridicule of Darryl's relatives only fosters his own sense of superiority, which in turn further invites his relatives' punishment and ridicule: "Pero el Darryl era un muchacho tan travieso y tan malcriado (rodando en el suelo y chillando como un marrano lastimado cuando no le cumplían sus deseos), que casi no podía uno resistir la tentación de darle una buena en su cabeza de hueso" (But Darryl was such a mischievous and difficult child (rolling on the floor and squealing like a wounded pig when he didn't get his way) that one could hardly resist the temptation to give him a good bop on his hard head) (Sagel 1983, 28, 29).

Yet in this short story, Sagel is not ready to give up on this hybrid youth and the upcoming generation for which he stands. The last moments of the narrative are devoted to Darryl's realization of his own strength—a twisted strength his relatives cannot understand. Taking a walk amid the rural poverty and decay characteristic of his rural landscape, Darryl sees models for strength in both nature and the social detritus of consumer society. Sagel writes:

> Andando por la basura, espantando a las gallinas y dando una patuda
> a una llanta gastada en su camino, fue hasta la puente que pasa por
> arriba del Rito de los Cañones. Mirando pa'bajo, vio a los carros
> "requendos" y tirados y comenzó a gozaren las formas curíosas del
> metal arrunendo y mojoso.

> —Como yo—pensó—Torcido, pero allí siempre.

> Y levantando los ojos pa'rriba, miró el Cerro Perdenal con su cima
> lisa brillando en el sol.

> —Diferente, pero sólido—pensó (Sagel 1983, 39, 41).

> Tramping through the garbage, spooking the chickens, and
> kicking a worn tire in his path, Darryl made his way to the bridge
> that spans the Rito de los Cañones. Gazing down, he saw the
> wrecked junk cars and took pleasure in the unusual forms the
> rusted metal created.

"Just like me," he thought, "Twisted but tough."

And, lifting his eyes, he looked up to the Cerro Pedernal with its flattened summit sparkling in the sun.

"Different but solid," he reflected. (Sagel 1983, 38, 40)

In this short story, Sagel struggles to find an alternative (if feminized) negative strength within the contradiction of emerging New Mexico culture. This vision stands in stark contrast to the less complicated admiration (almost adulation) of community elders. Nevertheless, as we shall see later in this essay, Sagel may have felt a stronger identification with the more painful tales of dialectical tension and negation.

Jaime Sagel (Sah HELL) aka Jim Sagel (Say Guell)

Sagel's literary reputation is largely based on his short stories, especially his collection *Tunomás Honey*, which won the 1981 Premio Casa de las Américas in Havana, Cuba. The prestigious honor catapulted him to the enviable position of a literary force to be reckoned with at the same time that it harmed Sagel's reputation beyond repair. Chicano writer Rolando Hinojosa won the award for his novel *Klail City y sus Alrededores* in 1976, and the judges believed that in awarding Sagel, they were recognizing another Chicano writer. Speaking of the award, the venerable Trinity professor and Charles Frankel prize winner Arturo Madrid told a *Denver Post* reporter of the award, "Jim Sagel permitted it be thought for the purposes of the (Premio Casa de Las Américas) competition that he is a Chicano. He didn't rise up and say, 'No, no, no, you have made a mistake,'" (*Denver Post* 1991).

Sagel maintained that the judges simply assumed he was Chicano, and Archuleta similarly insists he never made false claims to a Chicano identity. I have found no evidence to suggest Sagel, unlike some Anglo contemporaries, was explicitly engaged in a deliberate attempt to mask his actual ethnic/racial background. Nevertheless, Sagel's supposed masquerade darkened the remainder of his career. Enrique Lamadrid wrote in Sagel's obituary that much of the buzz around Sagel in Chicano literary circles was a debate over whether he deserved a place in the Chicano canon or was an interloper cashing in on Chicano chic (Lamadrid 1998). When I have discussed Sagel's work with critics of Chicano literature, in offhand remarks some have challenged the merit of his work purely based his status as an Anglo-American, casting him as some sort of charlatan. Archuleta is still stung by such charges and strongly asserts Sagel's love for his adopted home, the sincerity of his advocacy for Nuevomexicanos, and his acceptance among her family. Refuting the specific accusation of "cashing in" on "Chicano chic," Archuleta states that both she and Sagel believed that his focus on Chicana/os and his insistence on writing in Spanish prevented him from reaching a wide audience in the United States (Archuleta 2009).

Perhaps the virulence of literary critics' distrust of Sagel results from the fact that they had been burned before. Several contemporary twentieth-century Anglo authors deployed Spanish noms de plume in efforts to masquerade as Mexican American. For instance, as Amado Muro, the Anglo-American Chester E. Seltzer won fame as an early Chicano writer, and his deception extended to false biographic statements. To add insult to injury, Muro/Seltzer's work was included in the anthology *Mexican-American Authors*, edited by influential scholar Américo Paredes and literary critic Raymund Paredes (Paredes and Paredes 1976).[9] Similarly, as Danny Santiago, Daniel James received fame for his *Famous All Over Town* (Santiago 1983).[10]

Unlike Sagel's deceptive contemporaries, many would insist he does deserve a place in Chicano literature. For instance, in her documentary film *The Unexpected Turn of Jim Sagel*, filmmaker Pilar Rodríguez Aranda shows a litany of writers, including E. A. Mares, describing their admiration for Sagel's work (Rodríguez Aranda 2003).[11] The famous Chicana writer Sandra Cisneros told a reporter from the Denver Post, "'I think Jim Sagel is a Chicano writer because he is conscious in the most complete way, in his heart, of the struggle of Mexican-American people.'"

Others are less certain of his place in Chicano literature. The leading Chicano literary critic of the 1980s, Juan Bruce-Novoa, noted Sagel's significance and location within the Chicano literary canon with considerable ambivalence in his essay collection *RetroSpace* (Bruce-Novoa 1990):

> Our inability to submit authors to a *prueba de sangre* before
> nominating them for canonization can lead to embarrassing *faux pas*.
> La Casa de las Américas thought it was honoring another Chicano
> when it granted an award to Jaime Sagel (Sah HELL) aka Jim Sagel
> (Say Guell). . . . (Bruce-Novoa 1990, 140)

Similarly, his status seems to be controversial in Española proper, even though he was largely admired for his nuanced knowledge of the community and sometimes fierce defense of the valley's residents. He was occasionally reviled as an Anglo interloper. A well-known local politician who judged Sagel an outsider and his works as lacking significance for Española residents once challenged my interest in his work. Similarly, a local intellectual asked why I did not focus on "real" local writers. Even Sagel's defenders, such as Puerto Rican scholar Virginia Dessus Colón, cast the debate in terms of his insider/outsider status. In her thesis "El Mundo Chicano en *Tunomás Honey* de Jim Sagel," Dessus Colón argued that he deserved Chicano status because he was acculturated to Chicano culture and his stories were representative in form and content of Chicano narrative (Dessus Colón 1987, 1). In an attempt to resolve the problem, other Sagel supporters, like Rodríguez Aranda, place his work in the rather clumsy category of "Chicanesque" literature—works done about Chicanos but written by non-Chicanos.[12] Still, Sagel's own question of identity was framed in more complex terms than either Dessus or Rodríguez Aranda has elaborated.

I Am Somewhere Inside

In the course of their elopement, Sagel and Archuleta experienced a personal mythology that manifested a profound exchange. They also describe something unrepresentable. Here too he represents a comment thematic of critical modernism in that they suggest the historical discursive conditions of their production and open a space for the unrepresentable. In Bisbee, Arizona, on their way to Mexico's Pacific coast, Sagel and Archuleta encountered visions of a nineteenth-century incarnation of Sagel. These visions took on the form of a person Sagel and Archuleta could see and hear. In those visions, they learned that in a previous lifetime Sagel and Archuleta were lovers. Unable to accept their love, the father of Archuleta's antecedent opposed their union and ultimately was killed by Sagel's earlier incarnation.[13] The following account of their vision was drawn from an interview with Archuleta and Sagel's unpublished essay "Bisbee" and corroborated by a poem from Sagel's thesis similarly entitled "Bisbee" (Archuleta 2002c; Sagel n.d.a 1976).

Walking down a street in Bisbee, Arizona, they heard a noise coming from inside an abandoned building. Looking between the boards that covered the windows, Archuleta said, they saw a man behind bars in the manner of an old-fashioned jail; both Archuleta and Sagel knew that man was Sagel (Archuleta 2002c). Sagel wrote in the unpublished essay, "Peering through the decaying facade of the building, we hear a moan and I am somewhere inside. I am dying while you weep beyond these iron bars. An ache older than the night writhes between us like a dark fish" (Sagel n.d.a, 25). Archuleta said, "I looked at him and I said, 'Did you see that?' and he said, 'Yeah that was me in there'" (Archuleta 2002c). After walking for several more hours, they arrived at an old two- or three-story Victorian home. Sagel wrote:

> But our walk is not over, not until I find your house. If I don't climb those steps again, we will never be able to go on. I know your father is waiting for me. The fish knife in my right hand, I slowly ascend the wooden steps that are attached to the rear of the white Victorian house. There is no other way to that room on the second floor, no longer any way out. I climb to the top, my spine creaking and my tongue thickening in my coppery mouth. There is the door. This time, I must open it. As you watch from below, I pull the door toward me and glimpse inside. (Sagel n.d.a, 25)

Archuleta narrated similarly:

I wouldn't go close to [the house]. I was trembling and I was saying let's leave and he was compelled to go up there. It was an outdoor staircase. He went up . . . and I can't tell you how long he was gone but when he came back, he said that he had killed my father from that lifetime with a fish knife. With a knife that had a fish or a fish knife. I don't remember. And consequently that's why he landed up in jail. . . . And he was hung in that lifetime. (Archuleta 2002c)

Moreover, Archuleta told me that Sagel experienced a vision that evoked the murder of Archuleta's father. Sagel writes:

Later, I cannot tell you what I saw. Neither can I tell you at this moment what I am seeing, something blacker in the blackness of my own pupils regarding themselves in an instant outside of time that I will never be able to describe in the next instant that this instant has already become. All I can do is embrace you at the bottom of the steps as we start all over again. (Sagel n.d.a, 25)

Thus, Archuleta and Sagel saw that in a previous lifetime the two were lovers. In that lifetime, Sagel both killed Archuleta's father and suffered. Archuleta attributes Sagel's ability to express Nuevomexicano pain in his writing to this earlier suffering. Nevertheless, Sagel cannot tell you what he saw or is, at that moment, seeing.

As if some uncanny structuralist allegory, in Bisbee, Sagel and Archuleta experienced a profound mimetic exchange that seemingly brought fulfillment to their lives. Sagel envisioned a sense of magic and the supernatural in the New Mexican landscape, a "linda y rara brujería" in the eyes of his wife, and used both to face his personal demons and modernity. Within this exchange, Sagel's identity is truly the product of the couple's New Mexico mutual constitution. According to the *Denver Post*:

Sagel, a wiry, bearded man with blue-green eyes and a quick laugh, said he never felt alien in Española. "To tell the truth, I felt a sense of arriving where I belonged. I had a feeling that I had come home.

Added Teresa, "Sometimes I tell Jim he was a mejicano in an earlier life. His soul remembers. I truly believe it. He is sensitive—and I don't mean this in a cruel way—as other Anglos aren't." (*Denver Post* 1991)

In Archuleta, Sagel found a home and belonging. In Sagel, Teresa saw an escape that embodied her desire for something other than the working-class and irrevocably New Mexican lives of her parents.

Nevertheless, Sagel and Archuleta's mutual romance was an act of transgression that served as a rejection of their parents' visions of social order. It remains something not yet fully capable of articulation. Sagel wrote "something blacker in the blackness of my own pupils regarding themselves in an instant outside of time that I will never be able to describe in the next instant that this instant has already become." Within Sagel and Archuleta's mythology, Sagel murdered Archuleta's father. In this way, their past and present predicaments attained a tentative bargain that affirmed the aspirations of their present lives. As Sagel wrote, "All I can do is embrace you at the bottom of the steps as we start all over again."

A Little Pierced Heart

In the early 1990s, Jacobo Archuleta died, and Sagel's bouts with depression became more intense. He increasingly threw himself into his work, and his poetry took on an especially mournful quality. Archuleta said that he was in a chronic depression from 1991 or 1992 until his death. As time passed, and los viejitos died, Sagel was left only with the thoroughly modern landscape so distressing. His adopted home could no longer sustain the affirmative elements of his ambivalence. Hope and fear for a radically different future were invoked, producing an ambiguous textual form that encompassed at once death, suffering, horror, and redemptive transformation. In the 1990s, Sagel's dread remained. In a poem included in his poetry collection *Unexpected Turn*, he wrote:

The old apple orchards are ripening with doublewides, their
windows digitally lit by the Shopping Channel. How quickly I have
come to live too long, I think, as I drive through the night like a
man turning the pages of a family album filling up with pictures of
the dead. (Sagel 1997d, 52)

The ambivalent attraction that sustained Sagel's New Mexico romance
grew unbalanced as the traditional world of los viejitos faded into
memory. The Española Valley's younger generation seemed ever more
alienated from its ancestral life-style. In such a landscape negativity
proliferated, and the bargain struck in Sagel and Archuleta's elopement
was lost.

Meanwhile, Archuleta was confronting her own visceral rejection
of modernity: she became incapacitated by chemical and environmental
illness from the early to mid-1990s. She said, "I couldn't leave the
house too much because if I went out and someone was smoking or
women had perfume on or there were fumes from a gas pump or a
carpet that was new, it would affect me terribly" (Archuleta 2002c).
Moreover, Archuleta increasingly moved toward computer prints that
now depicted a much harsher and more ambivalent world than her
weavings. Even more than her early critical work, such as the weaving
"Crista," the computer prints from this period express a modernist
aesthetic with a critical—and often tortured—edge. In many works,
she uses Roman Catholic imagery, images that appear to be Archuleta
herself, and play with color and light that comment on both. For
example, in her piece *A Little Pierced Heart*, an image is half-filled by
a blending of reddish-brown, blue, and white colors. In the other half
of the piece, this form lyrically blends into a woman with a serene
expression holding a *malacate*, or spindle, that pierces a sacred heart.

One of Sagel's final works depicts a hopeful and tragic romance.
Sagel's bilingual novel *Always the Heart/Siempre el Corazón* (1998a) is the
unfulfilled love story of two couples, the teenagers Crescencia Marta
(C. M.) and Damián and C. M.'s great-grandmother Crescencia and
David. Written from C. M.'s point of view, the story is a retelling of the
Navajo story of Changing Woman, the Navajo goddess who represents
the cycles of the seasons and life. C. M. and Crescencia represent her

younger and older incarnations. Like Sagel and Archuleta, both couples fell in love at first sight. The parallels to real life are confirmed by the fact that Archuleta signed her high school poetry C. M. and her real first name is Marta (Archuleta 2009). In a voice that parallels Sagel's Bisbee vision, C. M. narrates as she gazes into Damián's eyes:

Se abre, se abre la puerta oscura que siempre está cerrada en mis sueños, se abre y los dos pasamos por ella, mano en mano, caminando por una pradera alfombrada de margaritas que se trasnorman en las nubes que miraba de niña acostada bajo el par de cerezos, y al abrir mis ojos, los veo refejados en los de él.

Por una pequeña eternidad nos quedamas abrazados, hablándonos sin decir palabra. Jamás en la vida me había acercado tanto a otra persona, pues si no fuera por nuestra piel, ni supiera dónde yo termino y él empieza.

It opens—the dark door that is always locked in my dreams swings open and the two of us pass through it, walking hand in hand through a meadow carpeted with daisies that turn into the clouds I used to gaze at as a child lying under the pair of cherry trees, and when I open my eyes, I see them reflected in his.

I remain in his arms for an endless moment as we speak without saying a word. Never in my life have I felt so close to another human being. If it weren't for our skin, I wouldn't know where I leave off and he begins. (Sagel 1998a, 126, 127)

In the novel's final chapters, it becomes clear that C. M. and Damián's romance is a continuation of Crescencia and David's. Damián leaves C. M. just as David did decades before.

As Sagel and Archuleta's real life love affair was ending, the literary version remained open, suggesting the possibility, if attenuated, that Sagel's New Mexico romance could continue. In the same moment that we later learn both the elderly Crescencia and now geographically distant David die, C. M. imagines her reunification with Damián/ David:

—Regresastes! Yo sabía ibas a regresear.
—Obligado de venir, tanto que me llamabas.
—Te miras lo mesmo. No te has cambiado nada.
—Y tú más hermosa que nunca.
—Siéntate conmigo, que la tarde es un sueño.
—Ya no queda tiempo. He regresado sólo para llevarte conmigo.
—Tanto que te he esperado. De veras que me llevas contigo?
—Sí vamos los dos.
—Ahora?
—Ahora mi vida. Súbete en el caballo que ya nos vamos.
(Sagel 1998a, 143, 145)

"You came back! I knew you'd be back."
"I had to return. You've been calling me for so long."
"You look the same. You haven't changed at all."
"And you are more beautiful than ever."
"Come sit beside me. The afternoon is a dream."
"We don't have time. I've come to take you with me."
"I've waited so long for you. Are you really going to take me with you?"
"Yes, the two of us will go together."
"Now?"
"Now, my love. Get on the horse—it's time to go." (Sagel 1998a, 142, 144)

Our Lady of Sorrows

Like many artists of his generation, Sagel came to New Mexico to find answers to what he believed to be wrong with the world and himself, but unlike many others, Sagel lived in a predominantly Latino New Mexico for the rest of his life. His writings were characterized by a vision of a culturally whole and sensuously spiritual New Mexico haunted by the community's ever-increasing incorporation into modernity and vice versa. As the reality of community fragmentation, poverty, and negation attained irrefutable reality, however, and as idealized visions of New Mexico as a traditional culture outside modernity became increasingly tenuous, the results were tragic and painful. Within this romance, Sagel's hope is matched by its negation. He wrote:

> The road deadends at Our Lady of Sorrows Church
> where a blue-robed Virgin beckons me to surrender
> to the amnesia inside. Shifting at the last moment,
> I turn toward the hills and search for your smile in
> the rocks. (Sagel 1997d, 37)

Whatever resolution Sagel had found had come undone. Similarly, a short poem included in his unpublished collection "Corazonazos" matches the love poem that opens this essay yet is, perhaps, even bleaker:

> Tu indiferencia es ensordecedora.
> Tu silencio ha roto los tímpanos
> de mi corazón. (Sagel n.d.b, 18)
> Your indifference is deafening.
> Your silence has broken the eardrums
> of my heart.
> (My translation)

In February 1998, Sagel asked Archuleta for a divorce and said he was seeing another woman. On April 6, 1998, a Game and Fish Department officer found Sagel's body hanging from a tree. He had hanged himself with his belt.

Commenting on the hurt of this time, Archuleta created a digital piece of art titled *Divorce*. Like many of her other computer art creations, this piece combines a deft use of color and form with an image of a woman that likely represents Archuleta and evokes a profound sense of isolation and sadness. With her back to the viewer and a hand against her cheek hiding her face, the woman stares at a piece of paper that contains a heart broken in two. The isolated figure is surrounded by primarily blue colors that are also a heart pierced with swords.

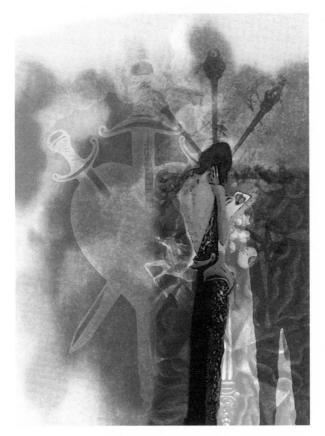

"Divorce." Digital artwork by Teresa Archuleta. *Reprinted with permission.*

For a time, Sagel's hunger and pain were confronted and sated, but such dreams proved fleeting and left others broken. Indeed, as understandings of dialectical tension and Archuleta's art would suggest, Sagel's presence would continue to be felt in his absence. While I lived in Española, I met many people who knew Sagel and greatly missed him. Moreover, I often used Sagel's former office while working part-time for the Adult Basic Education program at the University of New Mexico, Los Alamos. The custodian, an Española Valley man, told me that he sometimes felt drafts that they believed to be Sagel's presence.

After years of experiencing Sagel's continued presence and absence, in 2002 Archuleta remarried and moved to Colorado.

The next chapter explores another writer's examination of New Mexican identity. While Sagel traveled far from his birthplace to find, for a time, a sense of wholeness, social scientist and novelist G. Benito Córdova explores his own ancestry and its geography for the answers to modernity's contradictions.

CHAPTER SEVEN

The Secret of Why God Laughs

Fiction, representing the work of the imaginary, especially in its role of figuring an alternative symbolic mediation of the real, is the mode within which the critical work of folklore is enacted.

—Ramón Saldívar, *The Borderlands of Culture: Américo Paredes and the Transnational Imaginary*

"Think in reverse, vato loco. If you think something is good, and it's killing you, think the opposite. Do the *reverse*."

—G. Benito Córdova, *Big Dreams and Dark Secrets in Chimayó*

In the summer of 2004, I attended G. Benito Córdova's reading from his then-forthcoming novel *Big Dreams and Dark Secrets in Chimayó* (2006) at St. John's College in Santa Fe. I already knew Córdova's book *The 3½ Cultures of Española* (1990), and I was excited to hear him read from his current project. Córdova, then a professor at the University of New Mexico at Gallup, entered the room along with his wife and daughter. He was in a good mood and possessed the homespun aura of an organic intellectual. At the outset, the audience was clearly excited and looked forward to hearing a story with local color. In this respect, Córdova did not disappoint. His story, however, would prove to be more than the audience or I anticipated. Two years later, I would recognize the story as the *Big Dreams and Dark Secrets'* chapter "The Perfect Wall."

The chapter concerns a Chimayó man named Salvador "Flaco" Cascabel Natividad, his drunken hallucinations, and Georgia O'Keeffe's bizarre requirements for an adobe wall. Included are prodigious drinking, swearing, and examples of overblown machismo. The protagonist tells

O'Keeffe, "'The first thing you need to understand is that I'm a man and you're not. I have huevos, BALS' he misspells the word with capital letters, '*and* BIG ONES: bigger than John Wayne's weenie. Two of them'" (Córdova 2006, 119). The chapter then becomes Salvador's fantasy of challenging O'Keeffe to one of the most absurd of masculine competitions, the pissing contest, and the reality of Salvador wetting his own bed. It concludes, "Everything is soaked: his unmentionables, his blanket. Even his battered Tony Lama botas are a mess" (Córdova 2006, 121). That day I left the reading disturbed and disgusted, and the rest of the audience seemed to share my distaste. They quietly dispersed after a few polite questions and an interval of uncomfortable silence.

Upon later reading the novel, I recognized the story as a trickster tale and thus understood the author's broader, more hopeful project. The novel's prologue begins with Salvador still just a child. He asks his uncle to tell him the story of when Pedro de Urdemalas goes to hell. In Pedro, Córdova references a picaro and trickster renowned in Spanish-language literature and folklore (Lamadrid 1995) and signals to the reader that the novel is a trickster tale as well. Salvador, Pedro, and other tricksters are, according to one classic interpretation, the givers and negators, creators and destroyers, those who dupe others and are always duped themselves (Radin 1956, ix). The folktale's lesson is an important one for little Sal, as he grows up to become a trickster who, like Pedro, is a rogue hero who conveys lessons through shock, disgust, and distasteful ways. Like Pedro, the adult Salvador cheats (or wins) his way into heaven by doing the opposite of what he should. Ultimately, Salvador develops an alternative, liberating subjectivity that promises to transform Nuevomexicanos into the subjects of history.

A Trickster Cycle

Such tricksters have the double role of making use of humor and symbolic inversion to illuminate the inevitable social contradictions. They provide the engine for reinventing culture and later revitalizing it (Babcock-Abrahams 1975, 14; DeGuzmán 2001; Hyde 1998; Lamadrid 1995; Spinks 2001). Moreover, such inversion is often the subversive power of the folkloric and comedic (Babcock-Abrahams 1975). In the prologue to the English translation of Bakhtin's *Rabelais*, Michael Holquist describes this folkloric inversion of the dominant social order's ideal. For Bakhtin, the folk exist in opposition to the state's notions of "the people" and the appropriate behavior of the good citizen:

> [Bakhtin's] folk are blasphemous rather than adoring, cunning rather than intelligent; they are coarse, dirty, and rampantly physical, reveling in oceans of strong drink, pools of sausage, and endless coupling of bodies. In the prim world of Stalinist Biedermeier, that world of lace curtains, showily displayed water carafes, and militant propriety, Bakhtin's claim that the folk not only picked their noses and farted, but enjoyed doing so, seemed particularly unregenerate. The opposition is not merely between two different concepts of the common man, but between two fundamentally opposed worldviews with nothing in common except that each finds its most comprehensive metaphor in the "the folk." (Bakhtin 1984, xix)

This final chapter tells Salvador's story in the terms of its trickster narrative, demonstrates its satirical elements, and finally recounts the protagonists' remaking of the world and its implications for Nuevomexicanos. Like Bakhtin's folk, Salvador stands in opposition to good taste and idealized visions of Nuevomexicanos. In so doing, I will show, he offers a transformation of the social order and a sort of redemption.

Here, it is worthwhile to point out that Salvador's creator, Córdova, is a social scientist as well as a writer of fiction, and he is explaining through fiction the world that he really sees around him. In Foucault's terms, Córdova's work may be understood as the excavation of a subjugated knowledge of an already subjugated people (Foucault 1982). Many of the novel's characters and places are recognizable people and sites from the Española Valley and other northern New Mexican locations such as Española, Chimayó, Alcalde, Los Alamos, Abiquiú, Embudo, San Juan, and the Carson National Forest. Salvador, himself a Nuevomexicano from Chimayó, is an alcoholic, a former custodian at the Los Alamos National Laboratory, and an impenitent former

Penitente. He confronts problems immediately recognizable to many of us in the real world such as an unfulfilling job, lost love, alcoholism, and insecurity stemming from oversized machismo. Moreover, Córdova explicitly recognizes Salvador's experience as map for a more general regeneration. Speaking of his then–unfinished novel, Córdova said in an interview, "Salvador is a typical *norteño*. He wants to be in charge of his house and his woman. When things don't go his way, he drinks and gets in fights with people" (Pacheco 2004, 9). He explains to Pacheco:

> The Indians weren't happy when they had to give up their language and culture, and neither were the Hispanics when the American troops came in 1842 [*sic*]. Despite popular belief, everything is not hunky-dory. We're not all happy eating McDonald's hamburgers and doing American drugs. (Pacheco 2004, 9)

He tells Pacheco, "Our people are suffering; we're spiritually dead. We're a conquered people, and we've never come to terms with that" (Pacheco 2004, 9). Córdova tells her of his project's urgency, "We're drinking and drugging ourselves to death" (Pacheco 2004, 9). With New Mexico's contradictory reality in mind, Córdova's novel may be read on a number of different levels, each referencing the other. It is a retelling of the popular trickster genre of folktale, a comment on social (dis)order and sociocultural transformation, an expression of a transformative, if negative, Nuevomexicano condition.

Key to Salvador's subversive work is his genízaro transgression of racial boundaries that stands in stark contrast to the sterile purity of the prevandalized Oñate monument in Alcalde. In the text, readers come to find out that Salvador's grandmother was a Navajo woman who lived in Chimayó and thus was a *genízara*, or detribalized native woman.[1] Her individual experience stands in for New Mexico's long, fraught history of ethnic/racial boundary crossing. She is a genízara, and Salvador is, as her descendant, a genízaro too. In choosing such lead characters, Córdova sets his work apart from popular and academic works that would emphasize Spanish identity. Moreover, Salvador is at first ashamed of his grandmother, and *Big Dreams and Dark Secrets* may be read as Salvador's halting but ultimately successful recuperation of this ethnic/racial ancestry. It is in this context that the significance, contradiction, and promise of his full name, Salvador (Savior) Cascabel (rattle, as in rattlesnake) Natividad (Nativity), takes on its significance and meaning.

Like Paul Radin's classic telling of the Winnebago or Ho Chunk trickster cycle, the novel's story follows an overall trajectory of development that includes nineteen episodes of rejection, reversal, and transformation (Babcock-Abrahams 1975, 181; Radin 1956).[2] Córdova's story often parallels Radin's tale as both include episodes of ahistorical, abiological, and asocial acts that culminate in rejections, reversal, and finally, transformation (Babcock-Abrahams 1975, 181; Radin 1956). At the beginning of Radin's cycle, his protagonist is so unconscious of himself that his body is not a unity. His two hands fight each other. His sex is ambiguous. He does not even recognize his anus to be a part of himself (Jung 1956, 203). Through his adventures, he gains biological, psychic, and social awareness to the point where he returns to society and appears socialized and, further, assumes his role and identity as culture hero.

Big Dreams and Dark Secrets possesses a parallel trajectory of development that includes nineteen chapters that exist in a strange symmetry with Radin's cycle. Until the final pages of the text, Salvador possesses overblown machismo and great, uncontrollable anger, but he often does not know why. Córdova writes:

> Anger should have a reason for existing. But in Salvador's case, anger erupts when it chooses, 'cause it exists and has a life of its own. Salvador knows that he has a reason for being angry. Unfortunately, for the moment, he doesn't know why. (Córdova 2006, 124)

From the divorce of his wife, he emerges with an absurd masculinity:

> The product of this tragedy was that the walking ghost of Salvador resurrected as a Chimayó super macho, and a macho compounded with machismo, as everyone who has lived with one knows, is a tyranny that darkens the sun. Drinking became Salvador's life dance. Drinking became an outward sign that screamed, "I want to die and rest in peace, for eternity." (Córdova 2006, 21)

Salvador's misadventures include events such as an accidental marriage to his best friend's bride, doping the food of a gluttonous friend with Ex-Lax, the construction of an adobe wall for O'Keeffe, Salvador's death in the national forest, and an encounter with heaven's gatekeeper. At key moments in the text, he is inexplicably shadowed by a *duende,* or goblin, only he can see, and the narrative moves, sometimes seamlessly, from realistic events to alcohol-induced hallucinations and, finally, mythological truths.

His friend Tomás "No Más" Sánchez and his trusty dog Solo Vino often accompany Salvador, and the trio tool around in Sal's beat-up truck "The Brown Buzzard." Salvador's village antagonists include ex-wife Blanca Flor, don Wilberto B. C. Ferrán, and the village's Spanish-born priest, Padre Piedra. Salvador also encounters or reports encounters with supernatural figures such as Pedro de Urdemalas, Spider Woman, Saint Peter, a giant serpent that is actually a log and/or the dog Solo Vino, and a dead but supernatural tree. In the racially and class-charged situations throughout the novel, Salvador's Anglo antagonists include Dr. Carlisle Esmithenburgestein Johnson, a counselor at the alcohol treatment facility in Embudo, game warden Billy Bob Buford, the artist Georgia O'Keeffe, and his Los Alamos National Laboratory (LANL) boss, Mr. Wilhelm Hightower.

As the novel begins, Salvador appears to be a relatively well-adjusted rural New Mexican, although we quickly see that he is a heavy drinker. He is living in the village of Chimayó with his wife Blanca Flor, a woman who marries him by accident. Like many other aspects of Córdova's narrative, the reader is uncertain about the veracity of the story of Salvador's accidental marriage. According to the story, Salvador was to be the best man in his friend Tomás "No Más" Sánchez and Blanca Flor's wedding. After a night of revelry with Salvador and Tomás, the hungover, ill, and rushed priest mistook Salvador for the groom and married him to Blanca Flor. Like many of the events in the novel, however, the wedding events may be accurately depicted, a tall tale, or only the product of Salvador's skewed perception. Córdova writes, "Salvador loved retelling every exquisite detail of the wedding and when given an opportunity even bragged about the ceremony. Few believed Salvador's account. But tale or truth, it was still a great cuento" (Córdova 2006, 14). Blanca Flor will eventually leave him, taking their seven children with her, and here begins Salvador's descent into despair and alienation. Córdova writes, "Salvador's relation with the absent Blanca became a projection of his desires, his hatred, and his fears. He experienced her absence as though in a vacuum, but it was a vacuum that he filled with imagination" (Córdova 2006, 20). From this divorce, Salvador emerges a broken man and raging alcoholic who overcompensates and masks his frustrations with machismo.

The specific events of Salvador's death are set in motion midway through the novel, when Salvador is hunting in the national forest near Pedernal Mountain. After Salvador says, "'I'm, I'm so-o tired!'" and continues, "'I wish, I wish I were dead'" (Córdova 2006, 168), he is hit on the head by a falling tree. For the next five chapters, Salvador is pinned under the tree and undergoes a series of hallucinations/ adventures before he succumbs to hypothermia. The novel does not end with his death, however. Salvador's spirit, or anima, remains on earth for four more days and attends, among other things, his own funeral. Finally, Salvador reaches the gates of heaven, where he learns that the mysterious duende who followed him for much of the story is the trickster Pedro de Urdemalas, and that Pedro is transfigured as Saint Peter, the keeper of the keys to heaven.

The protagonist also inhabits a spiritual geography that provides a reservoir of traditional knowledge that will, if he heeds it, answer the most painful questions of his existence (Córdova 2006, 156–58). Chimayó's wise man, Wilberto B. C. Ferrán, tells Salvador that Chimayó's famed chapel, the Santuario de Chimayó, and its pocito, or hole containing healing dirt, and the mountain known as El Cerro de los Pedernales near Abiquiú are actually two parts of a single sacred place.[3] Ferrán explains that it is for this reason that the genízaros settled Chimayó and Abiquiú. Ferrán tells Salvador:

> "El Pocito is only half of the shrine. The holiest of all Genízaro shrines exists in two places at the same time, Salvador. They're one and the same, positive, and negative and at the same time both male and female. God, of course, is complete unto Him and Herself. God *is* both Male and Goddess." (Córdova 2006, 156)

The feminine pocito at Chimayó and the masculine peak at Abiquiú are joined by an underground river of brine that connects the two. Córdova writes:

> Don Wilberto B. C. Ferrán goes on to describe the complexity of the mesa vortex. How it connects the feminine pocito at Chimayó with the masculine peak at Abiquiú. "It's a body of water, an underground river of brine. The flow connects the two. The female pocito and the male Cerro de los Pedernales are like a car battery," the old man explains, "to be complete, the shrine must have a negative and a positive." (Córdova 2006, 157)

These assertions confirm Salvador's own maternal grandfather's teaching, knowledge he had forgotten. Córdova writes:

> [His grandfather had] described how the salty brine flowed into the ground near Chimayó and disappeared deep into the earth only to surface somewhere east of Los Alamos. The underground cavern connects the pocito to the Pedernales. His grandfather had explained how the brine waters drain into a green basin inside the Black-on-Red Mountain of El Cerro de los Pedernales. The underground vortex is a sacrarium, an inverted, upside-down basin where the spirits of unbaptized children rest. Salvador also had learned that the chamber's waters have regenerative power. Spirits that need healing or have lost their direction anoint themselves with soil from the pocito, and those afflicted with physical ills bathe in the salt water. (Córdova 2006, 157–58)

Córdova's Ferrán describes the stream as both the birthing channel and the navel of the world.

The Loco, the Sinner, the Fool

Guillermo E. Hernández's *Chicano Satire: A Study in Literary Culture* (1991) provides insights helpful for understanding *Big Dreams and Dark Secrets* and other Chicana/o uses of the trickster figure as social critique. Hernández states that in the western tradition, satire is associated with a number of stereotyped figures who are subjected to hostility, humor, or indifference (Hernández 1991, 2). These negative figures are often ultimately traced to marginal groups or individuals who are frequently subjected to censure or abuse. Thus, stigmatized members of a social group are the target of the antagonism or even the hatred of majorities who feel threatened. A more common response toward the marginal, when not perceived as an immediate threat, is censure, ridicule, or indifference. In this respect, satire fulfills the function of punishing those who, sometimes through no fault of their own, transgress the rules of appropriate social behavior. In Lamadrid's earlier telling of the Pedro de Urdemalas tale (Lamadrid 1995, 19–20), from an early age Pedro loses the shame, or *vergüenza*, that orders, pacifies, and ultimately limits the lives of the rest of humankind. To be *sin vergüenza* is of particular significance for Nuevomexicanos as it is for Latin Americans; the charge of being without shame or lacking honor or dignity suggests asociality (Valdez 1979). To be called shameless is an insult, and its significance is perhaps best illustrated by Chicana theorists' inversion of the insult in their critical engagement with an oppressive patriarchal social order. Karen Mary Dávalos illustrates this in her article "Sin Vergüenza: Chicana Feminist Theorizing," as does Edén Torres in *Chicana Without Apology: Chicana Sin Vergüenza: The New Chicana Cultural Studies* (Dávalos 2008; Torres 2003).

In his encounters with Anglo antagonists, our sinvergüenza, Salvador, is often the object of Anglo-American ethnic/racial marginalization and functions as the Chicano negative of the Anglo ideal. These differentials are particularly apt and potent with reference to the Los Alamos National Laboratory, an overwhelmingly Anglo institution, with an employment hierarchy in which almost all the scientists and administrators are Anglos, while blue-collar workers such as custodians are often Nuevomexicanos. Even if they do not work in Los Alamos themselves, most Española residents count relatives or friends among those who do. Joseph Masco writes that in the 1990s:

> Within the laboratory, a Hispanic Roundtable took on the issue
> of a glass ceiling in promotions and began a public discussion
> of institutional bias against Nuevomexicanos. Nuevomexicano
> employees argued that LANL was profoundly divided between
> scientists and management who are largely from out of state,
> on the one hand, and the support staff, which is made up
> predominantly of locals, on the other. They pointed out that of
> 2,760 LANL employees making over $60,000 a year, only 110 were
> Nuevomexicano, and attributed this disparity to a glass ceiling at
> the laboratory, and specifically to a LANL practice of hiring from
> outside the state rather than from within. (Masco 2006, 206)[4]

In 2006, LANL's longtime governing body, the Regents of the University of California, settled a class action lawsuit the Hispano Roundtable and other groups brought for racial and gender discrimination. The regents agreed to pay $12 million to current and former Hispanic and female employees at the lab.

Of the Anglos at LANL, Salvador complained, "'They're really prejudiced cabrones'" (assholes, literally billy goats) (Córdova 2006, 88) and, "'They really hate Chimayosos. Seventeen years, *seventeen years* I worked for the *cabrones* on the 'Hill,' and when I really needed them . . . and needed them bad, they fired my ass! *¡Pinche desgraciados!*'" (Córdova 2006, 39). Still, in even such power-laden and unequal interactions, Salvador is not blameless. For instance, it is in his confrontation with Hightower for his excessive use of profanity that he loses his job as a LANL custodian (Córdova 2006, 88–92). Called into Hightower's office, Salvador thinks to himself, "Oh, shit! *¡Me van a chingar!* This Gringo wants to screw my Chimayó *huevos. My miserable broom-pushing jale they call a 'career ladder,' Just 'cause I use a ladder to get supplies from the storage closets*" (Córdova 2006, 89). Relieved he is not facing accusations of on-the-job drinking, he decides that complete and vehement denial is his smartest course of action. Salvador responds to his boss's accusation of excessive profanity with the assertion, "'*Fuck, no!*'" He continues, "'Absolutely not, Mr. Hightower. I've never used no cuss words at work, Señor. Never! *Fuck—k no! No way sir!* Honest to God, Mr. Hightower!'" (Córdova 2006, 90). Not surprisingly, Hightower fires Salvador despite his denial.

The chapter titled "The Perfect Wall" that Córdova read aloud at that 2004 reading is another example of satire. It renders Salvador's machismo even more absurd. The chapter relates Salvador's drunken hallucination of an encounter between him and New Mexico's most famous artist, Georgia O'Keeffe (1887–1986). For decades after her definitive relocation to New Mexico in 1945, O'Keeffe lived in a house in the village of Abiquiú. As the ultimate butt of patriarchy's joke, Salvador fails to best O'Keeffe in one of the most basic, base aspects of masculinity, the pissing contest.[5] Upon hearing her compliments of his Chicano artistry, Salvador boasts that he is a man who possesses big balls while she has none. To show his contempt, he proceeds to unzip his fly in order to urinate on the wall. Before he can consummate the act, however, the artist forbids him to urinate on "her" wall. Córdova writes, "The brown emaciated Genízaro faces the Gringa *pintora*. The wily artist smiles at him and in a low hardboiled no-nonsense voice reproaches the waterman from Chimayó. 'No, no-o, no-o, you don't! Not on my wall,' she reprimands Flaco" (Córdova 2006, 120). Angered, Salvador challenges her to the contest, "'Vieja puta,' Salvador screams, 'When are you going to learn that you're never going to be able to piss like a real Chimayoso. Like an hombre! An hombre con huevos! BALS period'" (Córdova 2006, 120). To Salvador's surprise, the artist questions his masculine superiority, and Salvador therefore challenges her to the contest. Their argument continues:

> Her blue eyes are aglow with anticipation. After all, she's as obstinate as Flaco is and has had more practice. Salvador is shocked that a woman would have the audacity to challenge him at anything, much less at a pissing contest. Yet, here she stands before him ready and willing for action. "Yeah, for once and for all, I'm going to teach you the difference between a man and a woman," Flaco snarls at her, and Solo Vino yelps in the background. (Córdova 2006, 120)

Artist and vato loco square up for the dual. Despite Salvador's confidence, the contest ends badly for him. He "watches in impotent embarrassment as yellow fluid trickles down the front of his pants and onto his rattlesnake Durango boots" (Córdova 2006, 121). The "supermacho" is not only a failure in this test of masculinity, he is also incontinent. At this moment, Flaco awakens from his dream/fantasy to find himself wetting his bed. He realizes he has soaked his underwear, blanket, and even his prized, if battered, Tony Lama boots (Córdova 2006, 121). Still, as is already evident in the Hightower/LANL encounter, Salvador's antics are not the chief butt of the novel's joke.

Their Confessions, If You Heard Them

Like other satires, Córdova's novel also contains subversive potential. Radin states, "That those who gave the Wakdjunkaga cycle its present form intended . . . to make it a satire on man and on Winnebago society there is little question in my mind" (Radin 1956, 151). Such satiric elements include, among others, Wakdjunkaga's absurd war-bundle ritual, the trickster's marriage in transsexual disguise to the chief's son, and the trickster's misapprehension of his own tremendous penis and blanket for the chief's banner. The lampooning of the chief's banner is particularly effective. Radin states:

> The satire here is directed at one of the most important of the
> Winnebago feasts, that given by the chief of the tribe once a
> year, at which he raises his emblem of authority, a long feathered
> crook. It is his obligation at this feast to deliver long harangues
> admonishing his people to live up to the ideals of Winnebago
> society. (Radin 1956, 152)

Waking up one morning, Wakdjunkaga sees his blanket suspended high in their air on his own absurdly long and erect penis. Confusing the blanket and penis for the chief's long feather crook, thus rendering the chief's authority ridiculous, Wakdjunkaga exclaims, "'Aha, Aha! The chiefs have unfurled their banner! The people must be having a great feast!'" (Radin 1956, 152). Córdova's trickster narrative similarly renders the representatives of mainstream American culture and society, such as Salvador's Los Alamos boss, ridiculous.

The story of Salvador's firing from his custodial job at Los Alamos reveals that his boss and LANL's crimes are far greater and much worthier of social sanction than Salvador's relatively minor transgressions. Córdova states, "The National Lab perennially contaminates and poisons Mother Earth with its plutonium experiments, all in the belief that bombs and weapons of mass destruction will save and help spread democracy" (Córdova 2006, 91). Such statements are supported by recent academic texts such as Joseph Masco's *The Nuclear Borderlands* (2006) and Jake Kosek's *Understories* (2006). LANL has long been actively involved in its own experiments to trace the spread of LANL-produced toxins in the surrounding environment. LANL scientist P. Frésquez told Kosek:

> There is not a significant animal or plant that we have not tested
> in the region. I see the plants and animals as a medical researcher
> might see a petri dish—as a chance to better understand the
> nature and movement of toxic material in the environment. For
> us, the lab is everything around us. (Kosek 2006, 265)

The scientist said:

> You find the most interesting things in the strangest places. Some
> of the highest concentrations of radioactive materials were found in
> a fruiting apricot tree in the middle of town that has its roots right
> down into an old landfill. Similarly, you find that even when you
> think things seem stable and well-contained, you find surprises such
> as the forest of the Bayo Canyon. (Kosek 2006, 266)

Bayo Canyon leads from Los Alamos toward lower-elevation communities such as La Mesilla and Santa Clara, thus justifying many Española Valley residents' fears of contamination.

The narrator notes that Salvador's transgressions are small in comparison. "Toxic waste, after all, has a life span of more than twenty thousand years. Salvador, by contrast, if he's lucky, might live for fifty years" (Córdova 2006, 91). The comparative misdemeanor of Salvador's crimes is made even more emphatically clear in Córdova's statement, "In the history of the world, no one has ever been killed by eating badly roasted green chile and refried beans or suffered physical injury by listening to cuss words, including bilingual ones" (Córdova 2006, 92). Córdova satirically notes that Salvador has learned much from working at LANL. "On the positive side, Salvador worked at a very scientific laboratory and had caught on to the 'spirit of science' and elevated nontruths to a new level" (Córdova 2006, 88).

Córdova's description of artist Georgia O'Keeffe in "The Perfect Wall," and by extension the Santa Fe and Taos art communities that idolize her and her aesthetic choices, is even more devastating (Córdova 2006, 107–21). Córdova aptly demonstrates the ridiculousness of Santa Fe style and the art communities' desire to consume New Mexico's supposed premodernity. In reference to their desire for authentic native and Latino communities, Córdova states that O'Keeffe once drove all the way to the "Heart of Indian Country," Gallup, and stayed in a motel owned by a Hindu from India, to purchase a presumably Navajo and "genuine imitation plastic squash blossom necklace" from an Arab vendor (Córdova 2006, 119). Córdova tells the story of how she contracted a native of the Española Valley village of Alcalde to build a wall around her home. When the contractor built the wall in exact accordance with her specifications, she was horrified and angered by the wall's straightness and uniformity. She ordered the Alcalde man to tear it down and rebuild it. After these events were repeated, the flummoxed and angered contractor recommended the only man desperate and crazy enough to work for her, Salvador.

Although he never arrives at the jobsite, in a drunken delirium Salvador fantasizes building her a wall that she would like. In this dream, he outdoes New Mexico's most famous Anglo artist, bolstering his supermacho self-image. In a scenario that is perfectly plausible in the context of Santa Fe and Taos's faux-adobe style, Salvador imagines building the artist the wall she would want; in other words, "a wall more crooked and ugly than his mother-in-law." The wall would completely lack utility as it varies in height from six inches to taller than Salvador (Córdova 2006, 117). Upon surveying Salvador's handiwork, O'Keeffe, states:

"Sal . . . Sal, I'm here to personally congratulate you," she strums. "You're the only man in the universe to understand, truly understand . . . me. You alone understand that this wall is an aesthetic masterpiece. Art! Chicano art, which cries to blend with the contour of my quinta: it needs to complement my lesser canvas art, which is so esteemed by the world. You're a Genízaro genius. You're one of a kind. Chimayoso!" (Córdova 2006, 118)

O'Keeffe is beside herself and cannot hold back her praise. "The splendor of your wall will outlast the fame of all my creations. All of my canvas artwork!" (Córdova 2006, 119). Still, it is important to remember that Salvador is not only a catalyst of jokes; he is also a savior of sorts.

A Genízaro Walks in Two Worlds

Tricksters have the double role of making use of humor and symbolic inversion to illuminate the inevitable contradictions of societies and their institutions. In doing so, they provide the engine for reinventing culture and later revitalizing it (Babcock-Abrahams 1975, 14; Hyde 1998; Spinks 2001). When language cannot fully articulate experience, attention shifts to the margins and the possibilities of a new semiotic that produces a satisfactory (or dissatisfactory) match (Spinks 2001, 11). At such moments, trickster narratives proliferate in the form of dreams, hallucinogenic voices, neuroses, and psychoses. In the case of *Big Dreams and Dark Secrets*, Córdova posits a new/old genízaro way that is not bound by exclusionary, one-track thinking. This other way is also not prim and proper.

Córdova draws his hero as scatological, or, in Bakhtin's more empathetic terms, carnivalesque (Bakhtin 1984). In Córdova's words, "Flaco Salvador was skinny piñon size, a little larger than a small jalapeño, but he had a heart the size of a big bushel of small Chimayó red chile" (2006, 14). Here, Bakhtin's vision of the folk as opposed to state-sponsored discourses of appropriate behavior is relevant. Córdova states, "Salvador was *buena gente: Chico pero picoso*, small but snappy as his middle name, Cascabel—rattler—implied" (2006, 14). Upon his death,

Salvador is honored by his drinking friends, la plebe (common folks), for possessing the qualities of a real man.

> "Muy hombre," is La Plebe's technique of incorporating into
> one man the showmanship of former jailbird Freddy Fender, the
> sexuality of Don Juan, musical ability of Julio and Enrique Iglesias,
> and the *cojones* of Pancho Villa. Only one man in the whole world
> has all of these qualities in him and that person, as everyone knows,
> is Flaco Salvador. (Córdova 2006, 270)

Another genízaro, the older and wiser don Wilberto B. C. Ferrán, provides Salvador with a folkloric and subjugated theory of Nuevomexicano ethnic/racial identity. Córdova states, "Don Wilberto B. C. Ferrán was the acknowledged village elder." Playing on an Española joke that contends that the Española library only contains one book, Córdova writes that Ferrán gained much of his knowledge from that singular, fabulous text. "The libro brimmed with encyclopedic knowledge, and from it don Wilberto B. C. Ferrán pontificated, philosophized, and solved problems on every aspect of life" (Córdova 2006, 48). We learn that Ferrán is the son of a Navajo captive brought to Chimayó and purchased by the Ortegas, a well-known real family of weavers in Chimayó. Ferrán's father is a mystery. Many villagers suspect he is really the child of the village priest (Córdova 2006, 48). Through the story of Ferrán's mother, he asserts the reality of Nuevomexicana/o racial mixture and places it within New Mexico's genízaro historical specificities of forced incorporation and primal acts of gendered, sexual domination.

Ferrán does not seem to fret over his dual heritage. He has learned that his genízaro ancestry gives him the ability to move through multiple subjectivities. Ferrán explains, "'Mi madrecita was Navajo. She knew the Goddess and walked with Her to the freshness of the first rays of the morning'" (Córdova 2006, 150).[6] He continues, "'A Genízaro,' he chuckles, 'is a person who walks in beauty in different worlds, in different realities.'" By contrast, for Ferrán, "mestiza/o" is an ascribed identity and therefore lacks the choice integral to genízaro identity. Still, at this point midway in the novel, Salvador cannot yet fully comprehend Ferrán's genízaro reality:

Salvador thought he understood the significance of his words,
before don Wilberto B. C. Ferrán could finish his explanations,
the annoying borracho interrupted the old man "But . . . but . . .
I'm . . . I'm half Hispanic, half Indian. A mestizo!" The sage shook
his head in disgust and replied, "That's what you've *been anointed to
be, Salvador.* You can, if you choose, be a Genízaro. That's your right.
You can attempt to forget who you are, but it doesn't work that
way. You're a Genízaro! And as long as you live you shall remain a
Genízaro." (Córdova 2006, 151)

This genízara/o identity goes beyond mestizaje in another particularly
important respect.[7] Where mestizaje speaks of the creation of national
and ethnic subjects, genízaras/os remain denigrated even within those
traditions of national/ethnic identity that celebrate mestizaje (Contreras
2008, 30; Forbes 1973, 149).[8] Ferrán states, "'A mestizo surrenders his
right to choose. A mestizo throws himself at the mercy of the fry cooks
of the world. Just like you, Salvador'" (Córdova 2006, 153).

Indo-Hispano Heritage Has a Dark Side

In Miguel Gandert's *Nuevo Mexico Profundo*, Enrique Lamadrid draws
explicit connections to the negative, libratory powers of a genízaro past
(Gandert et al. 2000; Lamadrid 2000). In other words, there are nonfiction
and ritual texts that reference the same power. Up the Chama River, to
the north of Española in the village of Abiquiú, an annual celebration is
held to honor the village's genízaro heritage (Lamadrid 2000, 57). This
is especially relevant because Córdova lived here in his youth and traces
part of his own genízaro ancestry to this community (Córdova n.d.).
Each November, at the time of the feast of Santo Tomás the Apostle,
village children dressed in bright red cloth, buckskin, scarves, ribbons,
feathers, and Tewa-style face paint enact the memory of capture, ransom,
and incorporation (Gandert et al. 2000, 56–60).

  Among the songs and dances that speak to these origins is an acting
out of captivity and redemption. Lamadrid states that the dancers take
a prisoner from the crowd. The captives represent either indigenous

people being sold or a former village resident whose relatives must pay a ransom. After the ransom is paid, community members perform *El Borracho* (*The Drunkard*). In this dance, dancers circle around each other as though falling down drunk, and one waves a nearly empty whisky bottle. Lamadrid writes, "There is something strangely triumphant in these ironic antics and gestures. The people achieve communion and victory through sharing alcohol. Both women and men make ululations or 'war cries' during the dance" (Lamadrid 2000, 58).

Through another ritual dance form, Salvador's friends and kin chastise the overblown macho. Salvador is, after all, a sinvergüenza in both Anglo and Nuevomexicano terms. He has lost his way and is ritually castrated at Alcalde's matachines dance. The matachines dance as described in Córdova's chapter 3 "Matachín Magic" is ritually enacted at the Española Valley village on the day following Christmas, at Ohkay Owingeh Pueblo on Christmas Day, and on other days in many other Native American pueblos and Nuevomexicano villages (Romero 1993, 2006, 2007; Rodríguez 1996). At the Alcalde event, figures dressed in distorted buckskin masks enact, among other things, the ritual castration of a dancer known as the Torito, or little bull. In this act of mock castration, the ritual performers enforce the social mores of their community. There is a critical difference between their actions and Salvador's firing by Hightower, however. In the course of Salvador's conversation with Ferrán, he recognizes the matachines' origins in other, older social orders. Salvador wonders whether the dancers were Old Testament gods or Native American kachinas invading the world of Roman Catholicism and concludes that they exist in a different reality (Córdova 2006, 50). In other words, Salvador receives his comeuppance at the hands of the other/older ways of being that he has too often forgotten.[9]

While watching the dancers, Salvador's cousin Agustín tells him to be careful because "*they* [the performers] were ordered to even the score" (2006, 61). Suffering from a blackout, Salvador does not remember his offense. In the following chapter, Salvador's friend Tomás reminds him that in a drunken stupor he interrupted Christmas mass at Chimayó's Holy Family Catholic Church. In what can only be described as a Bakhtinian moment, he washed his face and combed his hair with holy water and then spat in the font (Córdova 2006, 67–70). Just as

Matachines Dancers and La Malinche. A ritual performance in Alcalde.
Photo by Miguel Gandert.

Abuelo. A ritual performer in Alcalde. *Photo by Miguel Gandert.*

The Abuelo y Toro. The torito and abuelo battle in an Alcalde
ritual performance. *Photo by Miguel Gandert.*

Abuelos y Toros. Two abuelos perform the ritual mock castration
of two toritos. *Photo by Miguel Gandert.*

Victory Abuelo. As the crowd looks on, an abuelo holds up a
walnut representing the castrated torito's testicles for all to see.
Photo by Miguel Gandert.

Padre Piedra was about to consecrate the Eucharist, Salvador grabbed
the sacramental bread and wine and gorged on each in succession. He
followed these acts with a tremendous fart and burp. Rendering his actions
even more ridiculous, he told the massgoers the "wine was 'exquisite' . . .
'charming' . . . 'an exceptional month!'" (Córdova 2006, 69).

At Alcalde, just as the *abuelos* disciplined wayward, unruly children,
Salvador must pay for his transgression by being symbolically castrated.[10]
The abuelos and matachin dancers descend upon him, and he becomes
the Torito, the victim of their mock castration. Córdova narrates:

> The twelve angry masked men, the two demented tricksters, the
> castrated and bleeding little bull, the hordes—the mob—look down
> and jeer him, Flaco Salvador. His legs are angrily jerked by the
> Abuelos, and finally he is rolled on his back. He yelps like a puppy
> that's been kicked by a cruel, unforgiving master. (Córdova 2006, 64)

In this way, the ritual dancers render the self-identified supermacho a
eunuch.

In an earlier conversation, with don Wilberto B. C. Ferrán at the Rock Bottom Bar, Salvador asks the elder about the matachines. "'*Esplain* to me . . . those *pinche* masked ones. What are they?'" (Córdova 2006, 55). Ferrán replies, "'Los Matachines are the laughter of God'" and that "'The Matachines were created at the dawn of time to make men laugh: to make the insolent and arrogant less stubborn. More humble!'" (Córdova 2006, 55). The wardens of the dances, the abuelos, we learn are "roguish pranksters" that pace like "hungry coyotes" among the matachin dancers to ensure that their costumes are in order and make certain all is as it should be in their "insanity dance" (Córdova 2006, 60). They also jeer and hurl sexual innuendos at the crowd and carry long buckskin chicotes, or whips, to enforce their brand of (dis)order. Córdova further states that they "resemble coyote tricksters from an age when the world was balanced differently" (2006, 60).

A Genízaro Is More than a Chameleon

Guillermo E. Hernández's *Chicano Satire* is helpful for understanding another element of *Big Dreams and Dark Secrets in Chimayó*. His study of Chicano literature offers the precedent of the *pocho* and the pachuco—the precursor to Española's Marco Cholo (Hernández 1991, 17–30). The pachuco has been seen to embody comic distortions of Mexican and Anglo-American cultural forms. In the 1970s and 1980s, however, the pocho and the pachuco were no longer treated comically as the *other*; they are now adopted, satirically, as the voice of the *subject* (Hernández 1991, 113). One variant that has become an icon in Chicana/o culture and Chicana/o studies is the character Pachuco, played by Edward James Olmos in Luis Valdez's play and film *Zoot Suit*. Another, more recent, manifestation may be found in Down AKA Kilo's popular song "Lean Like a Cholo" (Down AKA Kilo 2007; Valdez 1992).

New Mexico's regional tradition is richly populated with such folkloric figures (Lamadrid 1995). Examples include indigenous tricksters such as the Navajo coyote, to the picaros who arrived with the Spanish, and the mestizo traditions that developed in their wake. Other examples include the Pueblo clowns (rumored to have cut off Oñate's foot), Mano

Fashico, don Cacahuate and doña Cebolla, Pelón, and the abuelos of the matachines dance.[11] In her article "Turning Tricks: Trafficking in the Figure of the Latino," María DeGuzmán finds the trickster is a common figure in both Chicana/o and mainstream American literature (DeGuzmán 2001).[12]

Perhaps the most effective use of the trickster in recent Chicano literature resides in Sandra Cisneros's short story "Never Marry a Mexican" (Cisneros 1991). The story's protagonist, a Chicana, is having an affair with a married man. Her lover and his spouse are Anglo. Clemencia describes her lover as looking like Mexico's primal Spanish conqueror and colonizer, "Cortez," and his wife in terms of the archetypal Anglo-American woman, a "redheaded Barbie doll in a fur coat" (Cisneros 1991, 78, 79). In a provocative moment of transgression and violation, Clemencia hides Gummy Bears among her rival's most intimate possessions: in her rival's Lucite makeup organizer, nail polish, lipsticks, and in an extraordinary act of violation, in her "diaphragm case in the very center of that luminescent rubber moon" (Cisneros 1991, 81). In this way, Cisneros's Clemencia violates the most intimate boundaries and becomes the Malinche in her most subversive and fraught incarnation, exposing the contradictions and hypocrisy of late twentieth-century (Mexican) American society. In a similar way, Córdova offers the genízaro Salvador as the voice of an emergent and transformative, if negative, Nuevomexicano condition.

This genízaro power is founded in the indigenous experience that remains unarticulated in so-called "Anglo," "Spanish," or, even, "mestizo" ways of being. One day at the Cantina de los Rock Bottoms this earlier, indigenous social order becomes real for Salvador. He comes to discern it in the elder Ferrán. Córdova writes:

> Salvador studies the sage [Ferrán] and wants to glare at him and
> show the old man that his remarks don't faze him. But the elder
> has the greater power, and in keeping with tradition, Flaco lowers
> his gaze and looks away. A moment later Salvador looks at the elder
> and for the first time in his life really sees him. The sage's eyes are
> spherical black obsidian stones. His nose and mouth is an eagle's
> beak, and instead of a tongue, a jet blade protrudes from his face

resembling the warrior god of the dead. "A Genízaro," the bird-god pronounces, "is more than a chameleon. A Genízaro chooses what's best *and then* acts on that choice." (Córdova 2006, 152–53)

Despite this vision, Salvador does not yield to the choice of living as a genízaro. This story's dual resolutions must wait until Salvador's death and his journeys in his afterlife.

You're a Healer, Heal Quickly

In a manner that is indicative of his genízaro experience, Córdova's trickster tale follows two tracks. Salvador both wins his way into heaven in a retelling/inversion of the Christian narrative and must discover his own indigenous genízaro center. Córdova asserts that it is important to learn about genízaros like Salvador because most of the so-called Hispanos in New Mexico are of genízaro descent. He warns the reader that "you" may be a genízaro and unaware of it (Córdova n.d., 17).

In the final chapter, Salvador wanders in the afterlife for seven days in an interstitial purgatory. On the seventh day, he meets the duende who has shadowed him throughout his life. The duende tells Salvador that he is Pedro de Urdemalas himself. In the course of the conversation, Salvador comes to the realization that the duende/Urdemalas is at the same time Saint Peter, and all, the duende/Urdemalas/Saint Peter, transfigure into Chimayó priest Padre Piedra. In his Pedro apparition, this multifaceted figure guides Salvador by telling him that he, like Salvador, lived life in reverse and informs him of the "Law of Reverse Effects." Pedro then lists how Salvador's desires have almost always led him to acts that had the opposite of his desired effect. He tells Salvador:

> When you can't swim, you don't insist on walking in seawater or skin diving. You wait until the water freezes, then you walk over the ice. Yeah, Salvador, you love to swim upstream. And different in your case means the opposite. *That's* the solution. That's the answer. You would have been so much happier. (Córdova 2006, 303)

Pedro tells Salvador, "Think in reverse, vato loco. If you think something is good, and it's killing you, think the opposite. Do the *reverse*" (Córdova 2006, 304). Following Pedro's directive, Salvador takes a step backward. By his third step, he hits his stride, turns, and flips a backward somersault. He has learned that life, death, and resurrection are the same. In his death and his understanding of the Law of Reverse Effects, Salvador has come to a transcendent understanding of the universe. Córdova writes, "Yes, in his final adiós, Salvador discovered the hearth of his spiritual center—his inner still-point—solitude and peace—a place of harmony and bliss, where he dreams eternity very much awake" (Córdova 2006, 307).

Salvador's death, ninety pages earlier, contains another resolution of equal significance. We learn that on her deathbed, Salvador's mother, María Guadalupe, explained his name (Córdova 2006, 214). The word *salvador*, she told her then-seven-year-old son, means more than its English equivalent. "The name is Spanish, *sanador*: healer. A sanador mends. He makes whole . . ." (Córdova 2006, 214). Córdova adds that a sanador is more than a *curandero* because he liberates, aids the needy, and encourages the spiritually lame to walk in interior freedom (Córdova, 2006, 214). María Guadalupe wished the same for her son. "'Hijo mío,'" she said with telling ambiguity, "'You're a healer. Heal quickly'" (Córdova 2006, 214). Maria's son is a savior who must mend both others and himself. Ferrán offers a different but related view. Contesting María Guadalupe's Roman Catholic notion of savior and sin, Ferrán tells Salvador that his name was of Greek origins rather than Spanish. He said, "It comes from *soter*, one who sows seeds in the Earth's womb." He tells Salvador that, "At Chimayó we don't need to be redeemed from sin." Rather, Salvador is to teach the sick to exercise choice (Córdova 2006, 14). Similarly, in Salvador's own last hours on El Cerro de los Pedernales, he encounters another woman who pushes him toward assuming agency. As Salvador lies underneath the ocote where he will die, the tree becomes Spider Woman, the indigenous goddess who taught Navajos how to weave. She tells him "'Hijo, hijo mío, you have misunderstood. If you tangle your yarn, your web will become a trap'" (Córdova 2006, 218–19). Determined to reach Salvador, she continues, "Hijo, hijo mío, you are not dependent on the weaver.

You are the weaver'" (Córdova 2006, 218–19). María's son and Ferrán's wayward pupil and others like him are exhorted to become the *subject in* as well as *subject to* history.

The novel's conclusion provides Salvador with resolution, but as Córdova noted in his interview with Pacheco, it is a resolution that he only achieves in the afterlife (Pacheco 2004, 9). For those of us concerned with life on earth, Salvador's terrestrial struggles, transgressions, and their critical implications are of greater significance and carry a more critical edge. It is in these terrestrial struggles that Salvador teaches us to reconsider and recreate our world, and these are the dreams and secrets to which the book's title refers. Salvador is a genízaro savior who already carries the world and its subversion within him. He upsets a world that is unequal and demonstrates its absurdity. He moves Nuevomexicanos to become healers, weavers, and the subjects of their own contradictory history.

Conclusion

For how can rational discourses speak of the very processes they deny themselves access to, without contradiction or madness?

—Diana Coole, *Negativity and Politics: Dionysus and Dialectics from Kant to Poststructuralism*

The future will be an era of contradictions, just as parts of a wheel move backward so the front moves forward.

—G. Benito Córdova, *The 3½ Cultures of Española*

In writing this text, my goal is to challenge ethnography. Española and places like it—a place that plainly retains its alterity in the face of Santa Fe, the so-called City Different—are the test and measure of ethnography. Because, after all, the complex and internally differentiated subject positions epitomized in the negative by the stereotypical cholo who supposedly discovered Española have long been and are ever more increasingly part of The Land of Enchantment. Moreover, the implications of such a condition are wide. If the Española Valley is the supposed geographic locus that marks the eruption of the haunting inverse of the positive, there is a little bit of Española in every northern New Mexican community, and perhaps any community anywhere. Such a modernity is particularly Nuevomexicano, more broadly Latino, and especially North American as well. Our era is, after all, an era of contradictions.

Constant Subversion

According to influential cultural critic Slovoj Žižek, another way of thinking of negativity is as something undignified or inherently comic. Žižek would call it a little bit of the real (Žižek 2001, 43). Moreover, this suggests the subversive potential of Española jokes when told by G. Benito Córdova. This subversion is prompted by the even more disturbing joke in the social structure. Žižek writes, "Such an identification with the leftover, of course, introduces the mocking-comic mode of existence, the parodic process of the constant subversion of all firm symbolic identifications" (Žižek 2001, 43).

For a brief time in the 1980s, even the Española Valley Chamber of Commerce seemed to agree and took a joking attitude. The chamber produced an ad campaign that sought to turn the valley's reputation to their commercial advantage (Peterson 1984; Ward 2002). An ad from *New Mexico* magazine features a tourist trumpeting Española's lowriders and references the common practice of modifying these cars with hydraulics so they can bounce and thus "dance." Dressed in denim and a cowboy hat, the fictional (and definitely Anglo) tourist states, "'I've seen the Taj Mahal, a pacific sunset, and the northern lights, but not 'til I visited the Española Valley had I seen a '55 Chevy do a mating dance.' L-B (Formerly of New York.)" (Española Chamber of Commerce 1982). According to the *New York Times* article, the chamber of commerce intended to follow the first ad with a second that would depict a conquistador eyeing a lowrider and its driver and saying, "The natives seem friendly enough but they do ride strange mounts" (Peterson 1984). The Española Valley continues to be a place of such wondrous vehicles. On April 11, 2005, a group of men from Chimayó broke the world record for truck hopping at a car show in California. Jennifer L. Greff of the *Rio Grande Sun* writes:

> When it hops 82 inches in the air—almost seven feet from the ground to the front tire—the yellow Ford Ranger is practically perpendicular to the pavement. The truck, created by Ray's Auto shop in Chimayó, impressed onlookers from all over the world. (Greff 2005)

Chamber of Commerce bumper stickers from the 1980s period stated, "Española, when you're through kidding around," "Española, a great place, all joking aside," and, "Española, a great story. Have you heard it?"

I Am On My Way

Hegel comments that the musician who will revel in mad medleys will find a powerful note that restores spirit to itself, and, I suspect, he would agree that cars that move vertically as well as horizontally evoke the same feelings (Hegel 1977, 317–18). In this text and the accompanying journey, I too am searching for such notes. Indeed, this book may be read as a search for such notes of reconciliation and redemption. It is a mistake, however, to believe the specific acts along the way, such as Policarpio Valencia's embroidery, Sagel and Archuleta's visions, Oñate's passion, or drug use, provide the lessons to be learned. Similarly, this lesson does not lie in positive forms such as "culture" or the specifics of that something beyond culture that is expressed negatively—that something that Benjamin calls being thrown into ample handfuls to existence. As Diana Coole has pointed out, it must be approached circumspectly, through allusion, metaphor, and invocation (Coole 2000, 2). This is a lesson in form rather than content. On such journeys, we enter into history and find the significance in the transformation itself. The lesson lies in positivity and negativity's juxtaposition and dialectical tension. As Jean-Luc Nancy has stated, "It is thus not a point; it is the passage, the negativity in which the cutting edge of sense gets experienced as never before" (Nancy 2002, 6–7).

Such stories of embodied negativity and wildness are not limited to the Española Valley. For instance, Kathleen Stewart has described negativity as a central component of the redemptive violence that she calls a surge in the America dream and warns us that American dreams can be nightmares (Stewart 2000, 2007). Along these lines, in the wake of seeing Oñate's passion, I began to listen with more empathy to other insurgent tellings of Christ's suffering. Perhaps influenced by their Roman Catholic milieu and the upsurge of evangelical churches such

Reflecting Images. A painting on a car at the 2001 car show at the Ohkay Casino. An onlooker and another car may be seen reflected in the painting. *Photo by author.*

as the Española Christian Center, Victory Faith, and Rock Christian Outreach, I have heard drug users and sellers describe their own Bible meetings and claim Christ's suffering as their own.

Michael Trujillo, the addict and poet, finds redemption in his own, at least partially self-inflicted, suffering. He wrote the prayer on a yellow sheet of steno-pad paper and gave it to me more than a year before I saw the hypodermic-needle-bearing Oñate. Trujillo saw something other in the deaths of his friends and his own pain and claims a place for himself and other illicit drug users in Christ's suffering. He signed the prayer Micho Sicko. Such events offer an immanent critique, and in this manner, the dialectic remains open. In such prayers, we are witnesses to the world's entry into a history in which the point is transformation itself. He wrote:

Brother Christ. Forgive me.
Lord, grant me all the grace
to rejoice with you and
my brothers and sisters and loved
ones that have left this world
for death in this world is
only the beginning of eternal joy
and happiness made possible
by the death and resurrection
of your son in Jesus Christ
I claim the blood of the lamb
I am on my way.[1]

One suspects that Trujillo, a man who has spent much of his life incarcerated, would include both Carlos Herrera and his victims in this prayer. Perhaps this prayer would also include don Juan de Oñate, Policarpio Valencia, Darryl Francis Galván (also known as El Americano), Jim Sagel and Teresa Archuleta, the Friends of Acoma and the director of the Oñate Center, Charles Briggs, Paul Kutsche, and the Española ethnographers. Salvador Cascabel Natividad would be our savior.

Finally, despite Micho Sicko's references to leaving this world, like Salvador's his is an earthly dialectic not of his making, and for this reason, we should have compassion. Like Salvador's, his failures and his overcomings are our own. It is Salvador's hope of redemption that makes Córdova's book and his Salvador a fitting subject for the last chapter of this work and an exit point for this conclusion. Genízara/o subjectivity comes to understand a world of open contradictions and in so doing finds a sort of center even if it is in its absence. It is in the unresolved wounds of negativity and its implicit critique that this trickster tale gains its power.

Notes

Introduction

1. Oñate and his group of colonists first settled in the Native American Pueblo community of San Juan/Ohkay Owingeh and later at the neighboring village of San Gabriel. Today, a small, neglected monument within the bounds of San Juan Pueblo in the form of a cross on a concrete pedestal marks the spot of New Mexico's first capital.

2. James Diego Vigil defines cholo in the glossary to his book *Barrio Gangs: Street Life and Identity in Southern California* (Vigil 1988, 177). According to him, cholo is "a Chicano street style of youth who are marginal to both Mexican and Anglo culture; also used historically for cultural marginals and racial hybrids in Mexico and some parts of Latin America." Antecedents of cholo style include the Mexican-American pachuco style of the 1940s and 1950s that Octavio Paz denigrated (1985, 14–18). This attitude is often turned on its head in Chicana/o popular culture (Hernández 1991). See, for example, Luis Valdez's play and film *Zoot Suit* (Valdez 1992) and California-based rapper Down AKA Kilo's recent song "Lean Like a Cholo" from the album *Definition of an Ese* (Down AKA Kilo 2007). In AKA Kilo's album cholo is a term of admiration and self-identification.

3. A second and obvious reason that Española is the butt of jokes is the "-isms" (such as racism, classism, and sexism) that pervade U.S. society. Española is a largely Latino and working-class place and is therefore an easy target for jokes premised in racist and classist discourses.

4. The Rio Arriba region of New Mexico and southern Colorado roughly includes Taos, Rio Arriba, Santa Fe, and San Miguel counties in northern New Mexico and Conejos and Costilla counties in southern Colorado.

5. In the body of Lynn Rubright's lengthy thesis, she elaborates the evidence for all three, Native American, "Spanish," and non-Hispanic white, or "Anglo," cultural systems in the valley's landscape.

6. In 2005, San Juan Pueblo changed its official name from the Spanish term San Juan Pueblo to the Tewa term of Ohkay Owingeh. I will use the Tewa term throughout most of this text.

7. Interestingly, one group of non-Hispanic immigrants has increased since the
    1970s. The largely Anglo American Sikh community centered in the Española
    Valley community of Sombrillo has increased in size. Members believe in a
    syncretic mix of Sikhism and yogic traditions that also incorporate elements of
    New Age and counterculture thought (Elsberg 2003, xv). Nearly all the members
    of the area's Sikh community are followers of recently deceased Yogi Bhajan
    and are members of his organizations, the Happy Healthy Holy Organization
    (3HO) and Sikh Dharma. Anthropologist Constance Waeber Elsberg described
    3HO and Sikh Dharma on a national scale in her ethnography titled *Graceful
    Women: Gender and Identity in an American Sikh Community* (Elsberg 2003). 3HO
    is a teaching and outreach organization that sponsors courses in subjects such
    as kundalini yoga, meditation, nutrition, and spiritual healing (Elsberg 2003,
    xv). Sikh Dharma is the administrative and religious arm of the organization,
    consisting of an international network of ashrams whose affairs were, at the time
    Elsberg wrote, hierarchically organized under Yogi Bhajan's leadership (Elsberg
    2003, xv).

8. According to New Mexico Department of Education figures for 2003–4, the
    Española Valley School District had 4,946 students. In 2004–5, 90.2 percent of
    district students were Hispanic, 6.4 percent were Native American, 2.6 percent
    were Anglo, 0.5 percent were Black, and 0.2 percent were Asian (New Mexico
    Department of Education 2005).

9. The Atchison, Topeka and Santa Fe Railway arrived in nearby Santa Fe in 1880,
    a year before the arrival of the Denver and Rio Grande Railway in Española.
    A rail link between Santa Fe and Española was completed in 1887 (Gjevre
    1969).

10. In the specific terms of Rio Arriba County government, the northern village
    of Tierra Amarilla remains the county's nominal seat. In practice, most of
    county business is carried out in the county office annex in Española.

11. Chimayó is the center of a regional weaving tradition and the site of the
    Roman Catholic shrine called the Santuario de Chimayó. Numerous tourists
    stop in Chimayó to visit weaving studios, of which Ortega's Weaving Shop is
    the most well known. Helen Lucero's and Suzanne Baizerrman's dissertations
    as well as a book they co-wrote describe this weaving tradition in great depth
    (Baizerman 1987; Lucero 1986; Lucero and Baizerman 1999). The Santuario
    de Chimayó is a well-known pilgrimage site for Roman Catholics in New
    Mexico and beyond. Located within the church is a small hole that is said
    to contain healing dirt, as well as numerous photographs, crutches, and other
    objects left by people who hope to be cured or who have been cured.

12. The traditional economy may be of greater importance than these figures
    indicate. For example, as Jake Kosek's work demonstrates, in a place with both
    a high poverty rate and a harsh climate, the collection of firewood provides an

affordable source of both cooking fuel and heat in the winter (Kosek 2006).

13. According to a report by the United States Census Bureau, 22.4 percent of people in New Mexico lived in poverty during 1996, 1997, and 1999. While this average was slightly lower than the District of Columbia's 22.7 percent, these two averages are not statistically different, and both were significantly higher than the next poorest state, Louisiana, with an average rate of 18.6 percent (Dalaker 1999).

14. Some New Mexicans remember with fondness a Los Angeles neighborhood called Little New Mexico, and the famed bulldozed barrio Chávez ravine was named for a New Mexican. Perhaps because of the seeming ubiquity of lowriders and Chicano "urban" style, Española is sometimes called "little L.A."

15. Paige Penland, the author of the Lonely Planet guide to Santa Fe and Taos, is also a noted expert on lowriders (Penland 2004). She is a former writer and editor for *Lowrider* magazine and has written a popular social history of lowriding titled *Lowrider* (Penland 2003).

16. Sylvia Rodríguez made the comments cited in this book at a session titled Postmodern Mexicano at the 2002 American Anthropological Association Meeting. The comments were made in reference to my paper, "A Northern New Mexican 'Fix': Shooting Up and Coming Down in the Greater Española Valley" (Trujillo 2002). This paper formed the basis for this book's chapter 4.

17. Sylvia Rodríguez's comments also provocatively described the middle-class values as a strategic claim to whiteness and the lower-class foils as implicitly nonwhite embodiments. I find this contention particularly interesting and believe this analysis deserves a full-scale development in its own right.

18. Diana Coole also chronicles another genealogy of negativity that is descended from the work of Friedrich Nietzsche. Because Nietzsche himself rarely uses the word negativity and his concept seems significantly different, I forego this conceptualization of negativity. I instead follow the genealogy of negativity that passes more directly from Hegel, through western Marxism, to more contemporary cultural critics such as Žižek.

19. Following Colombia's racial structure, Taussig describes people of mixed European and indigenous ancestry as "white."

20. In this vein, George Marcus writes:

> Such ethnography is a comment on, a remaking of, a more standard, realist account. Therefore, the best subjects for modernist ethnography are those that have been heavily represented, narrated, and made mythic by the conventions of previous discourse. (Marcus 1998, 197)

21. Modernist ethnography's skeptical form also possesses dangers for those attempting to pose a transformative politics. José Limón argues that such a style must

be conscious of its own stance in the world if it is not to blur into a postmodern pastiche and thus simply reproduce the socially fragmenting effects of late capitalism (Limón 1994, 11). Mustering the power of negativity but heeding Limón's warning with care, this monograph will juxtapose divergent but integrated essays, each focused on a strategically chosen topic.

Chapter One

1. My account of the statue's dismemberment draws heavily on two messages mysteriously sent to the *Albuquerque Journal* and one to the *Santa Fe Reporter* (Calloway 1998; Larry Calloway, personal communication with author, 1999; *Santa Fe Reporter* 1998). Journalist Larry Calloway of the *Albuquerque Journal's* Santa Fe Bureau sent me photocopies of the two notes sent to the *Journal*. The note to the *Reporter* was a response to an August 26, 1998, editorial "Where's the Foot?" that requested an interview with those who severed the statue's foot. While the *Albuquerque Journal* received a photo of the severed foot with the first note, no such proof was sent to the *Reporter*. This note is similar in style and tone, however, and I strongly suspect it was written by the same person or people who wrote the first note.

2. Disputing Estevan Arellano's statement that the statue was intact the day before he received a call from the *Albuquerque Journal*, the "Friends of Acoma" wrote that they had cut the foot off days before anybody noticed.

3. Acoma's presence evokes the absence of so many other pueblos. Between 1598 and 1680, Pueblo settlements declined from 81 to 31. Similarly, between 1598 and 1660 the Pueblo people declined from sixty thousand to around seventeen thousand (Barrett 2002, 64).

4. Although not as contested as the terms for northern New Mexican Hispanics, terms for the group the U.S. census describes as "Non-Hispanic Whites" are also problematic. In local usage, this group is also often called Anglo. Many members of this group, particularly those who do not identify with descent from England, object to the term Anglo. For example, when asked of his ethnic identity, a man of Italian descent informed me that he was Sicilian and most definitely not Anglo.

5. In the following example, witness Enrique Lamadrid's movement between multiple terms in an effort to apparently describe the same population. He chose the term Indo-Hispano for the title of his text, *Hermanitos Comanchitos: Indo-Hispano Rituals of Captivity and Redemption*, but in the first sentence of the same text Lamadrid deploys two other terms:

> Village and urban festivals are part of living and coming of age in New Mexico, from the multitudinous State Fair and Santa Fe Fiestas, to the small-town rodeos and cook-offs, sports events, and

the *Funciones*, or patron saint's day feasts, in *Hispano* or *Mexicano*
barrios, towns, and Indian pueblos. (Lamadrid 2003)

In a footnote to this section, Lamadrid defines Hispano, Nuevomexicano,
Chicano, and the term Españoles Mexicanos (Spanish-Mexicans). Interestingly,
he notes that the term Españoles Mexicanos is used extensively in colonial
documents and could help resolve the "contemporary dilemma and controversy" surrounding Spanish versus Mexican origins (Lamadrid 2003, 240).

6. Ramón Gutiérrez's *When Jesus Came the Corn Mothers Went Away* (1991) is a
controversial book that received acclaim from historians and criticism from
Native American intellectuals and community leaders. Part of the criticism of
this work stems from Gutiérrez's depiction of the primal union of conquistador
and native women as an act of mutual desire. In this view, native women are
represented as willing participants in acts of colonial sexual domination. The
controversy continues to follow Gutiérrez. In a 2006 visit to the University
of New Mexico, native students accused Gutiérrez of representing Pueblo
women as "lustful" (Sánchez 2006).

7. The note writers' analysis requires a further shaking of the family tree. Such
an effort would reveal that Pueblos are also hybrid subjects who share mixed
roots with the Nuevomexicano communities that surround them. The cultural
borrowings of Pueblos from European sources has been well documented by
anthropologists and historians, including in the work of Santa Clara native
Edward Dozier (Dozier 1970, 65–71; Spicer 1962).

8. Timothy "Nasdijj" Barrus authored three well-received books under his false
identity (2000, 2003, 2005), including the Mountains & Plains Booksellers
Association's nonfiction 2001 Regional Book Award winner *The Blood Runs
Like a River Through My Dreams* (Lee 2001; Nasdijj 2000). In these books and
in their promotion, he claimed to be the child of a Navajo mother and Anglo-
American father but refused to reveal his full legal name. In 2006, Nasdijj was
unmasked as Timothy Barrus, a white man of no native ancestry and struggling
author of gay erotica (Fliescher 2006).

9. For a detailed description of the conflict between Nuevomexicano land
activists and environmentalists, see Jake Kosek's *Understories: The Political Life of
Forests in Northern New Mexico* (2006) and Laura Pulido's *Environmentalism and
Economic Justice: Two Chicano Struggles in the Southwest* (1996).

10. In her book *The Matachines Dance*, Sylvia Rodríguez shows the ways that
Pueblo clowns enact a "hidden transcript." This text illustrates how Pueblos
have defended their communities and negotiated with Spanish and Anglo-
American dominance (Rodríguez 1996).

11. The legend surrounding Starvation Peak also speaks to another period of
domination. According to a second version of the legend, the native peoples
surrounded a group of Americans crossing the Santa Fe Trail. Similar to the

Spaniards in the other version of the legend, these Americans starved to death on the peak.

12. The controversy surrounding the recent installation of a larger statue in El Paso, Texas, has garnered national attention and a nationally televised documentary (Pérez and Ortega 2008; *The Last Conquistador* 2008).

13. If Nuevomexicanos and Native Americans were to choose a positive icon, in the Hegelian sense, there is not a want of options. There is of course, Mexican Gov. José Gonzales. This man was briefly installed as New Mexico's governor in an 1837 insurrection by both Mexicans and Pueblos against the perceived threat ·of increased taxation and excesses of the previous governor, Albino Pérez (Lecompte 1985). Gonzales would be a particularly apt choice as he has been variously described as a *vecino* from the village of Taos and therefore likely a Mexican mestizo; a native from Taos Pueblo; and as a genízaro, or detribalized Indian from Ranchos de Taos. The rebellion that installed him as governor was centered in Santa Cruz and Chimayó (Lecompte 1985, 4, 19–21, 36). A second choice for such an icon could be either Pablo Montoya of Taos or Manuel Cortés of Mora. These men were central figures in the 1847 Rio Arriba revolt against the occupying American army and the government it installed. Their revolt united New Mexicans, Pueblos, and nomadic Indians against the American government. In this fight, New Mexicans and Pueblo Indians lost battles to U.S. Army regulars in the areas of Santa Cruz and Embudo. In the final battle of this conflict, 150 Pueblos and New Mexicans were massacred in Taos Pueblo's church. Estevan Arellano is known to take people to the site of the Embudo battle to see crosses that memorialize the dead.

Chapter Two

1. The area around the Guatemalan church that contains the original Nuestro Señor de Esquípulas is also known for the healing properties of a nearby hot springs. Pilgrims come to the area and consume dirt from the surrounding area that is similarly said to have healing powers.

2. Each year, many parents in the school districts that border the Los Alamos School District, such as the Española Valley and Pojoaque school districts, apply to send students to Los Alamos. The Los Alamos School District is far wealthier than the surrounding districts and has a much better reputation.

3. Lt. Leo Montoya and Herrera's mother, Joann Montoya, were later divorced.

4. At this time, Herrera was said to have weighed about 130 pounds, and this amount of cocaine seems excessive. Nevertheless, he likely consumed a very large amount of cocaine and alcohol that night.

5. Relying on information leaked to him concerning Herrera's confession, the *Rio Grande Sun's* crime reporter, Karl Moffat, reported the supposed drug debt.

Of all the reporters covering the murders, only Moffat explored the alternative explanation that questioned the victim's reported virtues. The victim's family reacted in anger at Herrera's claim and Moffat's coverage, and no other reporter delved into Herrera's claim, only reporting that no drugs were found in the murdered teen's system. Herrera's attorneys also failed to explore this explanation in court hearings. Nevertheless, in subsequent communications, Moffat, who went on to become an employee of an area drug-treatment program, expressed skepticism of Martínez's innocence (Karl Moffat, personal communication with author, 2002).

6. Many Native Americans are offended by festival's connection to the founding of the Spanish colony of New Mexico, and I suspect most stay away from this celebration. Still, I cannot say that no Native Americans were present at the 2004 parade as some Pueblos and Nuevomexicanos are difficult to distinguish by looks alone. In an offhand remark, a Navajo man I met in Española told me that, there, everything was mixed up and that many of the "Indians" appear "Spanish" and the "Spanish" appear "Indian."

7. As stated in chapter 1, in 2001 an area group of youth that called themselves La Verdad took away Oñate's armor and renamed the fiesta queen La Mestiza. In 2004, the festival's administration had been returned to civic leaders, and Oñate had been returned to his full grandeur: he wore his sword and armor, and his consort was again a queen.

Chapter Three

1. Montoya's statement obviously contains both Spanish and English slang. I did not translate the Spanish terms or define the English slang in the chapter's text because I did not want to disrupt the phrase's rhythm and word play. The statement means, "It's like the girls say, I need crack for my back, tokes (inhalations of marijuana) to joke . . . and chiva (heroin) in my vida (life)."

2. The names of illicit drug users in this chapter, such as Dolores Montoya and Joey Jaramillo, are pseudonyms.

3. The University of New Mexico study, "Tailoring Treatment Services to Drug Users' Needs," was conceived by Cathleen E. Willging, then a member of UNM's Department of Family and Community Medicine, who also served as the study's principal investigator. I worked as an ethnographic researcher on this project along with UNM sociology student Azul La Luz. The study resulted in a report submitted to the State of New Mexico Department of Health and Health Policy Commission and articles (Willging, Trujillo, and La Luz 2003, 2004, 2005). In this project, we combined participant observation in treatment, harm reduction, and drug use locales; unstructured interviews; and semistructured interviews. The semistructured interviews included forty-seven

interviews and eight "pilot test" interviews. Twenty-eight of the forty-seven interviewees were male and nineteen female. Nineteen were classified as current drug users and twenty-eight were classified as former drug users. While my fifth chapter is informed by Willging and W. Azul La Luz's research, unless otherwise stated, I collected the ethnographic materials related in this chapter.

4. New Mexico Department of Health epidemiologists state that, between 1995 and 2003, 397 people died of overdose deaths in New Mexico's Department of Health District Two. District Two includes Rio Arriba, Santa Fe, Taos, Los Alamos, Mora, San Miguel, Colfax, Harding, and Union counties. These epidemiologists state that 34 percent and 41 percent of those 397 deaths occurred in Rio Arriba and Santa Fe counties, respectively (Scharmen, Roth-Edwards, and Shah 2005, 7).

5. "Drug of choice" is a treatment concept referring to what treatment providers would consider the drug user's preferred drug or "core addiction." Perhaps because so many area drug users have had contact with treatment institutions, this concept has entered the vernacular and is understood by drug users even if they have never been in treatment.

6. Until the 1980s, most cocaine users produced a purer form of cocaine freebase through a method that used ether. Ether is a notoriously unstable chemical, and transforming powder cocaine into freebase this way is dangerous and potentially explosive. This method is perhaps best known for producing the fire that extensively burned comedian Richard Pryor.

7. Heroin is locally sold in units often called gorras or *papeles*. Residents are also familiar with the more general and national equivalent slang terms BB or paper. Ten BBs, papers, papeles, or gorras are equivalent to one gram (Willging, Trujillo, and La Luz 2003).

8. A heroin addict attempting to detox without tapering off or using medications may experience diarrhea, cramps, vomiting, aches, restlessness, chills, and insomnia, among other things. In contrast, cocaine freebase smokers describe their addiction to cocaine smoking as an intense desire to recapture the intense feeling of their first cocaine rush, and therefore more psychological than physical.

9. Jake Kosek's book *Understories: The Political Life of Forests in Northern New Mexico* (2006) was awarded the John Hope Franklin prize for the best book in American studies.

10. As Tierra Amarilla was and is a center of the land-grant movement in northern New Mexico, Angela García's evidence that a drug user from Tierra Amarilla would explicitly cite land loss as a reason for her drug use or as an explanation for widespread drug use does not surprise me (García 2006, 2007, 2008). I wonder, though, whether similar explicit statements concerning land loss were forthcoming from her other Española informants. In addition, I feel compelled to point out a specific error in Angela García's description of Tierra Amarilla's

settlement based on my own ancestral connections to Tierra Amarilla. She states, without citation, that "Tierra Amarilla was first settled as a land grant in the mid-1600s" (García 2008, 733). The mid-1600s would place Tierra Amarilla's founding deep within the Spanish era and prior to the Pueblo Revolt of 1680. While the land was likely grazed by families from the Abiquiú area since the beginning of the 1800s, the Tierra Amarilla land grant was issued in 1832—a time during the Mexican era and almost two centuries later than García stated (Ebright 1980; 1994, 73–83; Quintana 1991, 60–61).

11. Although we share the same name, the poet and heroin user Michael Trujillo is in no way related to the author of this paper. While I have used pseudonyms for the names of all other illicit drug users, I use Trujillo's actual name because he has appeared in public forums. Indeed, while he also told me the poetic line footnoted here, he also recited it on a *Nightline* segment aired January 29, 2001. The segment cited his actual name and featured footage of him using heroin.

12. Richard Klein's *Cigarettes are Sublime* (1993) writes of tobacco in a manner that evokes Michael Trujillo's comment "Dying will I rise." For Klein and the tobacco users he writes about, cigarettes' sublime power is their link to death. He writes:

> It is not the utility of cigarettes, however significantly useful they may be, that explains their power to attract the undying allegiance of billions of people dying from their habit. Rather the quality that explains their enormous power of seduction is linked to the specific forms of beauty they foster. That beauty has never been understood or represented as unequivocally positive; the smoking of cigarettes, from its inception in the nineteenth century, has always been associated with distaste, transgression and death. Kant calls "sublime" that aesthetic satisfaction which includes as one of its moments a negative experience, a shock, a blockage, an intimation of mortality. (Klein 1993, xi)

Chapter Four

1. In the works of anthropologists and cultural critics, an opposition may be found in experience- or "culturalist-" based microanalyses and "structuralist" or broader macroanalyses. Other times, scale renders clear differing research goals, such as normative approaches, that seek to depict positive or adaptive functions versus others that seek to render realist descriptions of social relations that include negativity.

2. There is a notable absence in Charles Briggs's review of the previous literature. Neither his dissertation nor his most ambitious work, *Competence in Performance*

(1988), addresses or even cites George I. Sánchez's 1940 study, *Forgotten People* (1940). This work describes the conquest, marginalization, and impoverishment of the Spanish-speaking population in Taos County and cannot be understood in the same terms as the sociological works Briggs described.

3. The very real political ramifications of anthropological work in northern New Mexico in the 1960s and 1970s are highlighted by the participation of anthropologists in government forums. For instance, anthropologist Francis Swadesh (she later became Francis Quintana) was called as a defense witness in a criminal trial against land grant activist Reies López Tijerina, Clark Knowlton was called to testify at a congressional subcommittee hearing immediately after the 1967 courthouse raid, and Kutsche himself represented Cañones residents at a state board of education meeting (Kutsche and Van Ness 1988, 192–96; Nabokov 1969, 140; Quintana 1991, 4).

4. Jiménez Núñez interviewed students at Española High School (EHS), Santa Cruz High School (SCHS), McCurdy Mission School, and at the Escuela Parroquial at Holy Cross Church in Santa Cruz. Today, EHS and SCHS have merged into Española Valley High School, and Escuela Parroquial exclusively serves elementary students. At least one additional high school affiliated with an evangelical church has been added, Victory Faith.

5. The specifics of Jiménez Núñez's attempts to measure structural assimilation are interesting. First, of the three hundred Nuevomexicano students Jiménez Núñez surveyed, he found that 63.47 percent of Hispano students' best friends were Hispanos and only 36.53 percent were Anglo (Jiménez Núñez 1974, 154). In particular, he found the highest percentage of Anglo friends, 57.03 percent, at the McCurdy Mission School and the lowest, 29.22 percent, at Española High School. He therefore believed there was some mixing across "ethnic" lines among school-age youth. Second, Jiménez Núñez found that during the years 1956–64 there were 520 marriages between Hispanos and only 56 were between Hispanos and Anglos (Jiménez Núñez 1974, 157–58). Still, he noted an additional 23 marriages where either the bride or groom was "coyote," that is, the child of an Anglo and Hispano parent. He found that in 41 of the 56 marriages between a Hispano and Anglo, the bride was Hispana and the groom was Anglo. Because of the significantly lower rate of intermarriage than school-age friendships, Jiménez Núñez believed social mixing between Nuevomexicanos and Anglos largely ended after residents graduated from high school.

6. *New York Times* exit poll states that 68 percent of New Mexico's "Hispanics/Latinos" voted for Obama and 30 percent for McCain. In contrast, 57 percent of "Whites" voted for McCain and 41 percent for Obama.

7. In my time as a newspaper journalist for Española's *Rio Grande Sun*, I saw firsthand the constant pressure on Española Valley School District administrators and teachers to improve students' low scores on standardized tests. The district is

notorious for its low scores as well as extremely high dropout rate. In that time I also learned that only a small number of the district's students are classified as English as a Second Language students. Most of these students are Mexican immigrants. Most students in the district, however, are English dominant but classified as "Lacking English Proficiency." As a result most of the funds for the district's bilingual education program are earmarked for maintenance of Spanish language skills.

8. The fact that the work of the village ethnographers is far more widely known than the work of their Española contemporaries may be partly explained by the economy of publication. Kutsche and Van Ness wrote a monograph that filled a gap in the ethnographic literature and was published in respected academic presses. Briggs's work was similarly printed in major academic presses and continues to be widely read for its theoretical and methodological significance in addition to ethnographic information. Meanwhile, Jiménez Núñez's work was published in Spanish in Spain; two of Whitecotton's articles were published in the relatively obscure *University of Oklahoma Papers in Anthropology*, and the third was published in an edited volume focusing on the politics of ethnicity in southern Mexico. Finally, while Ellis did publish some of his preliminary work in *University of Oklahoma Papers in Anthropology*, he did not publish the more mature work reflected in his dissertation.

9. Interestingly, Briggs himself lacks any reference to Jiménez Núñez's book in either *Competence in Performance* or his dissertation (Briggs 1981, 1988). What makes this particularly odd is that, although a decade apart, both Briggs and Jiménez Núñez were students at the University of Chicago. Moreover, the children from Briggs's field site, Córdova, attend middle school and high school in Española. Therefore, Jiménez Núñez's reporting of a generational decline in Spanish competency of students in the Española Valley has direct significance for the continuity of Briggs's verbal art and the fitness of Córdova's youths as the pedagogical object of that verbal art.

10. I was unaware of the Española ethnographies until Ronda Brulotte, who works in Oaxaca, happened across Whitecotton's article "Ethnic Groups in Southern Mexico and Northern New Mexico: A Historical Comparison of the Valley of Oaxaca and the Española Valley" in Howard Campbell's edited volume, *The Politics of Ethnicity in Southern Mexico* (Whitecotton 1996). Subsequently, University of New Mexico anthropologist Sylvia Rodríguez urged me to a deeper reading of Whitecotton and his students' work. Later, Whitecotton himself suggested Jiménez Núñez's monograph.

Chapter Five

1. Some materials from the folder were published in their entirety in "E. Boyd's Working Notes on Policarpio Valencia and his Alabado Embroidery" (Weigle, Larcombe, and Larcombe 1983).

2. In terms of Nuevomexicano arts and crafts, the most influential local manifestation of this larger arts and crafts revival was the Spanish Colonial Arts Society. This society was incorporated in 1929 and emerged from the earlier Society for the Revival of Spanish Colonial Arts founded by writer Mary Austin and artist Frank Applegate. Helen R. Lucero, herself a weaver, has been a longtime participant in the Spanish Colonial Arts Society. Lucero was the curator of Hispanic folk art at the Museum of International Folk Art in Santa Fe and, until recently, director of visual arts at the National Hispanic Cultural Center in Albuquerque.

3. The Inquisition in Mexico City ruled that the Santa Cruz poet Miguel de Quintana's mind was wandering with age and chose to admonish him and assign him to a confessor. This accusation of insanity overruled the New Mexican clergy's accusations of heresy and prompted the twentieth-century Nuevomexicano and Franciscan Fray Angélico Chávez to title his short article about the poet, "The Mad Poet of Santa Cruz" (Chávez 1948–49, 10–17). Still, Chávez's title belies his real opinion of the poet. His concluding remarks indicate that he was unconvinced by the assertion of insanity. Chavez instead credits Quintana with the brilliance of an artist and suggests he was the potential author of an important folk drama that continues to be performed in New Mexico. Chávez writes that Inquisition records tell us of the "talents of old and saintly Miguel de Quintana, who was not really mad but only so inclined (as what genius is not?), and who might be the author of many a verse or play that has survived as folklore—he might even be the author of Los Pastores" (Chávez 1948–49, 17).

4. E. Boyd presumably sought Rubén Cobos's interpretation, and the standard Spanish transcription is signed by Cobos with the salutation "Para mi amiga E. Boyd" (For my friend E. Boyd).

5. A four-page report on several of Valencia's embroideries is located in the Policarpio Valencia Folder of the E. Boyd archives in the New Mexico State Records Center. The report is undated and unsigned. A description of the folder's contents is located in the MOIFA library, however, describes the report as "possibly by Hester Jones." The report also contradicts several points Irene Emery convincingly argued in her 1953 article, suggesting the report was written before the publication of Emery's description of Valencia's work (Policarpio Valencia Folder n.d.).

6. Barela's astounding woodcarvings were exhibited along with the works of 171 artists at New York's Museum of Modern Art. Of the 171 artists who

participated in the show, Barela was specifically hailed by both the *New York Times* and *Time* magazine. Even for him, the admiration of art elites possesses a condescending quality. A newspaper article from the period states, "[Barela] is a real primitive and does not have to strive for effect. It is to be hoped that he may always retain this primitive simplicity that many sophisticated artists try to achieve" (quoted in Gonzales and Witt 1996, 176). In part because of his management by Federal Art Project administrators, Barela later sank back into poverty and relative obscurity.

7. Northern New Mexicans provided labor for the region's agricultural economy. Many heads of household traveled to Colorado and other southwestern locations to work as agricultural laborers and sheepherders. Before the 1930s, out of 592 families in the Santa Cruz complex of villages, 140 to 200 heads of family, on average, traveled to other communities for seasonal work for five to seven months each year. At the time of the study, in the 1930s, 15 heads of family continued work at a smelter in Leadville, Colorado.

8. At the time Emery wrote her article, the identity of the embroiderer was not yet established. Indeed, her article was the first to identify the embroiderer as Policarpio Valencia and established him as the creator of stylistically similar but unsigned pieces. Her article describes three pieces in depth and gives a cursory description of a fourth that was then only recently acquired. While she did not identify these pieces by their accession numbers, they correspond to pieces MOIFA MNMA 9.54 28 M, MOIFA B 89–13, and MOIFA MNM B89–48 (Emery 1953).

9. Key to Stuart Hall's analysis is under what circumstances a connection can be forced or made. Among the linkages that matter are between that articulated discourse and the social forces with which it can, under certain historical conditions, be connected.

10. According to Gaspar Martínez, the Christian message is about one mystery, the mystery of God. In turn, God is revealed in Jesus Christ, the order of nature, historical events, prophets, the Apostles, the early church, and through all the events, objects, and persons that constitute and shape human experience and history.

Chapter Six

1. I borrowed the title of this chapter from Sagel's short poem, "Cuando Hablan los Enamorados." This title means, "When those in love talk."

2. Jim Sagel's papers are now held at the University of Texas at Austin in the Benson Latin American Collection.

3. Included among Sagel's papers were notebooks written while he was hospitalized.

4. The research for this essay included interviews with Archuleta that took place in the spring and summer of 2002, a comprehensive review of Sagel's published work, and a short survey of his unpublished papers then in Teresa Archuleta's possession. This collection of materials is now located at the Benson Latin American Collection at the University of Texas at Austin.

5. Sagel appeared in the film version of *The Milagro Beanfield War* as a doctor, and Archuleta appeared as a nurse (Teresa Archuleta, personal communication with the author, 2005).

6. Sagel and Archuleta were married in the Roman Catholic Church four years later. At that time, Sagel, raised a Lutheran, converted to Roman Catholicism.

7. Several scholars have studied Río Grande and Chimayó weaving. In the Española area, Helen Lucero and Suzanne Baizerman's *Chimayó Weaving: The Transformation of a Tradition* (1999) represents the most thorough analysis.

8. For these essay portraits included in *Dancing to Pay the Light Bill*, Sagel states he interviewed the "ancianos" or Nuevomexicano elders, Native American, Anglo-American, and Black cultures of New Mexico. Nevertheless, as suggested by the Spanish term *ancianos*, Sagel's paradigmatic elder seems to be Latino like his father-in-law (Sagel 1992, ix).

9. Felipe de Ortego y Gasca writes in "Danny Santiago and the Ethics of Deception" that Chester E. "Amado Muro" Seltzer's actual identity was only discovered after Seltzer died (de Ortego y Gasca 1984).

10. Daniel "Danny Santiago" James was unmasked in John Gregory Dunne's *New York Review of Books* article, "The Secret of Danny Santiago" (Dunne 1984).

11. Pilar Rodríguez Aranda's *Unexpected Turn of Jim Sagel* was screened at the 2003 Santa Fe Film Festival. Rodríguez knew Sagel since 1991, and the press kit for the film characterizes it as a "homage to a lost friend, a visual and aural play with Jim's poetry, and an interpretative retelling of his life" (Rodríguez Aranda 2003).

12. According to Juan Bruce-Novoa, the category of Chicanesque literature was first coined by influential Chicano literary critics Francisco Lomelí and Donaldo Urioste for their 1976 annotated bibliography, *Chicano Perspectives in Literature* (Bruce-Nova 1990, 141; Lomelí and Urioste 1976). In an effort to illustrate the inadequacy of this term, Bruce-Novoa points out this category is not based on thematic or cultural criteria through which real Chicano works could be distinguished from Chicanesque works but on the blood of the author. He writes somewhat caustically that we need another category of "casi-casi," or "almost-almost," for those authors who cannot pass the blood test but whose writing is culturally and ethnically Chicano.

13. Archuleta considers herself to be psychic. As a child, she said she had many other psychic experiences. Since the early 1990s, in addition to her artwork, Archuleta has done psychic readings.

Chapter 7

1. The mixed race category of genízara/o is described in chapter 1.
2. The Winnebago Tribe of Wisconsin formally changed their name to the Ho Chunk Sovereign Nation in 1994.
3. El Cerro de los Perdenales is best known in the wider American national imagination through its representation in paintings by Georgia O'Keeffe.
4. One member of the Hispano Roundtable told Masco, "They didn't keep me poor and dumb and ignorant and now I'm saying I want more. I expect to be treated like anybody else that is working up here" (Masco 2006, 207).
5. Salvador also fails to satisfy another major measure of *machista* masculinity. While engaged in lovemaking with Blanca Flor, he is told, "'You . . . don't . . . you . . . don't satisfy me'" (Córdova 2006, 135).
6. Córdova states that anthropologist and Santa Clara Native Edward P. Dozier first taught him that it is acceptable to be a genízaro (Córdova n.d., 12).
7. The fictional Wilberto Ferrán theory of genízara/o identity parallels the views of mestizaje Chicana feminist theorists such as Gloria Anzaldúa or anthropologist Karen Mary Dávalos articulate (Anzaldúa 1987; Dávalos 2001). Dávalos writes that "we cannot consider mestiza/o experience from one perspective for it always originates from at least two places. Mestizaje is thus both an expression of affirmation and self-determination and a result of domination" (Dávalos 2001, 27).
8. In *Aztecas del Norte*, Jack Forbes makes the often-quoted claim that "Aztecas del Norte . . . compose the largest single tribe or nation of Anishinabeg (Indians) in the United States today" (Forbes 1973, 30).
9. In a related passage from his earlier article, Córdova writes:

   > There comes a time the student of culture must ask the difficult question, "What is the meaning of this comic opera?" Obviously, both the Hispanic and Indian communities look upon the *matachines* with a sense of wonderment, reverence, and awe. Both groups recognize that *matachines* fall into the domain of the holy, and sense that they function in the orb of the ancient sacred, a realm which the Western world seems to have forgotten. (Córdova 1997, 15)

10. Abuelo is a term of respect for wise elders, but, as Córdova tells us, matachin abuelos are wise with a difference. He states, these abuelos "wear distorted buckskin masks and flounder in a borderline senility, which may explain why their disguises resemble coyote tricksters from an age when the world was balanced differently" (Córdova 2006, 60).
11. As noted earlier in this chapter, don Cacahuate is the chief subject of one of Córdova's early publications (Córdova 1973).

12. As noted in chapter 2, Chicana feminists have reclaimed La Malinche as both a strong woman unbounded by patriarchal logic and the prototypical victim of Mexican and Chicano patriarchy (Alarcón 1989; Anzaldúa 1987, 44; Candelaria 1980; Contreras 2008, 105–32; Cypress 1991, 138–52; Del Castillo 1977; González 1991).

Conclusion

1. I have standardized the spelling in Trujillo's prayer.

Bibliography

Adorno, Theodor W. 1973. *Negative Dialectics*. New York: Seabury Press.

Agar, Michael. 1973. *Ripping and Running: A Formal Ethnography of Urban Heroin Addicts*. New York: Seminar Press.

Agoyo, Herman. 2009. Po'pay: A Pueblo Perspective on the Leader of the First American Revolution. In *Telling New Mexico: A New History*, ed. Marta Weigle with Frances Levine and Louise Stiver, 418–21. Santa Fe: Museum of New Mexico Press.

Alarcón, Norma. 1989. Traddutora, Traditora: A Paradigmatic Figure of Chicana Feminism. *Cultural Critique* 13 (Fall): 57–87.

Anzaldúa, Gloria. 1987. *Borderlands/La Frontera: The New Mestiza*. San Francisco: spinsters/aunt lute.

The Architect of the Capitol. 2009. The National Statuary Hall Collection: Po'pay. In *Telling New Mexico: A New History*, ed. Marta Weigle with Frances Levine and Louise Stiver, 415–17. Santa Fe: Museum of New Mexico Press.

Archuleta, Elizabeth. 2007. Memorializing Po'Pay and Oñate, or Recasting Racialized Regimes of Representation? *New Mexico Historical Review* 82 (3): 317–42.

Archuleta, Teresa. 2002a. Interview by author. Española, New Mexico. January 24.

———— 2002b. Interview by author. Española, New Mexico. February 28.

———— 2002c. Interview by author. Española, New Mexico. March 14.

———— 2009. Telephone interview by author. February 13.

Arellano, Juan Estevan. 1984. *Palabras de la Vista/Retratos de la Pluma*. Albuquerque: Academia.

———— 1992. *Inocencio: ni pica, ni escarda, pero siempre come el mejor elote*. Mexico City: Editorial Grijalbo.

———— 1997a. *Cuentos de Café y Tortilla*. Juárez: Universidad Autónoma de Ciudad Juárez.

———— 1997b. La Querencia: La Raza Bioregionalism. *New Mexico Historical Review* 72 (1): 31–37.

———— 1999. Interview by author. Embudo, New Mexico. October 12.

Babcock-Abrahams, Barbara. 1975. "A Tolerated Margin of Mess": The Trickster and His Tales Reconsidered. *Journal of the Folklore Institute* 11 (3): 147–86.

Baizerman, Suzanne. 1987. Textiles, Traditions, and Tourist Art: Hispanic Weaving in Northern New Mexico. PhD diss., University of Minnesota.

Baker, Deborah. 2000. Teen Shot Making Good Friday Pilgrimage to Northern New Mexico Church. Associated Press. April 21.

Bakhtin, Mikhail. 1981. Epic and Novel: Toward a Methodology for the Study of the Novel. In *The Dialogic Imagination*, ed. Michael Holquist, trans. Carly Emerson and Michael Holquist, 3–40. Austin: University of Texas Press.

———— 1984. *Rabelais and His World*. Trans. Helene Iswolsky. Bloomington: Indiana University Press.

Barrett, Annin. 2000. Policarpio Valencia's Embroidered Poetry. Proceedings of the Seventh Biennial Symposium of the Textile Society of America, Santa Fe, New Mexico.

Barrett, Elinore M. 2002. *Conquest and Catastrophe: Changing Rio Grande Pueblo Settlement Patterns in the Sixteenth and Seventeenth Centuries.* Albuquerque: University of New Mexico Press.

Barth, Fredrik. 1969. Introduction to *Ethnic Groups and Boundaries*. Boston: Little, Brown, and Company.

Benjamin, Walter. 1968. *Illuminations: Essays and Reflections*. Ed. Hannah Arendt. New York: Schocken Books.

———— 1978. Surrealism: The Last Snapshot of the European Intelligentsia. In *Reflections: Essays, Aphorisms, Autobiographical Writing*, ed. Peter Demetz, 177–92. New York: Schocken Books.

———— 2006. *On Hashish*. Trans. Howard Eiland. Cambridge, MA: The Belknap Press / Harvard University Press.

Blaut, J. M., and Antonio Ríos-Bustamante. 1984. Commentary on Nostrand's "Hispanos" and Their "Homeland." *Annals of the Association of American Geographers* 74 (1): 157–64.

Blum, Kenneth, John G. Cull, Eric R. Braverman, and David E. Commings. 1996. Reward Deficiency Syndrome. *American Scientist* 84:132–45.

Blumenthal, Ralph. 2004. Still Many Months Away, El Paso's Giant Horseman Keeps Stirring Passions. *New York Times*. January 10.

Bourgois, Philippe. 1995. *In Search of Respect: Selling Crack in El Barrio*. Cambridge: Cambridge University Press.

————, and Jeff Schonberg. 2009. *Righteous Dopefiend*. Berkeley: University of California Press.

Boyd, E. 1974. *Popular Arts of Spanish New Mexico*. Santa Fe: Museum of New Mexico Press.

Brady, Maggie. 1995. Culture in Treatment, Culture as Treatment: A Critical Appraisal of Development in Addictions Programs for Indigenous North Americans and Australians. *Social Science and Medicine* 41 (11): 1487–98.

Briggs, Charles L. 1974. A Functional Analysis of Youth Gangs in a Spanish-American

Village of North-Central New Mexico. Paper presented at the Rocky Mountain Social Science Association Annual Meeting, El Paso, Texas.

——— 1980. *The Wood Carvers of Córdova, New Mexico: Social Dimensions of an Artistic "Revival."* Knoxville: University of Tennessee Press.

——— 1981. "Our Strength is the Land": The Structure of Hierarchy and Equality and the Pragmatics of Discourse in Hispano ("Spanish-American") Talk of the Past. PhD diss., University of Chicago.

——— 1986. *Learning How to Ask: A Sociolinguistic Appraisal of the Role of the Interview in Social Science Research.* New York: Cambridge University Press.

——— 1988. *Competence in Performance: The Creativity of Tradition in Mexicano Verbal Art.* Philadelphia: University of Pennsylvania Press.

———, and John R. Van Ness, eds. 1987. *Land, Water, and Culture: New Perspectives on Hispanic Land Grants.* Albuquerque: University of New Mexico.

———, and Malaquías Romero. 1990. *Historia de la mina perdida de Juan Mondragón/ The Lost Gold Mine of Juan Mondragon: A Legend from New Mexico.* Ed. Charles L. Briggs and Julián Josué Vigil. Tucson: University of Arizona Press.

———, and Clara Mantini-Briggs. 2003. *Stories in the Time of Cholera: Racial Profiling During a Medical Nightmare.* Berkeley: University of California Press.

Bright, Brenda Jo. 1994. Mexican American Low Riders: An Anthropological Approach to Popular Culture. PhD diss., Rice University.

——— 1998. "Heart Like a Car": Hispano/Chicano Culture in Northern New Mexico. *American Ethnologist* 25 (4): 583–609.

Brodkin, Karen. 1998. *How Jews Became White Folks and What that Says Abut Race in America.* New Brunswick, NJ: Rutgers University Press.

Brooks, James. 2002. *Captives and Cousins: Slavery, Kinship, and Community in the Southwest Borderlands.* Chapel Hill: University of North Carolina Press.

Bruce-Novoa, Juan. 1990. *RetroSpace: Collected Essays on Chicano Literature.* Houston: Arte Público Press.

Bureau of Economic Analysis, United States Bureau of the Census. 1999. Regional Accounts Data. http://www.bea.doc.gov/bea/regional/reis.ca25 (accessed March 10, 2000).

Bustamante, Adrián. 1991. "The Matter Was Never Resolved": The *Casta* System in Colonial New Mexico, 1693–1823. *New Mexico Historical Review* 66 (2): 143–63.

Calkins, Hugh G. 1935. Preliminary Report on Concho. United States Department of Agriculture, Regional Bulletin No. 29. Conservation Economic Series No. 16.

——— 1937. Population of the Upper Rio Grande Watershed. United States Department of Agriculture, Regional Bulletin No. 43. Conservation Economic Series No. 16.

Calloway, Larry. 1998. Footnote: Careful Not to Offend. *Albuquerque Journal,* January 8.

Campa, Arthur L. 1979. *Hispanic Culture in the Southwest*. Norman: University of Oklahoma Press.

Candelaria, Cordelia. 1980. La Malinche, Feminist Prototype. *Frontiers* 2:1–6.

Cardoso, Patricia. 2002. *Real Women Have Curves*. HBO Home Video.

Carroll, Michael P. 2002. *The Penitente Brotherhood: Patriarchy and Hispano-Catholicism in New Mexico*. Baltimore, MD: The Johns Hopkins University Press.

Castañeda, Antonia I. 1993. Sexual Violence in the Politics and Policies of Conquest: Amerindian Women and the Spanish Conquest of Alta California. In *Building with Our Hands: New Directions in Chicana Studies*, ed. Adela de la Torre and Beatriz M. Pesquera, 15–33. Berkeley: University of California Press.

Cerney, Charlene. 1985. The *Blason Populaire* Northern New Mexico Style: The Española Joke. Unpublished manuscript.

———, and Christine Mather. 1994. *Textile Production in Twentieth-Century New Mexico*. In *Rio Grande Textiles: A New Edition of Spanish Textile Tradition of New Mexico and Colorado*, ed. Nora Fisher, 132–51. Santa Fe: Museum of New Mexico Press.

Chávez, Fray Angélico. 1948–49. The Mad Poet of Santa Cruz. *New Mexico Folklore* 3:10–17.

——— 1973. *Origin of New Mexico Families*. Albuquerque: University of New Mexico Press.

——— 1984. Rejoinder. *Annals of the American Association of American Geographers* 74 (1): 170–71.

Chávez, Lisa. 2002. Interview by author. Española, New Mexico. September 26.

Chipman, Donald E. 1977. The Oñate-Moctezuma-Zaldívar Families of Northern Spain. *New Mexico Historical Review* 52 (October): 297–310.

Cisneros, Sandra. 1991. Never Marry a Mexican. In *Woman Hollering Creek and Other Stories*, 68–83. New York: Vintage Books.

Cobos, Rubén. 1983. *A Dictionary of New Mexico and Southern Colorado Spanish*. Santa Fe: Museum of New Mexico Press.

Contreras, Sheila Marie. 2008. *Blood Lines: Myth, Indigenism, and Chicana/o Literature*. Austin: University of Texas Press.

Coole, Diana. 2000. *Negativity and Politics: Dionysus and Dialectics from Kant to Poststructuralism*. New York: Routledge.

Córdova, G. Benito. 1973. *Abiquiú and Don Cacahuate: A Folk History of a New Mexico Village*. Los Cerrillos, NM: San Marcos Press.

——— 1979. Missionization and Hispanicization of Santo Tomás Apostol de Abiquiú, 1750–1770. PhD diss., University of New Mexico.

——— 1990. *The 3½ Cultures of Española*. Albuquerque: El Norte/Academia Press.

——— 1997. The Twelve Masked Apostles. *La Herencia del Norte*, Winter.

——— 2006. *Big Dreams and Dark Secrets in Chimayó*. Albuquerque: University of New Mexico Press.

————— The Genízaro. Unpublished manuscript.

Cornish, Beatrice Quijada. 1917. The Ancestry and Family of Juan De Oñate. In
    The Pacific Ocean in History, ed. H. Morse Stephens and Herbert E. Bolton,
    452–66. New York: MacMillan Company.

Cowan, Bainard. 1981. Walter Benjamin's Theory of Allegory. *New German Critique* 22
    (Winter): 109–22.

Culture as a Cure/La Cultura Cura. 1997. VHS. Directed by Jonathan Lowe. Española,
    NM: Hands Across Cultures.

Cypress, Sandra Messinger. 1991. *La Malinche in Mexican Literature: From History to
    Myth*. Austin: University of Texas Press.

Dalakar, Joseph. 1999. *Poverty in the United States, 1999: Current Population Reports*.
    Washington, DC: U.S. Government Printing Office.

Dávalos, Karen Mary. 2001. *Exhibiting Mestizaje: Mexican (American) Museums in the
    Diaspora*. Albuquerque: University of New Mexico Press.

————— 2008. Sin Vergüenza: Chicana Feminist Theorizing. *Feminist Studies* 34 (1/2):
    151–71.

Dávila, Arlene. 2001. *Latinos Inc: Marketing and the Making of a People*. Berkeley:
    University of California Press.

————— 2004. *Barrio Dreams: Puerto Ricans, Latinos and the Neoliberal City*. Berkeley:
    University of California Press.

Davis, Deborah. 2003. Drug Users Offer Insights into Addictions, Treatment. *Santa Fe
    New Mexican*. October 25.

De Genova, Nicholas. 2008. "American" Abjection: "Chicanos," Gangs, and Mexican/
    Migrant Transnationality in Chicago. *Aztlan: A Journal of Chicano Studies* 33
    (2): 141–74.

de Ortego y Gasca, Felipe. 1984. Danny Santiago and the Ethics of Deception. *Nuestro*
    9:50–51.

De Guzmán, María. 2001. Turning Tricks: Trafficking in the Figure of the Latino. In
    Trickster Lives: Culture and Myth in American Fiction, ed. Jeanne Campbell
    Reesman, 168–84. Athens: University of Georgia Press.

DeKoven, Marianne. 1992. The Politics of Modernist Form. *New Literary History* 23
    (3): 675–90.

————— 2004. *Utopia Unlimited: The Sixties and the Emergence of the Postmodern*.
    Durham, NC: Duke University Press.

Del Castillo, Adelaida R. 1977. Malintzín Tenépal: A Preliminary Look into a
    New Perspective. In *Essays on la Mujer*, ed. Rosaura Sánchez and Rosa
    Martínez Cruz, 124–49. Los Angeles: Chicano Studies Center Publications,
    University of California, Los Angeles.

DeLoach, Dana Engstrom. 1999. Image and Identity at El Santuario de Chimayó in
    Chimayó, New Mexico. Master's thesis, University of North Texas.

Denver Post. 1991. Culture clash. September 1.

Dessus Colón, Virginia. 1987. El Mundo Chicano en *Tunomás Honey* de Jim Sagel. Master's thesis, Universidad de Puerto Rico.

Deutsch, Sarah. 1987. *No Separate Refuge: Culture, Class, and Gender on an Anglo-Hispanic Frontier in the American Southwest, 1880–1940*. New York: Oxford University Press.

Di Chiara, Gaetano. 1998. A Motivational Learning Hypothesis of the Role of Mesolimbic Dopamine in Compulsive Drug Use. *Journal of Psychopharmacology* 12:54–67.

Dilworth, Leah. 1996. *Imagining Indians in the Southwest: Persistent Visions of a Primitive Past*. Washington, DC: Smithsonian Institution Press.

Douglas, Mary. 1968. The Social Control of Cognition: Some Factors in Joke Perception. *Man* 3 (3): 361–76.

Down AKA Kilo. 2007. *The Definition of an Ese*. CD. Silent Giant.

Dozier, Edward P. 1970. *The Pueblo Indians of North America*. New York: Holt, Rinehart and Winston.

Dunne, John Gregory. 1984. The Secret of Danny Santiago. *New York Review of Books* 31 (13): 17–27.

Durán, Christina. 2007. Panaderías, Peluquerías, y Carnicerías: Re-Mexicanizing the Urban Landscapes of a Southwest City. PhD diss., University of New Mexico.

Ebright, Malcolm. 1980. *The Tierra Amarilla Grant: A History of Chicanery*. Santa Fe: Center for Land Grant Studies.

———. 1994. *Land Grants and Lawsuits in Northern New Mexico*. Albuquerque: University of New Mexico Press.

Edmonson, Munro S. 1957. *Los Manitos: A Study of Institutional Values*. New Orleans: Middle American Research Institute, Tulane University.

Ellis, Richard Stewart. 1980. Santa Cruz: Authority and Community Response in the History of a New Mexico Town. PhD diss., University of Oklahoma.

Elsberg, Constance, Waeber. 2003. *Graceful Women: Gender and Identity in an American Sikh Community*. Knoxville: University of Tennessee Press.

Emery, Irene. 1953. "Samplers" Embroidered in String. *El Palacio* 60 (2): 35–51.

Española Chamber of Commerce. 1982. Española Chamber of Commerce [advertisement]. *New Mexico Magazine*, August.

Espinosa, Aurelio M. 1985. *The Folklore of Spain in the American Southwest*. Norman: University of Oklahoma Press.

Espinoza, Angel, and James Espinoza. 1996. "El Corrido de Don Juan de Oñate." From *When Grandma was a Girl*. Santa Cruz, NM: Song Potter Records & Publishing Co.

Esquibel, Catriona Rueda. 2006. *With Her Machete in Her Hand: Reading Chicana Lesbians*. Austin: University of Texas Press.

Esquibel, José Antonio. 2006. The Formative Era for New Mexico's Colonial Population: 1693–1700. In *Transforming Images: New Mexican Santos*

In-Between Worlds, ed. Claire Farago and Donna Pierce, 64–79. University Park: Pennsylvania University Press.

Farago, Claire, and Donna Pierce, eds. 2006. *Transforming Images: New Mexican Santos In-Between Worlds*. University Park: Pennsylvania State University Press.

Fisher, Nora. 1979. *Spanish Textile Tradition of New Mexico and Colorado*. Santa Fe: Museum of New Mexico Press.

——— 1994. *Rio Grande Textiles: A New Edition of the Spanish Textile Tradition of New Mexico and Colorado*. Santa Fe: Museum of New Mexico Press.

Fleischer, Matthew. 2006. Navahoax: Did a Struggling White Writer of Gay Erotica Become One of Multicultural Literature's Most Celebrated Memoirists by Passing Himself off as Native American? *LA Weekly*. http://www.laweekly.com (accessed December 26, 2007).

Flores, Richard R. 2002. *Remembering the Alamo: Memory, Modernity, and the Master Symbol*. Austin: University of Texas Press.

Forbes, Jack. 1973. *Aztecas Del Norte: The Chicanos of Aztlán*. Greenwich, CT: Fawcett.

Forrest, Suzanne. 1987. The Preservation of the Village: The Origins and Implementation of New Mexico's Hispanic New Deal. PhD diss., University of Wyoming.

——— 1989. *The Preservation of the Village: New Mexico's Hispanics and the New Deal*. Albuquerque: University of New Mexico Press.

Foucault, Michel. 1982. *The Archaeology of Knowledge and the Discourse on Language*. New York: Pantheon Books.

Freise, Kathy. 2007. Contesting Oñate: Sculpting the Shape of Memory. In *Expressing New Mexico: Nuevomexicano Creativity, Ritual, and Memory*, ed. Phillip B. Gonzales, 233–52. Tucson: University of Arizona Press.

Freud, Sigmund. 1960. *Jokes and their Relation to the Unconscious*. Trans. James Strachey. New York: Norton.

Gandert, Miguel A., Lucy Lippard, Chris Wilson, Enrique Lamadrid, and Ramón Gutiérrez. 2000. *Nuevo México Profundo: Rituals of an Indo-Hispano Homeland*. Santa Fe: Museum of New Mexico Press.

García, Angela. 2006. Land of Disenchantment. *High Country News*. http://www.hcn.org (accessed February 5, 2009).

——— 2007. The Pastoral Clinic: Addiction and Absolution Along the Rio Grande. PhD diss., Harvard University.

——— 2008. The Elegiac Addict: History, Chronicity, and the Melancholic Subject. *Cultural Anthropology* 23 (4): 718–46.

García, Deborah D. 1998. The Statue of Don Juan de Oñate and Hispano Identity: A Turning Point in New Mexican History. Unpublished manuscript.

García Canclini, Néstor. 1995. *Hybrid Cultures: Strategies for Entering and Leaving Modernity*. Trans. Christopher L. Chiappari and Silvia L. López. Minneapolis: University of Minnesota Press.

———— 2005. *Imaginarios urbanos*. 3a ed. Buenos Aires: Eudeba.

Geertz, Clifford. 1973. *The Interpretation of Cultures: Selected Essays*. New York: Basic Books.

Gilbert, Elliot. 2001. San Juan Pueblo: The Ultimate Lowrider Competition Brings Out New Mexico's Finest Lows. *Lowrider* 23 (8): 105–6, 218.

Gisick, Michael. 2005. Popé Sent on His Way: Controversial Statue Unveiled at San Juan Pueblo. http://www.riograndesun.com (accessed May 30, 2005).

Gjevre, John A. 1969. *Chili Line: The Narrow Trail to Santa Fe*. Española, NM: Rio Grande Sun Press.

Glendinning, Chellis. 2005. *Chiva: A Village Takes on the Global Heroin Trade*. Gabriola Island, BC: New Society Publishers.

Gómez, Laura E. 2007. *Manifest Destinies: The Making of the Mexican American Race*. New York: New York University Press.

Gonzales, Edward, and David L. Witt. 1996. *Spirit Ascendant: The Art and Life of Patrociño Barela*. Santa Fe: Red Crane Books.

Gonzales, Phillip B. 1986. The Anti-Fraternity Bill of 1933. *New Mexico Historical Review* 61 (4): 281–99.

———— 1993. The Political Construction of Latino Nomenclature in Twentieth-Century New Mexico. *Journal of the Southwest* 35 (2): 158–85.

———— 1997a. The Categorical Meaning of Spanish American Identity Among Blue-Collar New Mexicans, circa 1983. *Hispanic Journal of Behavioral Sciences* 19 (2): 123–36.

———— 1997b. The Hispano Homeland Debate: New Lessons. *Perspectives in Mexican American Studies* 6:123–41.

———— 2000. La Junta de Indignación: Hispano Repertoire of Collective Protest in New Mexico, 1884–1933. *Western Historical Quarterly* 31 (Summer): 161–86.

———— 2001. *Forced Sacrifice as Ethnic Protest: The Hispano Cause in New Mexico and the Racial Attitude Confrontation of 1933*. New York: Peter Lang Publishing.

———— 2007. "History Hits the Heart": Albuquerque's Great Cuartocentenario Controversy, 1997–2005. In *Expressing New Mexico: Nuevomexicano Creativity, Ritual, and Memory*, ed. Phillip B. Gonzales, 207–32. Tucson: University of Arizona Press.

González, Deena. 1991 Malinche as Lesbian: A Reconfiguration of 500 Years of Resistance. *California Sociologist* 14 (1–2): 91–97.

González, Nancie L. 1969. *The Spanish-Americans of New Mexico: A Heritage of Pride*. Albuquerque: University of New Mexico Press.

Greff, Jennifer L. 2005. Truck Hopping Record Set by Chimayosos. http://www.riograndesun.com/news.asp (accessed May 5, 2005).

Gutiérrez, Ramón. 1991. *When Jesus Came, the Corn Mothers Went Away: Marriage, Sexuality, and Power in New Mexico, 1500–1846*. Stanford: Stanford University Press.

———— 2002. Background and Gestation: New Mexico Reinvented Charles Fletcher Lummis and the Orientalization of New Mexico. In *Nuevomexicano Cultural Legacy: Forms Agencies, and Discourse*, ed. Francisco A. Lomelí, V. A. Sorell, and Genaro M. Padilla, 11–27. Albuquerque: University of New Mexico Press.

———— 2003. Honor, Ideology, Marriage, Negotiation, and Class-Gender Domination in New Mexico, 1690–1846. In *Sexual Borderlands: Constructing an American Sexual Past*, ed. Kathleen Kennedy and Sharon Ullman, 5–26. Columbus: Ohio State University Press.

Halasan, Corazón, Michael Landen, Barbara Chatterjee, Phil Somervell, and Karen Johnson. 2001. Rio Arriba County Data Review on Drug, Alcohol and other Health-Related Issues. Unpublished manuscript.

Hall, Stuart. 1980. Cultural Studies: Two Paradigms. *Media, Culture, and Society* 2:57–72.

———— 1986. Gramsci's Relevance for the Study of Race and Ethnicity. *Journal of Communication Inquiry* 10(2): 5–27.

———— 1996. On Postmodernism and Articulation: An Interview with Stuart Hall. Ed. Lawrence Grossberg. In *Stuart Hall: Critical Dialogues in Cultural Studies*, ed. David Morley and Kuan-Hsing Chen, 131–50. New York: Routledge.

Hall, Thomas D. 1984. Rejoinder. *Annals of the Association of American Geographers* 74 (1): 171.

Hamon, Peter G. 1970. The Landholding System of Santa Cruz. *University of Oklahoma Papers in Anthropology* 11 (1): 21–40.

Hannan, Michael. 1979. The Dynamics of Ethnic Boundaries in Modern States. In *National Development and the World System*, ed. John Meyer and Michael Hannan, 255–56. Chicago: University of Chicago Press.

Hansen, Niles. 1981. Commentary: The Hispano Homeland in 1900. *Annals of the Association* of *American Geographers* 71 (2): 280–82.

Hegel, Georg Wilhelm Friedrich. 1977. *Phenomenology of Spirit*. Trans. A.V. Miller. Oxford: Clarendon Press.

Hendricks, Rick. 2009. Juan de Oñate, Colonizer, Governor. In *Telling New Mexico: A New History*, ed. Marta Weigle with Frances Levine and Louise Stiver, 101–6. Santa Fe: Museum of New Mexico Press.

Hernández, Guillermo E. 1991. *Chicano Satire: A Study in Literary Culture*. Austin: University of Texas Press.

Herrera Interrogation. 2000. Herrera Police Interview Transcript. Unpublished manuscript.

Homer, Sean. 1998. *Fredric Jameson: Marxism, Hermeneutics, Postmodernism*. New York: Routledge.

Howarth, Sam, Enrique R. Lamadrid, Miguel A. Gandert, Oscar Lozoya, and Cary Herz. 1999. *Pilgrimage to Chimayó*. Santa Fe: Museum of New Mexico Press.

Hurt, Wesley Robert. 1941. Manzano: A Study of Community Disorganization. Master's thesis, University of New Mexico.

Hyde, Lewis. 1998. *Trickster Makes the World*. New York: Northpoint Press.

Jameson, Fredric. 1971. *Marxism and Form: Twentieth-Century Dialectical Theories of Literature*. Princeton, NJ: Princeton University Press.

——— 1982. *The Political Unconscious*. Ithaca, NY: Cornell University Press.

Jiménez Núñez, Alfredo. 1974. *Los Hispanos de Nuevo México: Contribución a una antropología de la cultura hispana en USA*. Seville: Publicaciones de la Universidad de Sevilla.

Johansen, Sigurd. 1948. *Rural Social Organization in a Spanish-American Culture Area*. Albuquerque: University of New Mexico Press.

Jung, C. C. 1956. On the Psychology of the Trickster Figure. In *The Trickster: A Study in American Indian Mythology*, ed. Paul Radin, 195–211. New York: Schocken Books.

Kay, Elizabeth. 1986. *Chimayó Valley Traditions*. Santa Fe: Ancient City Press.

Keltz, Iris. 2000. *Scrapbook of a Taos Hippie: Tribal Tales from the Heartland of a Cultural Revolution*. El Paso: Cinco Puntos Press.

Klein, Richard. 1993. *Cigarettes are Sublime*. Durham, NC: Duke University Press.

Kluckhohn, Florence Rockwood, and Fred L. Strodtbeck. 1961. *Variations in Value Orientation*. Evanston, IL: Row, Peterson.

Knaut, Andrew L. 1995. *The Pueblo Revolt of 1680: Conquest and Resistance in Seventeenth-Century New Mexico*. Norman: University of Oklahoma Press.

Knowlton, Clark. 1961. The Spanish Americans of New Mexico. *Sociology and Social Research* 45:448–54.

——— 1962. Patron-Peon Pattern Among the Spanish-Americans of New Mexico. *Social Forces* 40 (4): 12–17.

——— 1967. Land Grant Problems Among the Spanish-Americans of New Mexico. *New Mexico Business* 20 (6): 1–13.

——— 1969. Changing Spanish-American Villages of Northern New Mexico. *Sociology and Social Research* 53:455–74.

———, ed. 1976. *Spanish and Mexican Land Grants in the Southwest: A Symposium*. Fort Collins, CO: The Social Science Journal.

Kojève, Alexandre. 1980. *Introduction to the Reading of Hegel: Lectures on the Phenomenology of Spirit*. Trans. James H. Nichols, Jr. Ithaca, NY: Cornell University Press.

Kosek, Jake. 2004. Deep Roots and Long Shadows: The Cultural Politics of Memory and Longing in Northern New Mexico Environment and Planning. *Society and Space* 22:329–54.

——— 2006. *Understories: The Political Life of Forests in Northern New Mexico*. Durham, NC: Duke University Press.

Kraemer, Paul. 2006. The Dynamic Ethnicity of the People of Spanish Colonial New

Mexico in the Eighteenth Century. In *Transforming Images: New Mexican Santos In-Between Worlds*, ed. Claire Farago and Donna Pierce, 80–98. University Park: Pennsylvania University Press.

Kutsche, Paul. 1976. A New Mexico Test of Modernization Theory. *University of Oklahoma Papers in Anthropology* 17 (2):138–49.

———. 1979. Introduction: Atomism, Factionalism, and Flexibility. *Colorado College Studies* 15:7–19.

———, ed. 1979. *The Survival of Spanish American Villages*. Colorado Springs: Research Committee, Colorado College.

———. 1983. Household and Family in Hispanic Northern New Mexico. *Journal of Comparative Family Studies* 14 (2): 151–65.

———, and John R. Van Ness. 1988. *Cañones: Values, Crisis, and Survival in a Northern New Mexico Village*. Salem, WI: Sheffield Publishing Company.

———. 1981. *Cañones, Values, Crisis, and Survival in a Northern New Mexico Village*. Albuquerque: University of New Mexico Press.

Lamadrid, Enrique R. 1982. Gallos y Gallineros. In *Hispanics of the United States: An Anthology of Creative Literature*, ed. Francisco Jiménez and Gary D. Keller, 62–63. Ypsilanti, MI: Bilingual Review/Press.

———. 1995. The Rogue's Progress: Journeys of the Pícaros from Oral Tradition Contemporary Chicano Literature of New Mexico. *MELUS* 20 (2): 15–34.

———. 1998. Pasó Por Aquí: Jim Sagel 1947 Brush, Colorado—1998 La Joya, New Mexico. *Poetry Flash* 277 (June/July): 6.

———. 2000. Abiquiú: Genízaros and the Price of Freedom. In *Nuevo México Profundo: Rituals of an Indo-Hispano Homeland*, ed. Miguel Gandert and Enrique Lamadrid, 57–58. Santa Fe: Museum of New Mexico Press.

———. 2003. *Hermanitos Comanchitos: Indo-Hispano Rituals of Captivity and Redemption*. Albuquerque: University of New Mexico Press.

Lamar, Howard R. 2000. *The Far Southwest, 1846–1912: A Territorial History*. Rev. ed. Albuquerque: University of New Mexico Press.

Lamphere, Louise, Patricia Zavella, Felipe Gonzales, and Peter B. Evans. 1993. *Sunbelt Working Mothers: Reconciling Family and Factory*. Ithaca, NY: Cornell University Press.

Landen, Michael. 2005. Overview of Drug Overdose Death in New Mexico. In *Drug Abuse Patterns and Trends in New Mexico: September 2004 Proceedings of the New Mexico State Epidemiology Work Group*, ed. Office of Epidemiology, New Mexico Department of Health, 7–9. Santa Fe: New Mexico Department of Health.

The Last Conquistador. 2008. DVD. Directed by John J. Valadez and Cristina Ibarra. Kitchen Sync Group. Wawick, NY.

Lecompte, Janet. 1985. *Rebellion in Rio Arriba 1837*. Albuquerque: University of New Mexico Press.

Lee, Morgan. 2001. Oñate's Foot: A Legend Grows. *Albuquerque Journal*, March 23.

Lende, Daniel H. 2005. Wanting and Drug Use: A Biocultural Approach to the Analysis of Addiction. *Ethos* 33 (1): 100–124.

Lenderman, Andy. 2003a. Bad Image Haunts Town. *Albuquerque Journal, Journal North*, November 6.

———— 2003b. Report: Drug Treatment is Fragmented. *Albuquerque Journal, Journal North*, December 26.

Lewis, Oscar. 1951. *Life in a Mexican Village: Tepoztlán Restudied*. Urbana: University of Illinois Press.

Leyva, Yolanda. 2007. Commemorating and Protesting Oñate on the Border. *New Mexico Historical Review* 82 (3): 317–42.

Lima, Lázaro. 2007. *Crisis Identities in American Literary and Cultural Memory*. New York: NYU Press.

Limón, José E. 1994. *Dancing with the Devil: Society and Cultural Poetics in Mexican-American South Texas*. Madison: University of Wisconsin Press.

———— 1998. *American Encounters: Greater Mexico, the United States, and the Erotics of Culture*. Boston: Beacon Press.

Logghe, Joan, and Jim Sagel. 1993. *What Makes a Woman Beautiful?* Tesuque, NM: Pennywhistle Press.

Lomelí, Francisco A. 2002. Background of New Mexico's Hispanic Literature: Self-Referentiality as a Literary-Historical Discourse. In *Nuevomexicano Cultural Legacy: Forms, Agencies, and Discourse*, ed. Francisco A. Lomelí, V. A. Sorell, and Genaro M. Padilla, 56–69. Albuquerque: University of New Mexico Press.

————, and Donaldo W. Urioste. 1976. *Chicano Perspectives in Literature: A Critical and Annotated Bibliography*. Albuquerque: Pajarito Publications.

————, V. A. Sorell, and Genaro M. Padilla. 2002. Introduction: Beyond the Land of Enchantment. In *Nuevomexicano Cultural Legacy: Forms, Agencies, and Discourse*, ed. Francisco A. Lomelí, V. A. Sorrell, and Genaro M. Padilla, 1–8. Albuquerque: University of New Mexico Press.

————, and Clark A. Colahan, eds. and trans. 2006. *Defying the Inquisition in Colonial New Mexico: Miguel de Quintana's Life and Writings*. Albuquerque: University of New Mexico Press.

López, Antonio. 1998. A Spanish View of History. *Santa Fe New Mexican*, April 19.

López Pulido, Alberto. 2000. *The Sacred World of the Penitentes*. Washington, DC: Smithsonian Institution Press.

Lucero, Helen R. 1986. Hispanic Weavers of North Central New Mexico: Social/Historical and Educational Dimensions of a Continuing Artistic Tradition. PhD diss., University of New Mexico.

————, and Suzanne Baizerman. 1999. *Chimayó Weaving: The Transformation of a Tradition*. Albuquerque: University of New Mexico Press.

Lummis, Charles F. 1893. *The Land of Poco Tiempo.* New York: C. Scribner's Sons.

Marcus, George E. 1998. *Ethnography Through Thick and Thin.* Princeton, NJ: Princeton University Press.

————, ed. 1999. *Critical Anthropology Now: Unexpected Contexts, Shifting Constituencies, Changing Agendas.* Santa Fe: School of American Research Press.

————, and Michael M. J. Fischer. 1986. *Anthropology as Cultural Critique: An Experimental Moment in the Human Sciences.* Chicago: University of Chicago Press.

Marez, Curtis. 2004. *Drug Wars: The Political Economy of Narcotics.* Minneapolis: University of Minnesota Press.

Martin, Arthur. 1998. Enchantment and Colonization: Modernity and Lifestyle Migrants in a New Mexico Town. PhD diss., University of New Mexico.

Martin, Douglas. 2004. Yogi Bhajan, 75, 'Boss' of Worlds Spiritual and Capitalist. *New York Times,* October 9.

Martínez, Gaspar. 2001. *Confronting the Mystery of God: Political, Liberation, and Public Theologies.* New York: Continuum.

Marx, Karl. 1978. The Eighteenth Brumaire of Louis Bonaparte. In The Marx-Engels Reader, 2nd ed. Ed. Robert C. Tucker, 594–617. New York: W. W. Norton and Company.

Masco, Joseph. 2006. The Nuclear Borderlands: The Manhattan Project in Post-Cold War New Mexico. Princeton, NJ: Princeton University Press.

McBrien, Richard P. 1980. *Catholicism.* Minneapolis: Winston Press.

McCarthy, Anna. 2006. From the Ordinary to the Concrete: Cultural Studies and the Politics of Scale. In *Questions of Method in Cultural Studies,* ed. Mimi White and James Schwoch, 21–53. New York: Blackwell.

McGeagh, Robert. 1990. *Juan de Oñate's Colony in the Wilderness: An Early History of the American Southwest.* Santa Fe: Sunstone Press.

McIlvoy, Kevin. 1998. A Dialogue: Rudolfo Anaya/John Nichols. In *Conversations with Rudolfo Anaya,* ed. Bruce Dick and Silvio Sirias, 53–80. Jackson: University of Mississippi Press.

Meinig, D. W. 1984. Rejoinder. *Annals of the Association of American Geographers* 74 (1): 171.

Meléndez, A. Gabriel. 1997. *So All Is Not Lost: The Poetics of Print in Nuevomexicano Communities, 1834–1958.* Albuquerque: University of New Mexico Press.

———— 2002. Contesting Social and Historical Erasure: Membership in La Prensa Asociada Hispano-Americana. In *Nuevomexicano Cultural Legacy: Forms, Agencies, and Discourse,* ed. Francisco A. Lomelí, Víctor A. Sorell, and Genaro M. Padilla, 28–55. Albuquerque: University of New Mexico Press.

———— 2007. Who Are the "Salt of the Earth"? Competing Images of Mexican Americans in Salt of the Earth and And Now, Miguel. In *Expressing New*

Mexico: Nuevomexicano Creativity, Ritual, and Memory, ed. Phillip B. Gonzales, 115–38. Tucson: University of Arizona Press.

——— 2008. Américo Paredes and Angélico Chávez: Sangre, Sotanas, Guitarras y Pistolas on the Camino Real to Aztlán. Paper presented at the Annual Meeting of the American Studies Association, Albuquerque, New Mexico.

Menchaca, Martha. 2002. *Recovering History, Constructing Race: The Indian, Black, and White Roots of Mexican Americans.* Austin: University of Texas Press.

The Milagro Beanfield War. 1988. DVD. Directed by Robert Redford. Universal Studios. Universal City, CA.

Mitchell, Pablo. 2005. *Coyote Nation: Sexuality, Race, and Conquest in Modernizing New Mexico, 1880–1920.* Chicago: University of Chicago Press.

Moffat, Karl F. 2000. Murder on the Road to El Santuario: Suspect Says Murders Were Over Drug Debt, Father Calls Claim Ludicrous, Youths were Special Teens. *Rio Grande Sun*, April 27.

Montgomery, Charles H. 2002. *The Spanish Redemption: Heritage, Power, and Loss on New Mexico's Upper Rio Grande.* Berkeley: University of California Press.

Montiel, Miguel, Tomás Atencio, and E. A. "Tony" Mares. 2009. *Resolana: Emerging Chicano Dialogues on Community and Globalization.* Tucson: University of Arizona Press.

Moore, Frank C. 1947. San Jose, 1946: A Study of Urbanization. PhD diss., University of New Mexico.

Moraga, Cherríe. 2000. *Loving in the War Years/Lo que nunca pasó por sus labios.* Cambridge, MA: South End Press.

———, and Gloria Anzaldúa. 1984. *This Bridge Called My Back: Writings by Radical Women of Color.* 2nd ed. New York: Kitchen Table—Women of Color Press.

Morgan, Kathleen O'Leary, and Scott Morgan. 2002. *Health Care State Rankings 2002: Health Care in the 50 United States.* Lawrence, KS: Morgan Quitno Press.

Morrison, Howard, Richard Ahlborn, Lisa Falk, Hank Grasso, Rayna Green, and Lonn Taylor. 1992. *American Encounters: A Companion to the Exhibition at the National Museum of American History.* Washington DC: Smithsonian Institution Press.

Mullin, Molly H. 2001. *Culture in the Marketplace: Gender, Art, and Value in the American Southwest.* Durham NC: Duke University Press.

Nabokov, Peter. 1969. *Tijerina and the Courthouse Raid.* Albuquerque: University of New Mexico Press.

Nancy, Jean-Luc. 2002. *Hegel: The Restlessness of the Negative.* Minneapolis: University of Minnesota Press.

Nasdijj. 2000. *The Blood Runs Like a River Through My Dreams: A Memoir.* Boston: Houghton Mifflin Company.

———— 2003. *The Boy and the Dog Are Sleeping. New York.* New York: Random House Publishing Group.

———— 2005. *Geronimo's Bones: A Memoir of My Brother and Me.* New York: Random House Publishing Group.

New Mexico Department of Education. 2005. *District Reports—Data Collection.* http://www.ped.state.nm.us/div/ais/data/dcrfactsheets.html (accessed March 18, 2005).

Nichols, John Treadwell. 1974. *The Milagro Beanfield War.* New York: Holt, Rinehart, and Winston.

———— 1978. *The Magic Journey.* New York: Holt, Rinehart, and Winston.

———— 1981. *The Nirvana Blues.* New York: Holt, Rinehart, and Winston.

Nieto-Phillips, John M. 2004. *The Language of Blood: The Making of Spanish-American Identity in New Mexico, 1880s–1930s.* Albuquerque: University of New Mexico Press.

Nora, Pierre. 1989. Between Memory and History: Les Lieux de Mémoire. *Representations* 26:7–24.

Northsun, Nila, Jim Sagel, and Kirk Robertson, eds. 1982. *Small Bones, Little Eyes.* Fallon, NV: Duck Down Press.

Nostrand, Richard L. 1980. The Hispano Homeland in 1900. *Annals of the Association of American Geographers* 70 (3): 382–96.

———— 1981. Comment on Reply (to Hansen). *Annals of the Association of American Geographers* 71 (2): 161–69.

———— 1992. *The Hispano Homeland.* Norman: University of Oklahoma Press.

Ochoa, Gilda L. 2004. *Becoming Neighbors in a Mexican American Community: Power, Conflict, and Solidarity.* Austin: University of Texas Press.

Office of Epidemiology, New Mexico Department of Health, ed. 2005. *Drug Abuse Patterns and Trends in New Mexico: September 2004 Proceedings of the New Mexico State Epidemiology Work Group.* Albuquerque: New Mexico Department of Health.

Omi, Michael, and Howard Winant. 1994. *Racial Formation in the United States: From the 1960s to the 1990s.* 2nd ed. New York: Routledge.

Ortiz, Alfonso. 1969. *The Tewa World: Space, Time, Being, & Becoming in a Pueblo Society.* Chicago: University of Chicago Press.

———— 1988. Indian/White Relations: A View from the Other Side of the "Frontier." In *Indians in American History: An Introduction,* ed. Frederick E. Hoxie, 1–16. Arlington Heights, IL: Harlan Davidson, Inc.

———— 2009. Popay's Leadership: A Pueblo Perspective on the 1680 Revolt. In *Telling New Mexico: A New History,* ed. Marta Weigle with Frances Levine and Louise Stiver, 107–13. Santa Fe: Museum of New Mexico Press.

Ortner, Sherry. 1998. Identities: The Hidden Life of Class. *Journal of Anthropological Research* 54 (1): 1–17.

Pacheco, Ana. 2004. G. Benito Córdova. *La Herencia* 41 (Spring): 8–9.

Paredes, Américo. 1993. Folk Medicine and the Intercultural Jest. In *Folklore and Culture on the Texas—Mexican Border*, ed. Richard Bauman, 49–72. Austin: CMAS Books.

———, and Raymund Paredes. 1976. *Mexican-American Authors*. Boston: Houghton Mifflin Co.

Parsons, Jack, and Jim Sagel. 1990. *Straight from the Heart: Portraits of Traditional Hispanic Musicians*. Albuquerque: University of New Mexico Press.

———, Carmella Padilla, and Juan Estevan Arellano. 1999. *Low 'N Slow: Lowriding in New Mexico*. Santa Fe: Museum of New Mexico Press.

Paz, Octavio. 1985. *The Labyrinth of Solitude and Other Writings*. New York: Grove Press.

Penland, Paige R. 2003. *Lowrider: History, Pride, Culture*. Saint Paul, MN: Motorbooks International.

——— 2004. *Santa Fe and Taos*. Footscray, Australia: Lonely Planet Publications.

Pérez, Frank G., and Carlos F. Ortega. 2008. Mediated Debate, Historical Framing, and Public Art: The Juan de Oñate Controversy in El Paso. *Aztlán: A Journal of Chicano Studies* 33 (2): 121–40.

Pérez-Torres, Rafael. 2006. *Mestizaje: Critical Uses of Race in Chicano Culture*. Minneapolis: University of Minnesota Press.

Peterson, Iver. 1984. Española, N.M., Embraces Española Jokes and Laughs Last. *New York Times*, May 22.

Pihl, Robert O., and Jordan B. Peterson. 1995. Alcoholism: The Role of Different Motivational Systems. *Journal of Psychiatry and Neuroscience* 20:372–96.

Policarpio Valencia Folder. N.d. E. Boyd Collection. New Mexico State Records Center, Santa Fe.

Preble, Edward, and John J. Casey. 1969. Taking Care of Business—The Heroin Addict's Life on the Street. *International Journal of the Addictions* 4:1–24.

Pulido, Laura. 1996. *Environmentalism and Economic Justice: Two Chicano Struggles in the Southwest*. Tucson: University of Arizona Press.

Quintana, Frances Leon. 1991. *Pobladores: Hispanic Americans of the Ute Frontier*. South Bend, IN: University of Notre Dame Press.

Rabinow, Paul, and George E. Marcus, with James D. Faubion and Tobias Rees. 2008. *Designs for an Anthropology of the Contemporary*. Durham, NC: Duke University Press.

Radin, Paul. 1956. *The Trickster: A Study in American Indian Mythology*. New York: Schhocken Books.

Rael, Juan Bautista. 1951. *The New Mexican Alabado*. Stanford: Stanford University Press.

Rael-Gálvez, Estevan. 2002. Identifying Captivity and Capturing Identity: Narratives of American Indian Slavery. Colorado and New Mexico, 1776–1934. PhD diss., University of Michigan.

Ravenscroft, Alison. 2003. A Picture in Black and White: Modernism, Postmodernism, and the Scene of 'Race.' *Australian Feminist Studies* 18 (42): 233–44.

Redfield, Robert. 1930. *Tepoztlán, a Mexican Village: A Study of Folk Life.* Chicago: University of Chicago Press.

Reed, Maureen. 2005. *A Woman's Place: Women Writing New Mexico.* Albuquerque: University of New Mexico Press.

Reich, Alice Higman. 1977. The Cultural Production of Ethnicity. PhD diss., University of Colorado, Boulder.

Reichelt, Lauren. 2001. *Substance Abuse, Culture and Economics in Rio Arriba County, Northern New Mexico: An Analysis of Impacts and Root Causes.* Española, NM: Rio Arriba Department of Health and Human Services.

Rio Arriba: Tragedy and Hope. 2000. VHS. Directed by Joe Day and Manuel Machuca. Santa Fe: Daylight Productions.

Robins, Lee N. 1974. *The Vietnam War Drug User Returns.* SAODAP Monograph. Washington, DC: GPO.

Robinson, Terry E., and Kent C. Berridge. 1993. The Neural Basis of Drug Craving: An Incentive-Sensitization Theory of Addiction. *Brain Research-Brain Research Reviews* 18:247–91.

Rodríguez, Sylvia. 1987. Land, Water, and Ethnic Identity in Taos. In *Land, Water, and Culture: New Perspectives on Hispanic Land Grants*, ed. Charles L. Briggs and J. R. Van Ness, 313–403. Albuquerque: University of New Mexico Press.

——— 1989. Art, Tourism, and Race Relations in Taos: Toward a Sociology of the Art Colony. *Journal of Anthropological Research* 45 (1): 77–89.

——— 1992. The Hispano Homeland Debate Revisited. *Perspectives in Mexican-American Studies* 3:95–114.

——— 1994. The Tourist Gaze, Gentrification, and the Commodification of Subjectivity in Taos. In *Essays on the Changing Images of the Southwest*, ed. Richard Francaviglia and David Narrett, 105–26. College Station: University of Texas at Arlington / Texas A&M University Press.

——— 1996. *The Matachines Dance: Ritual Symbolism and Interethnic Relations in the Upper Rio Grande Valley.* Albuquerque: University of New Mexico Press.

——— 1998. Fiesta Time and Plaza Space. *Journal of American Folklore* 111 (439): 39.

——— 2001. Tourism, Whiteness, and the Vanishing Anglo. In *Seeing and Being Seen: Tourism in the American West*, ed. David M. Wrobel and Patrick T. Long, 194–210. Lawrence: University Press of Kansas.

——— 2003. Tourism, Difference, and Power in the Borderlands. In *The Culture of Tourism, the Tourism of Culture: Selling the Past to the Present in the American Southwest*, ed. Hal K. Rothman, 185–205. Albuquerque: University of New Mexico Press.

——— 2007. Honor, Aridity, and Place. In *Expressing New Mexico: Nuevomexicano*

Creativity, Ritual, and Memory, ed. Phillip B. Gonzales, 25–41. Tucson: University of Arizona Press.

Rodríguez Aranda, Pilar. 2003. *The Unexpected Turn of Jim Sagel: La Vuelta Inesperada de Jim Sagel*. VHS. Santa Fe: Anaraca Films.

Romero, Brenda Mae. 1993. The Matachines Music and Dance in San Juan Pueblo and Alcalde, New Mexico: Contexts and Meanings. PhD diss., University of California, Los Angeles.

———. 2006. Sound, Image, and Identity: The Matachines Dance Across Borders. In *Transforming Images: New Mexico Santos In-Between Worlds*, ed. Claire Farago and Donna Pierce, 187–91. University Park: Pennsylvania University Press.

———. 2007. *La Dance Matachines* as New Mexican Heritage. In *Expressing New Mexico: Nuevomexicano Creativity, Ritual, and Memory*, ed. Phillip B. Gonzales, 61–83. Tucson: University of Arizona Press.

Rubright, Lynnell. 1967. A Sequent Occupance of the Española Valley, New Mexico. Master's thesis, University of Colorado, Boulder.

Sabatini, Rafael. 1921. *Scaramouche: A Romance of the French Revolution*. Boston: New York: Houghton Mifflin Company.

Sagel, Jim. 1976. Rebuilt. Master's thesis, University of New Mexico.

———. 1980. *Hablando de brujas y la gente de antes*. Austin, TX: Place of the Herons Press.

———. 1981. *Foreplay and French Fries*. San Jose, CA: Mango Publications.

———. 1983. *Túnomas Honey*. Ypsilanti, MI: Bilingual Press/Editorial Bilingüe.

———. 1984. *Los cumpleaños de Doña Agueda*. Austin, TX: Place of the Herons Press.

———. 1988. *Sabelotodo entiendelonada*. Tempe, AZ: Bilingual Press/Editorial Bilingüe.

———. 1990. *On the Make Again: Otra vez en la movida*. Santa Maria, CA: Archer Books.

———. 1991. *Más que No Love It*. Albuquerque: West End Press.

———. 1992. *Dancing to Pay the Light Bill: Essays on New Mexico and the Southwest*. Santa Fe: Red Crane Books.

———. 1993. *Where the Cinnamon Winds Blow/Donde Soplan Los Vientos de Canela*. Minneapolis: Sagebrush Education Resources.

———. 1994. *Remedios: Poemas curativas*. Caracas, Venezuela: Editorial la Espada Rota.

———. 1996a. *El santo queso/The Holy Cheese*. Albuquerque: University of New Mexico Press.

———. 1996b. *Garden of Stories/Jardín de cuentos*. Santa Fe: Red Crane Books.

———. 1997a. *Choque*. Córdova, Argentina: Ediciones Radamanto, Plaquetas del Herrero.

———. 1997b. *Doña Refugio y su comadre*. San Sebastián, Spain: Kutxa Fundazioa/Fundación.

——— 1997c. My Real Education. Commencement speech for University of New Mexico, Los Alamos. Box 87, Jim Sagel Papers. Benson Latin American Collection, University of Texas Libraries, University of Texas at Austin.

——— 1997d. *Unexpected Turn*. Albuquerque: University of New Mexico Press.

——— 1998a. *Always the Heart/Siempre el corazón*. Santa Fe: Red Crane Books.

——— 1998b. *Remedios e irremediables: Remedies and the Remediless*. Mexico City: Papeles Privados.

——— N.d.a. Bisbee. Box 76, Jim Sagel Papers. Benson Latin American Collection, University of Texas Libraries, University of Texas at Austin.

——— N.d.b. Corozonazos: Poemas por Jim Sagel. Box 59–61, Jim Sagel Papers. Benson Latin American Collection, University of Texas Libraries, University of Texas at Austin.

Saldívar, Ramón. 2006. *The Borderlands of Culture: Américo Paredes and the Transnational Imaginary*. Durham, NC: Duke University Press.

Sánchez, Christopher. 2006. Provost Candidate Defends his Book: Ramón Gutiérrez's Ability to Run Diverse University Questioned. http://media.www.dailylobo.com/media/storage/paper344/news/2006/03/06/News/Provost.Candidate.Defends.His.Book-1656367.shtml (accessed July 12, 2007).

Sánchez, George Isidore. 1940. *Forgotten People: A Study of New Mexicans*. Albuquerque: University of New Mexico Press.

Sánchez, Joseph P. 1990. *The Spanish Black Legend: Origins of Anti-Hispanic Stereotypes/La Leyenda Negra Española: Orígenes de los Estereotipos Antihispánicos*. Albuquerque: National Park Service, Spanish Colonial Research Center.

Santa Fe Reporter. 1998. Proud Actions. September 9.

Santiago, Danny. 1983. *Famous All Over Town*. New York: Simon and Schuster.

Santiago-Irizarry, Vilma. 1996. Culture as Cure. *Cultural Anthropology* 11 (1): 3–24.

Saunders, Lyle. 1954. *Cultural Difference and Medical Care*. New York: Russell Sage Foundation.

Scharmen, Thomas N., Lisa Roth-Edwards, and Nina Shah. 2005. Drug Overdose Deaths in New Mexico's Public Heath Districts: 1995–2003. In *Drug Abuse Patterns and Trends in New Mexico: September 2004 Proceedings of the New Mexico State Epidemiology Work Group*, ed. Office of Epidemiology, New Mexico Department of Health, 10–15. Santa Fe: New Mexico Department of Health.

Schroeder, Albert H. 1972. Rio Grande Ethnohistory. In *New Perspectives on Pueblos*, ed. Alfonso Ortiz, 41–70. Albuquerque: University of New Mexico Press.

Shadow, Robert D., and Maria J. Rodríguez-Shadow. 1994. Clase y etnicidad entre los rancheros mexicanos del norte de Nuevo México. In *Rancheros y sociedades rancheras*, ed. Esteban Barragán, Odile Hoffman, Thierry Linck, and David Skerritt, 153–71. Zamora, Mexico: CEMCA, Colegio de Michoacán.

———. 1997. Rancheros, Land, and Ethnicity on the Northern Borderlands: Works on Social and Agrarian History in the Last Decade. *Latin American Research Review* 32 (1): 171–98.

———. 1998, Rituales y símbolos de identidad étnica entre los mexicanos del norte de Nuevo México. *Antropología* 49:27.

Simmons, Marc. 1984. Rejoinder. *Annals of the Association of American Geographers* 74 (1): 169–70.

———. 1993. *The Last Conquistador: Juan de Oñate and the Settling of the Far Southwest.* Norman: University of Oklahoma Press.

Singer, Merrill. 2008. *Drugging the Poor: Legal and Illegal Drugs and Social Inequality.* Long Grove, IL: Waveland Press.

Spicer, Edward H. 1962. *Cycles of Conquest: The Impact of Spain, Mexico, and the United States on the Indians of the Southwest, 1533–1960.* Tucson: University of Arizona Press.

Spinks, C. W. 2001. Trickster and Duality. In *Trickster and Ambivalence: Dance of Differentiation*, ed. C. W. Spinks, 7–19. Madison, WI: Atwood Publishing.

Steel, Thomas J., SJ. 1978. The Spanish Passion Play in New Mexico. *New Mexico Historical Review* 53 (3): 239–59.

Stewart, Kathleen. 1996. *A Space on the Side of the Road: Cultural Poetics in an Other America.* Princeton, NJ: Princeton University Press.

———. 2000. Real American Dreams (Can Be Nightmares). In *Cultural Studies and Political Theory*, ed. Jodi Dean, 243–56. Ithaca, NY: Cornell University Press.

———. 2007. *Ordinary Affects.* Durham, NC: Duke University Press.

Stocking, Jr., George W. 1989a. The Ethnographic Sensibility of the 1920s and Dualism of the Anthropological Tradition. In *Romantic Motives: Essays on Anthropological Sensibility*, George W. Stocking, Jr., 208–76. Madison: University of Wisconsin Press.

———. 1989b. Romantic Motives and the History of Anthropology. In *Romantic Motives: Essays on Anthropological Sensibility*, ed. George W. Stocking, Jr., 3–9. Madison: University of Wisconsin Press.

Strong, Pauline Turner. 1999. *Captive Selves, Captivating Others: The Politics and Poetics of Colonial American Captivity Narratives.* Boulder: Westview Press.

Swadesh, Frances Leon. 1968. The Alianza Movement: Catalyst for Social Change in New Mexico. Proceedings of the 1968 Annual Spring Meeting of the American Ethnological Society, 162–77.

———. 1974. *Los Primeros Pobladores: Hispanic Americans of the Ute Frontier.* South Bend, IN: University of Notre Dame Press.

Taussig, Michael. 1983. *The Devil and Commodity Fetishism in South America.* Chapel Hill: University of North Carolina Press.

———. 1987. *Shamanism, Colonialism, and the Wild Man: A Study in Terror and Healing.* Chicago: University of Chicago Press.

———. 1999. *Defacement: Public Secrecy and the Labor of the Negative.* Stanford, CA: Stanford University.

———. 2004. *My Cocaine Museum.* Chicago: University of Chicago Press.

———. 2006. *Walter Benjamin's Grave.* Chicago: University of Chicago Press.

Thompson, Ginger. 2002. As Sculpture Takes Shape in Mexico, Opposition Takes Shape in the U.S. *New York Times,* January 17.

Tijerina, Reies López. 1978. *Mi Lucha por la Tierra.* Mexico City: Fondo de Cultura Económica.

———. 2000. *They Called Me "King Tiger": My Struggle for the Land and our Rights.* Houston: Arte Público Press.

Toomey, Don. 2002. Teresa Archuleta Sagel. *Tradición Revista* 7 (2): 64–69.

Torres, Edén E. 2003. *Chicana Without Apology/Chicana Sin Vergüenza: The New Chicana Cultural Studies.* New York: Routledge.

Tracy, Sarah W., and Caroline Jean Acker, eds. 2004. *Altering American Consciousness: The History of Alcohol and Drug Use in the United States, 1800–2000.* Amherst: University of Massachusetts Press.

Trujillo, Michael L. 1998. Tierra Amarilla, Reterritorialization, and Place: Imagining the Borderlands. Master's thesis, University of Texas at Austin.

———. 2000. Anglo Environmentalists in a Chicano Homeland. Paper presented at the Annual Meeting of the American Ethnological Society, Tampa, Florida.

———. 2002. A New Mexico "Fix": Shooting Up and Coming Down in the Greater Española Valley. Paper presented at the Annual Meeting of the American Anthropological Association, New Orleans, Louisiana.

———. 2006. A Northern New Mexico "Fix": Shooting Up and Coming Down in the Greater Española Valley. *Cultural Dynamics* 18 (1): 89–112.

———. 2008. Oñate's Foot: Remembering and Dismembering in Northern New Mexico. *Aztlán: A Journal of Chicano Studies* 33 (2): 91–119.

———, and Cathleen E. Willging. 2005. "All Our Pain Gone": Comorbidity and Poly Drug Use in North Central New Mexico." Paper presented at the Annual Meeting of the American Society for Applied Anthropology, Santa Fe, New Mexico.

Twitchell, Ralph Emerson. 1909. *The History of the Military Occupation of the Territory of New Mexico from 1846 to 1851 by the Government of the United States Together with Biographical Sketches of Men Prominent in the Conduct of the Government During that Period.* Denver: Smith-Brooks Company.

U.S. Bureau of the Census. 1995. 1990 Census Lookup. http://venus.census.gov/cdrom/lookup (accessed February 7, 2000).

———— 2005. American Fact Finder, Española Urban Cluster Tables. http://factfinder.census.gov/servlet/DTSubjectShowTablesServlet?_ts= 129237448588 (accessed June 5, 2005).

U.S. Congress. Senate. Committee on Appropriations. Subcommittee on Commerce, Justice, State, the Judiciary, and Related Agencies. 1999. Rio Arriba County Strategy to Combat Heroin Addiction: Hearing before a Subcommittee of the Committee on Appropriations. 106th Cong., 1st sess., Special Hearing. Washington DC: U.S. Government Printing Office.

Usner, Donald J. 1996. *Sabino's Map: Life in Chimayó's Old Plaza*. Santa Fe: Museum of New Mexico Press.

———— 2001. *Benigna's Chimayó: Cuentos from the Old Plaza*. Santa Fe: Museum of New Mexico Press.

Valdez, Facundo. 1979. Vergüenza. *Colorado College Studies* 15:99–106.

Valdez, Luis. 1992. *Zoot Suit and Other Plays*. Houston: Arte Público Press.

Valencia, Paul. 2002. Interview by author. Española, New Mexico, August 14.

Valle, Victor M., and Rodolfo D. Torres. 2000. *Latino Metropolis*. Minneapolis: University of Minnesota Press.

Van Ness, John. 1976. Spanish American vs. Anglo American Land Tenure and the Study of Economic Change in New Mexico. *Social Science Journal* 13 (3): 45–51.

———— 1979. Hispanic Village Organization in Northern New Mexico: Corporate Community Structure in Historical and Comparative Perspective. *Colorado College Studies* 15:21–44.

————, and Christine M. Van Ness, eds. 1980. *Spanish and Mexican Land Grants in New Mexico and Colorado*. Manhattan, KS: Sunflower University Press.

Vigil, James Diego. 1988. *Barrio Gangs: Street Life and Identity in Southern California*. Austin: University of Texas Press.

Vila, Pablo. 2000. *Crossing Borders, Reinforcing Borders: Social Categories, Metaphors, and Narrative Identities on the U.S.-Mexico Frontier*. Austin: University of Texas Press.

Villagrá, Gaspar Pérez de. 1933. *Historia de la Nueva México/History of New Mexico*. Los Angeles: Quivira Society.

———— 1992. *Historia de la Nueva México, 1610: A Critical and Annotated Spanish/English Edition*. Albuquerque: University of New Mexico Press.

Waggoner, Laura. 1941. San Jose: A Study of Urbanization. Master's thesis, University of New Mexico.

Wallerstein, Immanuel Maurice. 1974. The Rise and Future Demise of the World-Capitalist System. *Comparative Studies* 16:387–415.

———— 1979. *The Capitalist World-Economy*. Cambridge: Cambridge University Press.

Walter, Paul A. F. 1938. A Study of Isolation and Social Change in Three Spanish
      Speaking Villages of New Mexico. PhD diss., Stanford University.

Ward, Dave. 2002. Interview by author. Española, New Mexico, January 2002.

Weber, David J. 1982. *The Mexican Frontier 1821–1846: The American Southwest Under
      Mexico*. Albuquerque: University of New Mexico Press.

Weigle, Marta, ed. 1975. *Hispanic Villages of Northern New Mexico: A Reprint of
      Volume II of the 1935 Tewa Basin Study, with Supplementary Materials*. Santa
      Fe: Lightning Tree.

——— 1976. *Brothers of Light, Brothers of Blood: The Penitentes of the
      Southwest*. Albuquerque: University of New Mexico Press.

——— 2007. *A Penitente Bibliography*. Santa Fe: Sunstone Press.

———, Claudia Larcombe, and Samuel Larcombe, eds. 1983. *Hispanic Arts and
      Ethnohistory in the Southwest: New Papers Inspired by the Work of E. Boyd*.
      Santa Fe: Ancient City Press.

———, and Kyle Fiore. 1994. *Santa Fe and Taos: The Writer's Era, 1916–1941*. Santa
      Fe: Ancient City Press.

Westphall, Victor. 1983. *Mercedes Reales: Hispanic Land Grants of the Upper Rio Grande
      Region*. Albuquerque: University of New Mexico Press.

Weyerman, D. 2000. Chimayó's Curse: Rural NM City, Long Held in Deadly Grip
      of Heroin, Wages a Battle to Break Free. *Dallas Morning News*, April 17.

White, Hayden. 1978. The Forms of Wildness: Archaeology of an Idea. In *Tropics
      of Discourse: Essays in Cultural Criticism*, 150–82. Baltimore: The Johns
      Hopkins University Press.

Whitecotton, Joseph W. 1970. The Social History of a New Mexican Region: A
      Preliminary Analysis. *University of Oklahoma Papers in Anthropology*
      10:1–20.

——— 1976. Tradition and Modernity in Northern New Mexico. *University of
      Oklahoma Papers in Anthropology* 17 (2): 121–37.

——— 1996. Ethnic Groups and Ethnicity in Southern Mexico and Northern
      New Mexico: A Historical Comparison of the Valley of Oaxaca and the
      Española Valley. In *The Politics of Ethnicity in Southern Mexico*, ed. Howard
      Campbell, 1–32. Nashville: Vanderbilt University.

Willging, Cathleen E., Michael Trujillo, and W. Azul La Luz. 2003. *Final Report:
      Ethnography of Drug Use, Help-Seeking Processes, and Behavioral Health Care
      Needs*. Santa Fe: New Mexico Department of Health and Health Policy
      Commission.

——— 2004. Ethnography of Drug Use and Barriers to Care in the Española
      Valley of New Mexico. *New Mexico Epidemiology Report* 5:1–3.

——— 2005. Ethnography of Drug Use and Barriers to Care in the Española
      Valley of New Mexico. In *Drug Abuse Patterns and Trends in New Mexico:
      September 2004 Proceedings of the New Mexico State Epidemiology Work Group*,

ed. Office of Epidemiology, New Mexico Department of Health, 35–37. Santa Fe: New Mexico Department of Health.

Williams, Gerry. 1985. Dependency Formations and the Spanish-American Community: An Interpretative and Theoretical Study of Modernization in New Mexico. PhD diss., University of Oklahoma.

Williams, Raymond. 1977. *Marxism and Literature*. Oxford: Oxford University Press.

Williams, Terry. 1993. *Crackhouse: Notes From the End of the Line*. New York: Viking Penguin.

Wilson, Chris. 1997. *The Myth of Santa Fe: Creating a Modern Regional Tradition*. Albuquerque: University of New Mexico Press.

Winn, Russell. 2005. Drug Use Among Arrestees in Rio Arriba County, New Mexico. In *Drug Abuse Patterns and Trends in New Mexico: September 2004 Proceedings of the New Mexico State Epidemiology Work Group*, ed. Office of Epidemiology, New Mexico Department of Health, 47–46. Santa Fe: New Mexico Department of Health.

Zavella, Patricia. 1997. Feminist Insider Dilemmas: Constructing Ethnic Identity with "Chicana" Informants. In *Situated Lives: Gender and Culture in Everyday Life*, ed. Louise Lamphere, Helena Ragone, and Patricia Zavella, 42–61. New York: Routledge.

Zinberg, Norman E. 1984. *Drug, Set, and Setting: The Basis for Controlled Intoxicant Use*. New Haven, CT: Yale University Press.

Žižek, Slavoj. 1993. *Tarrying with the Negative: Kant, Hegel, and the Critique of Ideology*. Durham, NC: Duke University Press.

———. 1999. *The Žižek Reader*. Ed. Elizabeth Wright and Edmond Wright. Malden, MA: Blackwell.

———. 2001. *The Fragile Absolute: Or, Why is the Christian Legacy Worth Fighting For?* New York: Verso.

Index

Page numbers in italic text indicate illustrations.

Abeyta, Bernardo, 61, 62
Abiquiú, 189–90; ritual enactment
   of capture/ransom/incorporation,
   199–200, 228n6
abuelo (elder), *201–3*, 203–5, 228n10;
   Archuleta, Jacobo, 161–68
acculturation, 116, 118, 119–20, 186. *See
   also* assimilation, structural
Acoma Pueblo, 217n3; Oñate's
   expedition to, 1, 29, 32–34. *See also*
   Friends of Acoma
adobe building, 196–97. *See also* "The
   Perfect Wall"
African American, 115
agropastoral economy: loss of, 9, 11,
   86–90, 100–102, 116, 142, 215n12,
   226n7; Valencia's references to, 127,
   137–40

alabado (hymn), 137
Alamo, 36–37, 50. *See also* Los Alamos;
   Los Alamos National Laboratory
Albuquerque, 41, 50–51
Albuquerque Journal, 31, 53–54, 63, 217n1
Alcalde, 196; *matachines* dance/ritual
   enactment, 200, *201–3*, 204
allegory: Christian: suffering and
   redemption, 58, 153, 211–12;
   contemporary: Martínez and
   Castañón's Passion, 63–69; Oñate's
   Passion, 69–72, *71*; in Valencia's work,
   128–29, 151–55
Anglo, as problematic term, 217n4
Anglo-American worldview, xvi, 36,
   38–39, 44–47, 50, 123, 210, 218n10;
   on craft production, 134; "cultural
   abyss," 100, 105–6, 116; exotic/pristine

New Mexico, 101, 123, 133–34, 160; "*Salvador*" v. ideals of, 191; village culture as barrier to assimilation, 98, 100. *See also* ethnographic studies; Eurocentric history/thinking

annexation, 9–10, 26–27, 50, 127. *See also* land rights

anthropological works, 96, 222*n*1, 223*nn*3–5

Anzaldúa, Gloria, 228*n*7

Archuleta, Jacobo, 161–68

Archuleta, Teresa, 26, 156, 161–68, 227*n*13, 227*nn*5–6; "Crista," 163–65, *164*; works of dialectical tension, 180–81, *181*

Arellano, Juan Estevan, 16, 48, 54, 55, 217*n*2, 219*n*13; on Oñate statue, 46–47, 55–56

Arroyo Seco, *2*

assimilation, structural: Jiménez Núñez's studies, 111–13, 116, 118; Rodríguez on identity formation v., 14–15, 100, 113–14, 216*nn*16–17, 218*n*10; village culture as barrier to, 98, 100; Whitecotton's studies, 112–13

Atencio, Tomás, 154

Baizerman, Suzanne, 133–34

Bakhtin, Mikhail, 17–18; on folkloric inversion of dominant ideal, 185, 197, 200, 204

Barela, Patrociño, 141, 225*n*6

Barrus, Timothy "Nasdijj," 218*n*8

Bayo Canyon, 195–96

Benjamin, Walter, 46; on "trance" from drug use, 80

Big Dreams and Dark Secrets in Chimayó (Córdova), 183–84; Catholicism in, 200, 204, 206–7; Española Valley in,

185–86; *genízaro* "Salvador" in, 186–87, 197–99; healing dirt and regenerative water in, 190–91; Santuario de Chimayó in, 189–90; sociocultural transformation, 186; spiritual geography of, 189, 205–8; subversive humor in, 183–85, 197–99, 207–8; trickster as social critique, 191, 204–6; two tracks in, 206

"Billy Bob Buford," 188

bitterness, time of, 122, 125

Black Legend, 45

"Blanca Flor," 188, 189

Bond, Frank, sheep-raising system of, 142–43

borracho perdido (hopeless drunk), 15, 200

Boyd, E., 130–31, 135, 137, 149–50, 225*n*4

Briggs, Charles, 96, 133–34, 222*n*2, 224*nn*8–9; village culture recast, 97–107, 120–23

"The Brown Buzzard," 188

bulletproof person, 93–95

Bustamante, Adrián, 39–40

caballero (horseman/gentleman), 102

California, 12; *cholo*, 214*n*2; colonization, 43; Regents of University of California, 192

Calloway, Larry, 31–32, 217*n*1

Cañones: Values, Crisis, and Survival in a Northern New Mexico Village (Kutsche and Van Ness), 102–3, 104–7

Cañones village, 96, 98, *99*, 102–3, 106

capitalist economy, 105–6, 113–15, 155; contradictions of late, 94–95, 102–3

"Carlisle Esmithenburgestein Johnson," 188

casino industry, 9, 12, *110*

casta (caste), 39–40

Castañón, Karen, 58, 63–69

castration: *matachines* dance ritual enactment of, 200, *201–3*, 204; "Salvador's" firing and mock, 192–93, 200

Catholic Church/Catholicism, *60*, 226*n*10; in *Big Dreams and Dark Secrets*, 200, 204, 206–7; Friends of Acoma to, 49; source of Valencia's moral order/ continuity, 134–45, 137; Virgin Mary, 51, *212*

Cerny, Charlene, 15–16, 129, 134, 146–47

Chávez, Angélico, 225*n*3

Chávez, Lisa, 82

Chicana/o identity/culture, 28–29, 43, 47; pocho and pachuco, 204–5; problematic terminology, 41–43, 217*nn*4–5; Sagel's status in, 171–73; sociolinguistic, 114–15, 117, 223*n*7; trickster tales, 204–5

Chicana/o movement, 48, 96, 117, 154; land-grant activists' courthouse raid, 47

Chicanesque literature, 227*n*12

Chicano Satire: A Study in Literary Culture (Hernández), 191, 204

Chimayó, 57, 124, *125*, 133–34, 215*n*11; home of "Salvador 'Flaco' Cascabel Natividad," 188; Santo Niño *bulto* at, 61–62; El Señor de Esquípulas at, 61, 218*n*1; wisdom from, 189–90, 198–99

Chimayoso, 192, 193

choice, exercise of, 198–99, 207–8, 228*n*7

cholo, 16, 77, 214*n*2; Marco Cholo, 1–2, 3–4, 18, 23

Christianity: suffering and redemption, 58, 153, 211–12. *See also* Catholic Church/Catholicism

cigarettes, 222*n*12

Cisneros, Sandra, 205

Clinton, Hillary Rodham, 115

clowns, Pueblo, 204–5, 218*n*10

Cobos, Rubén, xv, 137

cocaine, 77, 221*n*7

colcha embroidery, 131, 144, 149–50

Colombia, 216*n*19

colonialism, in New Mexico: *casta*, 39–40; gendered domination, 43; slaving economy, 39, 56, 199–200

colonizing myths, 21, 32; Pueblos' resilience/endurance v., 34–35

Colorado, 214*n*4, 226*n*7

Competence in Performance: The Creativity of Tradition in Mexicano Verbal Art (Briggs), 98, 103–7, 122–23

Conejos county, 214*n*4

confession: Herrera's, 67–69, 219*n*5; LANL's v. "Salvador's," 195–96

conquistadors, 44–47. *See also* don Juan de Oñate Monument and Visitors Center; Oñate, don Juan de

contradictions: drug use "fixing" of, 91–95; New Mexico's reality as, 186, 209; socioeconomic, 94–95, 102–3; trickster tales illuminating, 183–85, 197–99; Valencia's working through of, 148, 151–55; women's identities having, 85

Coole, Diana, 18–19, 23, 209, 211, 216*n*18

Córdova, G. Benito, 16–17, 26, 40; Abiquiú and genízaro ancestry of, 199–200, 228*n*6; *Big Dreams and Dark Secrets*, 183–200, 204–8; on LANL's toxic waste, 195–96; Marco Cholo joke, 1–2, 3–4, 18, 23; on *matachines*, 228*n*9; "The Perfect Wall," 183–84, 193–94; satiric humor, 195–97; "think in reverse," 183, 207

Córdova village, 96, 98–106, *99*

Cortés, Manuel, 219*n*13

Costilla county, 214*n*4

"*coyote*" (Anglo and Hispano parentage), 223n5

coyotes, 204

coyote tricksters, 204–5, 228n10

Coyote village, 102, 121, 162

crack cocaine, 84–85

criollos (Spaniards born in New World), 44

"Crista" (Archuleta), 163–65, *164*

Cuartocentenario, 29, 32–34

"Cultural Studies and the Politics of Scale" (McCarthy), 107–8

culture loss, 86–90, 100–101, 124–25

culture reinvention, 184–85

The 3 1/2 Cultures of Española (Córdova), 183

Dávalos, Karen Mary, 191, 228n7

Day, Joe, 63

defacement, 22–23, 52–53

Defacement: Public Secrecy and the Labor of the Negative (Taussig), 52

DeKoven, Marianne, 157

Denver and Rio Grande Railway, 10, 108

descansos (markers for accident victims), 72–73

despedimiento (farewell, sung at wakes for dead), 137

dismemberment, of Oñate statue, 28–29, 217n1; Friends of Acoma on, 27, 31–32, 35–36; options for statue's foot, 48–52

"Divorce" (Archuleta), 180–81, *181*

don Juan de Oñate Monument and Visitors Center, *31*, 55, 186; allegory of The Passion, 69–72, *71*; in El Paso, 210n12; Friends of Acoma deconstructing, 50; reframed in

Chicano and Hispanic terms, 47–48, 213

Douglas, Mary, 17

Down AKA Kilo, 214n2

"drug of choice," 78–79, 221n5

drug use/addiction: "because I like it," 74–86; from "culture loss," 86–90; "drug(s) of choice," 78–79, 221n5; "fixing" the contradictions, 91–95; Hegel on fulfilling desires v., 75–76; overdose deaths, xii, 3, 75, 76–77, 221n4; as passive v. active mentality, 79–86; as transgenerational tradition, 95

duende (goblin), 188, 206

El Borracho dance, 200

El Cerro de los Pedernales, 189–90, 228n3

Ellis, Richard Stewart, 96, 106–18, 123–26

El Paso, 50–51, 210n12

Embudo, battles at, 219n13

Emery, Irene, 132, 144–45, 153, 226n8

employment, 11, 226n7; Española: reservoir of cheap labor, 14, 142, 226n7; LANL hierarchy, 191–92; loss of agropastoral, 9, 11, 86–90, 100–102, 116, 142, 215n12, 226n7; "Wilhelm Hightower" firing of "Salvador," 192–93; working-class, 9, 10, 11, 14

Española (city): Americanness in, 119–20; "anti-Santa Fe," 8–15; ethnography, 106–18, 123–26; Jiménez Núñez on, 120; Main Street, *110*; as reservoir of cheap labor, 14, 142, 226n7; Spanish v. English language, 111–12; Valencia's embroidering, 129–30

Española High School, 223n4, 223n7

Española Valley, *13*; *Big Dreams and Dark Secrets* sites, 185–86; commemorative fiesta, *19*, *20*, 29–32, 51–52, *71*; drug use v. transformation of, 74–75; economy, 11–12, 14, 76, 142–43; ethnographic studies, 96; fear of toxic waste contamination, 195–96; geography, 6; jokes about, 15–18; *matachines* dance/ritual enactment, 200; Rubright on, 6, 214*n*5; social geography, 5–10

Española Valley School District, 98, 215*n*8, 219*n*2, 223*n*7

Españoles Mexicanos, 217*n*5

ether, 221*n*6

"ethnicity v. race" issue, 114–17. *See also* terminology, racial/ethnic group

ethnographic studies, 96–97; Española, 106–18, 123–26; McCarthy on methodologies, 107–8; village ethnography, 97–106, 120–23. *See also* identity and self-concept

Eurocentric history/thinking, 4–5, 35, 36, 152; Oñate as first European colonizer v., 38–39. *See also* Anglo-American worldview

feminists, Chicana, 43; "Crista," 163–65, *164*; gender discrimination lawsuit, 192; "La Malinche" reclaimed by, 51–52, 205, 229*n*12; on self-determination, 228*n*7; *When Jesus Came the Corn Mothers Went Away*, 218*n*6

Fiesta parade, *71*, *72*, 220*n*6

Flores, Richard R., 36–37, 46

Foucault, Michel, 185

fragmentation, 101, 152–55, 157, 166

Fragua, Cliff, 51

freedom, interior, 207–8

Freud, Sigmund, 17

Friends of Acoma, 27, 31–32, 35–36, 217*nn*1–2; deconstructing Oñate icon, 50; identity mystery, 48–49

Gallup, city of, 196

gang-banger, 15

García, Angela, 89–90, 124–25, 221*n*10

García Canclini, Néstor, 96, 130

gender dominance, 43; *When Jesus Came the Corn Mothers Went Away*, 218*n*6

generational gap, xii

genízara/o (Hispanicized native peoples), 39, 40, 219*n*13; dark side of, 199–204, *201–3*; interior freedom of, 207–8; *mestiza/o* identity compared to, 198–99; redemption through ritual performance, 199–200, *201–3*, 204; self-healed, healing others, 206–8; two-track thinking of, 197–99; "Wilberto B. C. Ferrán" on living as, 205–6, 228*n*7. *See also* "Salvador 'Flaco' Cascabel Natividad"

God, transcendent wholeness, 137, 151–54, 190

Gonzales, José, 219*n*13

Good Friday pilgrimage, 57–61, *60*, 63

gorra (unit of heroin), 79

Gramscian analysis, 105, 124

Greff, Jennifer L., 210

Gutiérrez, Ramón, 39–40, 218*n*6; on Spanish colonialism, 43

Hall, Stuart, 127, 149, 226*n*9

Happy Healthy Holy Organization, 215*n*7

Harvey, Fred E., 5

healer, self-healed, 206–8

healing dirt, 57, 61, 215*n*11, 219*n*1; in *Big Dreams and Dark Secrets*, 190
healing salt water, in *Big Dreams and Dark Secrets*, 190–91
Hegel, Georg Wilhelm Friedrich, xvi, 18, 57, 153, 216*n*18, 219*n*13; on fulfilling desires, 75–76
Hernández, Guillermo E., 191, 204
heroin, 77, 79–84, 221*n*7
Herrera, Carlos, 58, 63–66, 213, 219*n*4; confession from, 67–69, 219*n*5
Hispano: *coyote*, 223*n*5; as problematic term, xv, 41–43, 217*nn*4–5
Hispano Roundtable, 192, 228*n*4
Historia de la Nueva México (Villagrá), 33
"historical loss," 90
Holquist, Michael, 185
Holy Week, 57–59
humor. *See* jokes/humor
hypodermic needle(s): giant, in Fiesta parade, *71, 72*, 212; Good Friday pilgrimage path, 61

icon: Alamo: ethnic/racial subjugation, 36–37; conquistadors as, 44–47; Flores on, 36–37; La Verdad's, 51–52; "La Mestiza," 51–52; Oñate statue: ethnic/racial subjugation, 36; Oñate statue: New Mexico's George Washington, 38–39; options for Nuevomexicano/Native American, 219*n*13; preserving continuity with past, 46
identity and self-concept, 39, 40–43, 44–47; *cholo*, 1–2, 3–4, 16, 18, 23, 77, 214*n*2; "ethnicity" v. "race," 114–17; healer and self-healed, 206–8; Lamadrid on, 217*n*5; *mestizo*, 55; more than chameleon, 204–6; political mobilization and, 47–48; Rodríguez

on dialectical process, 14–15, 113–14, 216*nn*16–17, 218*n*10; Whitecotton on reconstruction/intensification of, 112–13. *See also* ethnographic studies; Sagel, Jim
Iglesia de Santa Cruz de la Cañada, 7
Indians. *See* Native Americans
Inquisition, Mexico City, 225*n*3
inversion, symbolic, 184–85, 197–99, 200, 204
irrigation district, 142–43

Jameson, Fredric, 97
Jaramillo, Joey, vii, 24, 74, 79, 95, 220*n*2
Jiménez Núñez, Alfredo, 14, 96, 106–18, 123–26, 223*nn*4–5, 224*nn*8–9; repelled by Española's Americanness, 119–20
Jokes and Their Relation to the Unconscious (Freud), 17
jokes/humor: Cerny's typology of, 15–16; *Chicano Satire: A Study in Literary Culture*, 191, 204; about Española, 210–11, 214*n*3; Marco Cholo, 1–2, 3–4, 18, 23; negativity as undignified/inherently comic, 210; options for statue's foot, 48–52; subversive, 18, 127–28, 183–85, 197–99, 207–8, 218*n*10; trickster cycle, 183–85
joven (young men), 125–26; disruptive/negative behavior of, 121

Kant, Immanuel, 222*n*12
Klein, Richard, 222*n*12
Kosek, Jake, 114, 124–25; on LANL's toxic waste, 195–96

Kutsche, Paul, 96; village culture recast, 97–107, 120–23

Lamadrid, Enrique, 21–22, 58–59, 161, 217n5
La Mesilla, 195
Land of Enchantment concept, 4–8, 18
land rights, xii, 47, 221n10, 222n10; activists of, 54–56, 125; culture loss and, 86–90, 100–101, 124–25; loss of, 9, 11, 86–90, 100–102, 116, 142, 215n12, 226n7; traditional economy loss, 100, 142
LANL. See Los Alamos National Laboratory
Latina/o, as problematic term, 42, 217nn4–5
Latino Metropolis (Valle and Torres), 12
La Verdad, 51–52, 220n7
"Law of Reverse Effects," 183, 206–7
liberating power, 72–73, 126; trickster tales, 183–85
Límon, José E., 24, 116–17, 216n21
Little New Mexico, 216n14
López, Cruz, 21
Los Alamos, 1, 10, 12, 14, 17, 195–96
Los Alamos National Laboratory (LANL), 185, 188; confession from, 195–96; employment hierarchy, 191–92
Los Alamos School District, 219n2
lowrider, 12, 15, 42, 88, 115, 124, 216n15
Lucero, Charlie, 79, 81–82
Lucero, Helen R., 133–34, 225n2
Lummis, Charles, 4–5

machismo, 183–84, 187, 188, 189, 193, 196, 228n5; "Salvador's," 187, 192–93, 200
Machuca, Manuel, 63
"La Malinche," 51–52, 205, 229n12
Mann, E. B., 5
Marco Cholo joke, 1–2, 3–4, 18, 23. See also jokes/humor
Marcus, George, 23–24, 216n20
Mares, E. A. "Tony," 154
"María Guadalupe," 207–8
Martínez, Gaspar, 152, 226n10
Martínez, Lonnie, 91–93
Martínez, Raymond, 65, 66, 68, 72
Martínez, Ricky, 58, 63–67
Marxism, 37, 97, 105, 216n18
Masco, Joseph, 192, 195–96
masculine strength, 168–71. See also machismo
matachines, 115, 124; realm of ancient and sacred, 228nn9–10; ritual enactments by, 200, 201–3, 204; "Salvador's" mock castration, 200, 203; subversive humor of, 218n10
Mather, Christine, 129, 134, 146–47
McCain, John, 115, 223n6
McCarthy, Anna, 107–8
mejicano, -na (Mexicano, Mexican), xv
memory: Benjamin on, 46; Nora on, 45–46
"La Mestiza," 51–52, 220n7
mestiza/o (person of mixed race), 28, 44, 55, 219n13; as ascribed identity, 198–99; "La Mestiza" as festival queen, 51–52, 220n7
metropolitan style/features, 112–13
Milagro Beanfield War (Nichols), 6, 90, 160–61, 227n5
modern art, 128–29, 130, 153, 163–65, 173–74
modernist ethnography, 23–24, 216nn20–21

modernization/modernity: "analysis
of, without solace of closure," 127;
fragmentation yearning for wholeness,
94, 101, 152–55, 157, 166; masculine
strength v. pain of, 168–71, 176–77;
metropolitan style/features, 112–13; as
ruptures in traditional and ancient, 130,
209; urbanization and impoverishment,
11, 80, 116, 155, 215*n*12, 216*n*13; world
systems theory of, 109, 111
Moffat, Karl, 65–66, 219*n*5
Montiel, Miguel, 154
Montoya, Alfredo, 47
Montoya, Dolores, 79, 220*nn*1–2
Montoya, Joann, 219*n*3
Montoya, Leo, 67, 219*n*3
Montoya, Pablo, 219*n*13
Morales, Moisés, 47
mystery: Christian, 226*n*10; defacement's
role in animating, 53, 56; Friends of
Acoma identity, 48–49

Nancy, Jean-Luc, 211
Native American ancestry, 22, 218*n*7,
220*n*6; revival of knowledge from,
189–90, 198–99; valorization of
Spanish ancestry over, 39, 40. See
also *genízara/o* (Hispanicized native
peoples)
Native Americans, 6, 186, 220*n*6,
228*n*8; Navajo, 177–78, 198, 207–8;
Towa é (two of six primal brothers), 62;
Winnebago (Ho Chunk), 187, 228*n*2;
wisdom of, 189–90, 198–99
Navajo: enslaved, 198; Spider Woman,
207–8; story, 177–78
needle, hypodermic: giant, in Fiesta
parade, *71*, 72, 212; on Good Friday
pilgrimage path, 61

negativity/negative, xvi, 115–16, 177,
211; as creative/destructive force,
19–21, 23; *genízaros'* "dark side,"
199–204, *201–3*; Hegel on, xvi,
18, 57, 75–76, 153, 216*n*18, 219*n*13;
horrible and liberating power of,
72–73, 126, 199–200, *201–3*, 204;
in Nuevomexicano culture, 19–23,
76–77, 96, 118–20, 120–23, 125–26,
209; Taussig on, 18, 21–22, 52;
trickster tales, 183–85; urbanization
and poverty, 11, 80, 116, 155, 215*n*12,
216*n*13; wildness of youth, 121–22;
"You know what? It's humanity,"
158–59; Žižek on, as inherently comic,
210
New Mexico: annexation of, 9–10,
26–27, 50, 127; loss of agropastoral
economy, 9, 11, 86–90, 100–102, 116,
127, 137–40, 142, 215*n*12, 226*n*7; out-
of-state seasonal work, 226*n*7
New Mexico: Land of Enchantment (Mann
and Harvey), 5
New York Times, 223*n*6; art of lowriding
(1984), 15
Nichols, John, 6, 90, 160–61
Nietzsche, Friedrich, 18, 216*n*18
Nora, Pierre, 45–46
norteño, 183–86
The Nuclear Borderlands (Masco), 195–96
Nuestro Señor de Esquípulas, 61, 219*n*1
Nuevomexicano culture, 44–47, 106–18,
219*n*13; Chicana/o identity, 28–29,
43, 47, 204–5; negative cultural forms,
19–23, 76–77, 96, 118–20, 120–23,
125–26, 209; newly emergent, 118–20;
problematic term, 41–43, 217*nn*4–5;
reinventing, 184–85; Rodríguez
on, 100; Sagel's status in, 171–73;
sociolinguistics of, 114–15, 117, 223*n*7;
Spanglish cultural dynamics, 169–71;

"structure of feeling," 130, 148–49;
trickster tales, 204–5

O'Bama, Barack, 115, 223n6
Ohkay Casino, 12, 110
Ohkay Owingeh Pueblo, 6, 12, 42;
matachines dance/ritual enactment,
200; Po'pay, 49–50, 51; San Juan
Pueblo renamed (2005) as, 214n6
O'Keeffe, Georgia, 183–84, 188,
193–94, 196–97, 228n3
Omi, Michael, 114–15
Oñate, don Juan de: criticism and
banishment of, 36; expedition to
Acoma Pueblo (1598), 1, 29, 32–34;
La Verdad's version of, 51–52; Native-
Spanish bloodline of, 44; as New
Mexico's George Washington, 38–39;
at San Juan Pueblo community,
214n1
Oñate Monument and Visitors Center,
27–29, 31, 35; Arellano on, 46–47,
55–56; dismemberment of Oñate
statue, 28–29, 217n1; options for
statue's foot, 48–52
Ortega family, 198
overdose deaths, xii, 3, 75, 76–77, 221n4

Pacheco, Ana, 186
"Pachuco," 204
"Padre Piedra," 188, 200, 204, 206
Paredes, Américo, 17
Parsons, Jack, 158
The Passion narrative, 58; Christ's, 59,
60; Ricky and Karen, 63–66
Pedernales. See El Cerro de los
Pedernales

"Pedro de Urdemales," 183–85, 188, 191;
on "Law of Reverse Effects," 206–7
peninsulares (Spaniards born in Spain), 44
Penitentes, 59, 186
Penland, Paige, 12–13, 216n15
Pérez-Torres, Rafael, 55
"The Perfect Wall" (Córdova), 183–84,
188, 193–94, 196–97
pilgrimage, 57–61, 60, 63, 215n1
pissing contest, 193–94
pocito (little hole), 189–90
Po'pay, 49–52
poverty: heroin addicts and, 80; irrigation
district/taxation of farmers, 142–43;
New Mexico, 216n13; Rio Arriba
County, 11, 215n12; urbanization and,
11, 80, 116, 155, 215n12, 216n13
"primitivist" art, 133–34, 141–42, 225n6
Pueblo clowns, 204–5, 218n10
Pueblo Indians: battles of Embudo and
Santa Cruz, 219n13; identity/self
conception, 218n7; negotiating Anglo-
American dominance, 218n10; Oñate's
expedition to Acoma (1598), 1, 29,
32–34; resilience and endurance, 34–35

Quintana, Miguel de, vii, 137, 225n3
Quintana, Seferina, 40

Rabelais (Bakhtin), 185
race and hybridity, 114–17; in California,
43; Chicano studies on, 28–29, 39–43,
217n5; New Mexican ancestry, 39–43;
Oñate's, 44; Pueblo, 218nn6–7. See also
terminology, racial/ethnic group
Radin, Paul, 187
railroads, 142–43; Atchison, Topeka and

Santa Fe Railway, 10, 215n9; Denver and Rio Grande Railway, 10, 108
rancher-farmer-gatherer economy: loss of, 9, 11, 86–90, 100–102, 116, 142, 215n12, 226n7; Valencia's references to, 127, 137–40
redemption: Christian, 58, 153, 211–12; genízara/o's, through ritual performance, 199–200, 201–3, 204; through trickster's subversion, 185
Regents of University of California, 192
Resolana: Emerging Chicano Dialogues on Community and Globalization (Montiel, Atencio, Mares), 154
Rio Arriba: Tragedy and Hope, 63
Rio Arriba county/region, 11, 214n4, 219n13; drug use, 74–75, 76–77, 221n4; ethnographic studies, 96
The Rio Grande Sun, xiii, xvi, 223n7
la risa de Dios (laughter of God), vi, 183; "Wilberto B. C. Ferrán" on, 204
Rodríguez, Sylvia, 14–15, 113–14, 216nn16–17, 218n10; on cultural identity and land loss, 100
Rubright, Lynn, "A Sequent Occupance of the Española Valley, New Mexico," 6, 214n5
ruptures, from modernization/urbanization, 130

Sabatini, Rafael, 1
sacrarium, 190
sacred geography, 58–62, 59, 60; Santuario de Chimayó, 189–90
Sagel, Jim, 171–73, 227n8, 227n11, 227nn5–6; Archuleta family and, 26, 156–61, 161–68; personal mythology/transformation, 173–76; Spanglish cultural dynamics, 169–71

"Saint Peter," 188, 206
Saldívar, Ramón, 183
"Salvador 'Flaco' Cascabel Natividad": confession from, 195–96; as *genízaro*, 197–99; inhabiting spiritual geography, 189, 205–8; machismo and anger of, 187, 189, 192–93, 200; *matachines* mock castration of, 200, 203; misadventures of, 188; *sin vergüenza*, 191, 200; as typical *norteño*, 183–86; "Wilhelm Hightower" firing of, 192–93, 200
sanador (healer/liberator), 207–8
Sánchez, George I., 117, 222n2
San Gabriel, 3
San Gabriel Pueblo, Oñate at, 214n1
San Juan Pueblo, 62, 214n1; renamed "Ohkay Owingeh" (2005), 214n6
San Miguel county, 214n4
Santa Clara, 195
Santa Clara Pueblo, 6, 62
Santa Cruz, 7, 112–13, 134; battles at, 219n13; Valencia's embroidering of, 129–30
Santa Cruz High School, 223n4
Santa Fe, 101, 214n4, 215n9, 221n4; Anglo-American worldview and, 133–34; Atchison, Topeka and Santa Fe Railway, 10, 215n9; Córdova's satire of art community, 196–97; Española compared to, 1, 8–15; U.S. Army invasion of, (1846), 9–10, 219n13
Santa Fe Reporter, 217n1
Santo Niño *bulto* (Christ Child statue), 61–62
Santo Niño village, Valencia's hometown, 127, 129, 134
Santuario de Chimayó, 57, 59, 60, 61–62, 215n11; *Big Dreams and Dark Secrets in Chimayó*, 189–90
satire, 191; Córdova's, 195–97
scale, ethnographic, 97, 107–8

El Señor de Esquípulas, 61, 218*n*1
"A Sequent Occupance of the Española Valley, New Mexico" (Rubright), 6, 214*n*5
Serra, Junipero, 43
"si, es cierto" (yes, it is true), 105
Sikh population, 215*n*7
sin vergüenza (without shame/lacking dignity), 191, 200
slaving economy, 39, 56, 198; ritual enactment of capture/ransom/incorporation, 199–200
"Solo Vino," 188, 193
source of moral order in Valencia's work, 134–37, 151–53
Spanglish, 169–71
Spanish- and Mexican-era settlers, 9, 222*n*2
Spanish Colonial Arts Society, 131, 225*n*2
Spanish ethnicity: problematic term, 41–43, 217*nn*4–5; valorization of, 39, 40, 186
Spanish language: Nuevomexicano shift to English, 111–12, 116–17, 159, 169–71; Sagel's use of, 156–57; trickster tales literature, 183–85; in Valencia's works, 137–39
"Spider Woman," 188, 207–8
spirits, of unbaptized children, 190
spiritual geography, 189, 205–8
Starvation Peak, 218*n*11
Stewart, Kathleen, 211
Stocking, George, 133
subversive humor, 3–4, 18; *Big Dreams and Dark Secrets in Chimayó*, 183–85, 197–99, 207–8; *matachines'*, 218*n*10; Valencia's, 127–28
surumato (undocumented Mexican worker), 15
symbolic inversion, 184–85, 197–99, 200, 204

"Tailoring Treatment Services to Drug Users' Needs," 75, 220*n*3
Taos, 101, 113, 214*n*4, 219*n*13, 222*n*2; Anglo-American worldview and, 133–34; Córdova's satire of art community, 196–97; faux-adobe style, 196–97
Taos Pueblo, 219*n*13
Taussig, Michael, 18, 21–22, 24, 96, 97, 216*n*19; on defacement, 27, 52–53
tecato (drug addict), 15
Tepoztlán, 100
terminology, racial/ethnic group, 114–17; Anglo, 217*n*4; Chicana/o, 41–43, 217*nn*4–5; Hispano, 41–43, 217*nn*4–5, 223*n*5; Latina/o, 42, 217*nn*4–5; Nuevomexicana/o, 41–43, 217*nn*4–5; Spanish ethnicity, 41–43, 217*nn*4–5; White, 217*nn*4–5. See also *genízara/o* (Hispanicized native peoples)
Tewa Basin Study (1935), 142–43
Tewa-speaking people, 62, 199, 214*n*6
"think in reverse," 183, 206–7
Tierra Amarilla, 47, 113–14, 215*n*10; land grant, 222*n*10
Tijerina, Reies López, 117
"Tomás 'No Más' Sánchez," 188, 200
Torres, Rodolfo, 12
tourist industry, 11, 101
Towa é (two of six primal brothers), 62
transformation, recreating one's world, 186; through drug use, 86, 91, 93–95; Martínez and Castañón as Passion play, 64–66; Valencia's articulation, 141–46; Winnebago (Ho Chunk) trickster tales, 187
Trapp, Robert Braiden, xiii
treasure stories, 122
Treaty of Guadalupe Hidalgo, 10
trickster tales: abuelo/coyote tricksters

and Pueblo clowns, 204–5, 218*n*10; in Chicano literature, 204–5; illuminating contradictions, 183–85, 197–99

tricultural harmony concept, 4, 7, 15, 18

Truchas village, 124

Trujillo, Michael, 94–95, 212–13, 222*n*11, 229*n*1

Understories: The Political Life of Forests in Northern New Mexico (Kosek), 124–25, 195–96

Unexpected Turn (Sagel), 166–68, 176–77

U.S. Army, invasion of Mexico (1846), 9–10, 219*n*13

urbanization: and impoverishment, 11, 80, 116, 155, 215*n*12, 216*n*13; as ruptures in ancient and traditional, 130

Valdez, Alex, 7–8, 15

Valencia, Policarpio, 26, 127, 133–35, 137–41, 225*n*5, 226*n*8; allegorical, 128–29, 151–55; articulating transformation, 141–46; embroidered works of, *131, 136, 138, 147, 150*; moral order and continuity, 134–45; subversive humor, 127–28; working through of contradictions, 148, 151–55; works of dialectical tension, 146–50

Valle, Víctor, 12

Van Ness, John R., 96, 97–106, 120–23

Varela, Maria, xii, 53–54

Velásquez, Beth, xiii

vernacular speech, 117

Vigil, James Diego, 214*n*2

village ethnography, 97–106, 120–23

Villagrá, Gaspar Pérez de, 33–34, 44

Virgin Mary, 51, *212*

voting, 114–15, 223*n*6

Wallerstein, Immanuel, 109, 111

waters, regenerative, 190–91

weaving, 163–65, *164*, 215*n*11, 227*n*7; Ortega family, 198; Spider Woman on, 207–8

Weigle, Marta, 42

When Jesus Came the Corn Mothers Went Away (Gutiérrez), 218*n*6

Whitecotton, Joseph W., 96, 106–18, 123–26, 224*n*8, 224*n*10; reconstruction/intensification of ethnic identity, 112–13

Whites: in Colombia, 216*n*19; problematic term, 217*nn*4–5

"Wilberto B. C. Ferrán," 188, 204; on laughter of God, 204; on living as *genízaro*, 205–6, 228*n*7; traditional Chimayó wisdom via, 189–90, 198–99

"Wilhelm Hightower," 188, 192–93, 200

Williams, Gerry, 108

Williams, Raymond: on "rural community" concept, 134–35; on "structure of feeling," 148–49

Williams, Terry, 80

Winant, Howard, 114–15

Winnebago (Ho Chunk), 187, 228*n*2

working-class economy, 9, 10, 11, 14, 76, 142, 228*n*4

world systems theory, 109, 111

Zaldívar, Juan de, 32–33

Zaldívar, Vicente, 33–34

Žižek, Slavoj, 18, 210, 216*n*18